The Invention of Religion

The Invention of Religion

RETHINKING BELIEF IN POLITICS AND HISTORY

EDITED BY

DEREK R. PETERSON

DARREN R. WALHOF

Rutgers University Press

New Brunswick, New Jersey, and London

Library of Congress Cataloging-in-Publication Data

The invention of religion: rethinking belief in politics and history / edited by
Derek R. Peterson and Darren R.Walhof.
    p. cm.
    Includes bibliographical references and index.
    ISBN 0-8135-3092-X (cloth : alk. paper) — ISBN 0-8135-3093-8 (pbk. : alk. paper)
    1. Religion and politics—History. I. Peterson, Derek R., 1971– II. Walhof, Darren R.,
1969–

BL65.P7 I58 2002
291.1'7—dc21

                        2001 058681

British Cataloging-in-Publication information is available from the British Library.

Manufactured in the United States of America

CONTENTS

ILLUSTRATIONS

Preface and Acknowledgments

To write about religion and politics is to enter into a field that has already been dichotomized, in which the stakes are seemingly clearly marked out: secular freedom of choice versus religious obedience to authority; tolerance versus absolutism; reason versus faith; reality versus belief. This book argues that these oppositions are products of history, not natural categories. Moreover, we hope to show that representing the relation between religion and politics in this way serves particular discursive ends, at particular historical junctures. Our aim, then, is to study religion as a part of history, to show how definitions of and struggles over theology and ritual play into and contest particular political projects.

This book grew out of a May 2000 conference we organized under the auspices of the MacArthur Interdisciplinary Program on Global Change, Sustainability and Justice at the University of Minnesota. The university's College of Liberal Arts, the Department of History, the program in Early Modern History, the Graduate and Professional Student Assembly, and the Graduate Christian Fellowship provided financial and logistical support. We want to thank our colleagues Ana Gomez and Christopher Chiappari for their intellectual and organizational contributions and Raymond Duvall, acting director of the MacArthur Program, who gave vital advice in the formative stages of the conference.

We gratefully acknowledge the insights of Celia Chazelle, Jo-Ann Gross, and an anonymous reviewer, who offered helpful comments on various parts of the manuscript. Steven Bishop translated Enrique Dussel's essay, for which we are thankful. We owe special thanks to David Myers and the staff at Rutgers University Press, who enthusiastically supported this project. Finally, we thank the contributors for their patience, diligence, and good humor.

Gauri Viswanathan's essay in this volume was previously published as "Literacy and Conversion in the Discourse of Hindu Nationalism," *Race and Class* 42 (June 2000): 1–20, © 2000 Institute of Race Relations. Reprinted with permission. Publication of this book was made possible through a grant from the Office of Research and Development at the College of New Jersey.

The Invention of Religion

CHAPTER 1

Rethinking Religion

⚜

DEREK R. PETERSON AND DARREN R. WALHOF

*I*n his recent book *Manufacturing Reli-gion*, Russell McCutcheon illuminates the social and political consequences of certain representations of religion in scholarship.[1] McCutcheon particularly criti-cizes the anthropologist Mircea Eliade, whose work was foundational to the field of comparative religion, for regarding religion as sui generis, an irreducible sys-tem distinguished from all other aspects of human life. In Eliade's view reli-gious symbols and actions are meaningful because they correspond to an absolute referent, the sacred; the study of religion, then, is to be segregated from the study of history and politics.[2] McCutcheon argues that placing priority on the sacred obscures the local or situational meanings of religious symbols and silences the ways that religious actions comment on political and social processes. Instead of viewing religion as sui generis, McCutcheon suggests, scholars should ex-plore religion as one among a spectrum of human practices embedded within historical and political contexts.[3]

Like McCutcheon, the essays collected in this volume argue that repre-senting religion as sui generis, personal, unique, and autonomous from all other facets of human life suppresses the political meanings of religious actions. But where McCutcheon and other critics of religious studies argue that "it is the study of religion that invented 'religion,' " the present collection demonstrates that in-venting religion was never purely an academic project.[4] Creating, redefining, and standardizing religion has long been a political strategy linked to the mak-ing of national identities and the exercise of colonial power. In precolonial south-ern Africa, for example, Europeans denied that Africans possessed religion in order to deny their humanity, a potent means of legitimating colonial conquest. After colonial enclosure, Africans were suddenly found to possess religions that

1

could be inventoried and used in colonial administration.[5] Discovering African religion was an aspect of colonial knowledge production. Studying the invention of religion in Africa and elsewhere therefore means studying how modernizing elites standardized and inventoried human practices as a strategy of political control.

The present volume traces the contested processes through which nationalists, colonial officials, and secular scholars formalized religious practices and doctrines in order to define political constituencies and claim authority. The book is organized in three sections. The first section explores the invention of religion as a strategy of marginalization, a way of hollowing out the political thought of others. Representing religious practices and ideas as otherworldly and apolitical is a useful means of truncating their political meanings and social functions, as the essays on Buddhism, African Traditional Religion, and Haredism demonstrate. But while some religions were defined as apolitical belief systems, others were made into templates for nation building. As the essays on the Ottoman Empire, Japan, and India in the second section show, the reformation of religion was often coextensive with the imagination of nationalism. Nation builders purged religions of their divisive elements in order to define religious practice as patriotic duty. The third section explores how tourists, pilgrims, and others resist elites' efforts to categorize and contain the meanings of religious symbols and ideas. In secular Turkey and in the southern United States, pilgrims and tourists deconstruct museum exhibits by turning religious displays into objects of spiritual veneration. Taken together, the essays collected in this volume reconstruct these contrary, contested genealogies of religion as a way of linking the study of religion to the study of national and colonial governmentality.[6]

Modernity, Religion Scholarship, and Politics

Seeing the invention of religion as an aspect of governmentality illuminates connections between the sui generis account of religion and the consolidation of national and colonial power. Modernization theory predicted that religion would gradually disappear from public discourse: religion was the past; rationality was the future. The definition of religion as archaic, personal, and nonpolitical went hand in hand with the definition of the state as rational, secular, and modern. As a way of creating a public sphere governed by rationality, confining religion to the private sphere of belief helped nation builders define a constituency, a citizenry, from which to expect civil conduct. Defining religion as primitive and archaic also helped to legitimate Europe's colonial expansion. As Enrique Dussel argues in this volume, its secularity was one means by which Europe distinguished itself from ostensibly primitive religious others in an era of colonial expansion. Secular modernity, then, was never the natural outgrowth of historical development—although it was often represented that way.

Defining secular modernity as the end of history was an aspect of Europe's self-definition, an ideology that legitimated the civilizing mission by making colonialism seem a noble, morally necessary project.

Our argument, then, is that the sui generis model of religion helped fashion the distinctions between private and public, past and future, which were at the heart of the formation of European states. These distinctions can be traced at least back to seventeenth-century England, where debates over the toleration of religious dissenters produced a new understanding of the nature of religion, as evidenced by John Locke's *Letter Concerning Toleration.* At a time of religious conflict spawned by the persecution of dissenters by the established church, Locke claimed that "Liberty of Conscience is every man's natural right."[7] Drawing a distinction between the purposes of a commonwealth and the purposes of a church, Locke thought religious uniformity unnecessary for the stability of a political society; indeed, attempts to enforce uniformity would inevitably produce conflict. If the civil government would restrict its actions to the protection of civil interests—life, health, liberty, and possessions—and if the churches would restrict theirs to the salvation of souls, there would no longer be conflict on the basis of religion. Members of different traditions would be able to coexist in civic harmony.

This institutional differentiation of church from government was an important development in Western political thought. What is often overlooked, however, is that Locke's argument depended upon the definition of *religion* as personal belief. Locke distinguished between "speculative" and "practical" articles of faith. The former were those that "terminate simply in the Understanding" and which were "required only to be believed."[8] Speculative articles of faith—Locke's example was the doctrine of transubstantiation—had no consequences in action; they were merely a matter of belief. Thus, they fell completely within the jurisdiction of the church, not within that of the civil government, and ought to be tolerated. Practical articles of faith, on the other hand, were those that had to do with living a good life and, thus, necessarily involved practices that had social and political consequences. Because they affected the interests of others, practical articles of faith potentially conflicted with government-mandated restrictions meant to ensure civic harmony. Locke managed to avert this intractable conflict by appealing to reason. If all practical articles of faith were governed by reason, harmony would prevail, since reason also taught that citizens were not to infringe on the civil interests of others. Reasonable faith traditions would support the same set of moral practices, eliminating conflicts on the basis of religion. Locke's exclusion of Catholics from his model of a tolerant society is instructive here: their belief in the authority of the pope in this world had social and political consequences that affected the civil interests of others. Catholics thus failed to govern their practical articles of faith by reason and could not be tolerated.

Locke's work defined a public sphere, governed by reason, in which civic discourse could take place without the threat of violence. As part of the same process, Locke redefined *religion* itself, equating it with speculative matters of faith. Although Locke did not dismiss the pragmatic, bodily or "practical" elements of religion outright, his approach stipulated that such practices were acceptable only to the extent that they were irrelevant to social and political realities. The importance of this development is evident when contrasted to the forms of embodied discipline practiced by pre–Enlightenment Christians. In medieval monastic Christianity, as Talal Asad shows, religious practices were not formulaic expressions of participants' interior beliefs. Rather, correctly performed ritual disciplines constituted individual virtue and were themselves virtuous. Penance, for example, could involve self-flagellation, fasting, and exacting vigils. Such practices were "medicine for the soul"; bodily pain prescribed by church authorities purged the sufferer and restored him to spiritual health.[9] Ascetic practices such as chastity similarly called on the discipline of the monastic community to watch, test, and protect the ascetic against transgression. Such practices, argues Asad, were not merely means of subjection and domination. They were means of producing truths, ways of creating virtuous individuals and defining religious communities.

Locke's definition—part of larger trends in European thought after the Reformation—divested religion of its bodily and pragmatic dimensions.[10] Confining religion to the speculative realm of faith was for Locke and other intellectuals of the Enlightenment a way of managing religious conflict. Disembodied and made into an internal affair between God and believer, religion was the template by which nineteenth-century Europeans made sense of the ideas and practices of other people in an era of colonial expansion. The anthropologist E. B. Tylor's influential *Primitive Cultures,* to take one example, was published in 1871 at the beginning of systematic missionary activity in sub-Saharan Africa. Tylor argued that religion—which he defined as "a belief in Spiritual Beings"—was a universal element in human culture.[11] The "primitive" cultures of the rest of the world, argued Tylor, were continuous with that of Europe, albeit at an earlier stage on the evolutionary scale: they were corollaries to the Old Testament sacrifices of the Hebrews.[12] Their future, the fullest stage of their development, was thus supposed to be Christianity.

Later anthropologists were much more attentive than the "intellectualist" Tylor to the practices and rituals of non-Western religions. But, like Tylor, they thought religion drew its meaning from a sacred, otherworldly realm. E. E. Evans-Pritchard's important 1956 study *Nuer Religion,* for example, concluded with a reminder to readers of the priority of the sacred: "Though prayer and sacrifice are exterior actions, Nuer religion is ultimately an interior state. This state is externalized in rites which we can observe, but their meaning depends finally on an awareness of God and that men are dependent on him and must be resigned to his will. At this point the theologian takes over from the anthropologist."[13] For Evans-Pritchard, as for other anthropologists, ritual was symbolic activity opposed to the instrumental behavior of everyday life. Classically defined by Victor Turner as "formal action directed at the Sacred," rituals were supposed to draw their capacity for meaning from their reference to the otherworldly, divine realm.[14] Nuer ritual action, for example, was supposed to be meaningful because it called on a God that was itself outside time to mediate human relations. What these rituals themselves constituted, how Nuer religion commented on and created social and political relationships in the here and now, was not of interest to Evans-Pritchard.

Nineteenth-century anthropologists shared with Locke and other Enlightenment thinkers a conjoined genealogy of religion. Seeking to limit conflict and create a space for civil discourse, Locke differentiated the personal domain of religion from the pragmatic public sphere. The differentiation of private from public divested religious actions of their embodied, practical, and political meanings; religion was "speculation." Intellectualist definitions of *religion* follow directly from these distinctions between religion and the real. For Evans-Pritchard and Tylor, the meanings of religious practices ultimately derive from their reference to an otherworldly, sacred realm. By defining religion as sui generis, Evans-Pritchard, Tylor, and other anthropologists distinguished the study of religion from the study of historical change, social conflict, or political struggle.

For colonial anthropologists no less than for Locke, sui generis religion was a strategy of political and intellectual containment. Colonial rule in sub-Saharan Africa, Mahmood Mamdani argues, worked by standardizing certain African social practices as invariant.[15] By formalizing African law, for example, colonial officials created mechanisms through which to govern their subjects indirectly, through the supposedly timeless institutions of tribal authority. Studying and inventorying African knowledge systems as timeless, changeless, and disembodied religions were aspects of the larger process by which colonial officials sought to freeze and formalize Africans' political thought. Defining religion as changeless and archaic, we can conclude, was for Locke and for nineteenth-century anthropologists a useful strategy of control. By placing the priority on the sacred, the sui generis definition extracted religious actions out of their social and political contexts, truncating their meanings and segregating religion from the real.

Intellectualist models of religion have not gone unchallenged. At least since Émile Durkheim, anthropologists have vigorously debated whether religion amounts to a system of belief or a system of practice. The most interesting intervention in this debate has recently come from Malcolm Ruel. Ruel studies Kuria religion (on the Kenya-Tanzania border) without depending on Tylorean preoccupations with theological reasoning and spiritual beings.[16] His work demonstrates that Kuria rituals do not invoke the existence of a divine realm opposed to the human but, instead, engage humanity directly with the natural world. The ritual killing of animals, for example, is a formal process in which an elder suffocates the animal, opens a hole in its distended paunch, and takes the chyme from it. The chyme is then eaten by other elders or sprinkled over a person who had been rendered unpropitious by some misfortune. For the Kuria, eating the chyme is eating the life of the animal; it transfers to the taker the vital force of the slaughtered beast. This transaction does not depend on the presence of a God for its meaning. As Ruel puts it, what is at issue for Kuria in the taking of the chyme "is not the life *of* the animal—a life offered in surrogate as part of a morally conceived relationship—but rather the life *in* the animal, a life that derives from the natural world and is here mediated to the homestead through the animals that are associated with it."[17] Slaughtering an animal and consuming its chyme bring Kuria people in touch with the vital life forces of the natural world. Kuria religion, Ruel concludes, is oriented not toward the supernatural but to the constitution of productive social relationships.

It is not our purpose in this volume to ask whether religion is essentially practice or essentially belief. Our agenda, rather, is to understand when and why some religions seem to amount to a set of privately held beliefs, while others demand correct, embodied practices as essential to the development of social harmony, political solidarity, and religious virtue.[18] What purposes does defining religion as a privately held system of belief serve? Conversely, why and how are some religions defined not as private practice but as an index of patriotic citizenship? How do performances described as religious form certain sorts of subjects and create different kinds of publics? Asking questions like these links the study of religion to the study of the sociology of power. The invention of religion, we argue, was never simply an abstract exercise in theology. Making and remaking religion is a political enterprise, intimately linked to the imagination of new social and intellectual communities.

The essays in the first section examine the political consequences of representing religion as a timeless system of belief. Richard Cohen highlights how the prevailing scholarly model of Buddhism as pure soteriology plays into the agenda of Hindu nationalists. Defining Buddhism as otherworldly allows Hindutva activists to define India as naturally and organically Hindu, leaving non-Hindus with little voice in public affairs. Cohen argues that scholars need to recover local histories that complicate such universal definitions of Buddhism. Examining inscriptions and other archaeological evidence at the Ajanta caves dating from 400 C.E., Cohen demonstrates that, for the Ajanta community, Buddhism was more than an otherworldly belief system. What scholars today call Buddhism was, at Ajanta, a means of negotiating kin and trade relationships with local political rulers. The nature of Buddhism at Ajanta, Cohen suggests, highlights the need for locally specific histories that attend to the political functions of religion.

Cohen argues that defining Buddhism as interior and otherworldly is for Hindu nationalists a means of marginalizing religious minorities. Derek Peterson's essay suggests that the construction of religion as otherworldly follows from a prior construction of religion as a set of propositions, to be believed in subjectively. Peterson argues that "traditional religion" in central Kenya was a colonial invention, created as missionaries attempted to rope Africans into conversations about contending principles and dogmas. Searching for dogmas against which to preach, missionaries represented Gikuyu social thought as religious, structured by codified, systematic theology. But the Gikuyu understood the world to be too fluid to be rendered into timeless propositions. As befitting a culture of forest-clearing pioneers, their thought was experimental and corporeal. Confronted with missionary preaching about another world, the Gikuyu deconstructed Christian rituals and ideologies, dwelling on the techniques of missionary evangelism instead of the meanings that missionaries sought to convey. This struggle over technique, Peterson suggests, was a struggle over religion itself. By refusing to engage in debates about disembodied dogma, the Gikuyu also refused to be drawn into the colonial order of objects and subjects, the hierarchy of reality through which British power worked.

Cohen and Peterson demonstrate that inventing religion was for colonial elites and nation builders alike a strategy of containment, a means of pinning down and managing the ideas and practices of their subjects. Jeremy Stolow shows that contemporary academics participate in the political act of containing the meanings of religious ideas. Examining haredi religious and political writing in Jewish journals, Stolow compares contemporary scholarship on Jewish religion with the haredim's self-representation. Scholarly interpreters treat statements by haredi authorities as evidence to help explain the rise of Jewish "fundamentalism." But haredi authors continually challenge the right of academics to speak for them by proposing alternate interpretations of their history. Stolow argues that this field of encounter is the proper field for scholarly inquiry. Instead of treating haredi texts as evidence to be assembled and interpreted, scholars should explore the discursive strategies through which leaders, adherents, and secular academics make and legitimate claims about Haredism.

These three essays suggest that inventing religion was and is an act of power, a means by which scholars, politicians, nationalists, and colonialists truncated the social and political meanings of certain human practices. In these contexts, naming a certain practice or disposition religious rendered it something other than real. Inventing African religion was a potent means by which colonial officials ossified the social practices of Gikuyu people in Kenya. Defining Buddhism as an otherworldly religion similarly allows Indian nationalists to claim this world for the practical, this-worldly religion of Hinduism. And defining Haredism as fundamentalism permits secular scholars to claim scientific authority for themselves, thereby delegitimizing the haredim's own understandings of truth and authority. Defining religion as sui generis was and is a useful strategy of political and intellectual control.

Reforming Religion, Imagining Nationalism

We have argued that representing religion as archaic and irrational was a critical dimension of Europe's self-definition. But, as the essays in the second section show, religion was never only modernity's other. In Japan, India, and the Middle East nation builders defined religious rituals as patriotic duty. Just as inventing traditions helped nation builders create an inspirational and unifying past, so too did inventing or formalizing religious rituals help create ideologies of patriotism.[19] But before they could claim Shinto, Islam, or Hinduism as national religions, nation builders had first to fight internal battles against uncivil forms of popular religious practice. By divesting religions of their divisive or heterodox elements, nation builders crafted templates for nationalism, unifying sets of rituals and ideas that defined new political communities.

Understanding the nationalist imagination in these historical terms is particularly important given current scholarly consensus about the relation of nationalism to religion. Eric Hobsbawm's *Nations and Nationalism since 1780,* together with Benedict Anderson's *Imagined Communities,* are the most important examples of what has come to be called the modernist tradition of nationalism scholarship.[20] In the view of the modernists European nationalisms, now pirated abroad, were nineteenth-century inventions—indeed, Hobsbawm thinks it "pointless" to trace their histories prior to 1780. For both Hobsbawm and Anderson, nationalism developed as a theory of political legitimacy requiring that dynastic subjects become national citizens in order to participate in government. Bound together horizontally by common linguistic and experiential ties, European and American nationalisms were "imagined communities" called into existence as the consequence of print capitalism, industrialization, and the privatization of religion.

Anderson and Hobsbawm make it possible to think of nationalisms as created, historically shaped, political communities. The question that they do not sufficiently answer, however, is, created from what? What shared ideas and practices did nationalists elaborate on in proposing new forms of political association? Answering these questions links the study of nationalism to the study of religious discourse. Because they focus almost exclusively on the modern period, Hobsbawm and Anderson do not explore the role of Christian discourse in the making of national identities. Hobsbawm does devote several pages to the discussion of religion and "protonationalism," describing the fusion of nation and religious identities in various regions.[21] But he thinks such fusions "paradoxical," since religions tend either to supersede nationalisms in their claims to universal authority or to undermine national solidarities by dividing citizens. Anderson similarly thinks nationalism a consequence of the decline of Latin, the language of the church, and the rise of vernacular publishing. Nationalism was for Hobsbawm and Anderson a modern phenomenon, arising once the medieval church had lost its hold on European politics. Their chronology makes it difficult to understand nationalism as anything but a linear successor to religion and, therefore, closes off investigation into the political nature of religious discourse.

No one has probed the premodern religious history of European nationalisms more fully than Adrian Hastings. In his recent book *The Construction of Nationhood* Hastings traces how ethnic communities in medieval Europe and colonial Africa became internally more diverse, externally more active nations.[22] Hastings focuses on the history of medieval England, which he regards as Europe's prototypical nation. In one of his most provocative arguments, Hastings contends that the intellectual template for the English nation was the nation of Israel. Reading King Alfred's translation of the Venerable Bede's *Ecclesiastical History of the English People* and tracing fourteenth-century Wyclifite translations of the Latin Vulgate, Hastings argues that Israel provided a model for English intellectuals of what it meant to be a nation, with a unity of people, language, religion, territory, and government. By the later Middle Ages, well before the periods that Anderson and Hobsbawm study, both the word and the concept of nationhood were already active in English self-imagining and expressed in the English language. Taught widely through clerical schooling, recited daily in Latin church services and in vernacular public readings, the history of the nation of Israel provided a theological model for the expansion of local ethnicities to a wider English nationalism. A widely used Christian vernacular literature, concludes Hastings, fostered a national political imagination in England and elsewhere by enabling readers to imagine themselves as sharers of a common future.

Hastings's study makes it possible to see nationalism not as a successor to religion but as a historical product of religious discourse. English nationhood, like the other nationalisms that Hastings studies, was imagined on templates already established through Christianity. Other scholars have similarly challenged secularization theory by demonstrating how religious rituals and ideas shaped national imaginations. Peter van der Veer and Hartmut Lehmann's important collection *Nation and Religion,* for example, highlights how entangled the nationalist imagination was with religious symbology.[23] Tracing the ways that religious rituals cross into the sphere of national politics, the essays in their volume show how the lines between the secular and the religious are blurred by phenomena such as Dutch war memorials or Hindu ideas of martyrdom. Nationalism, they argue, feeds on a symbolic and ideational repertoire already available in religion. Far from fading into the abstracted past forecasted by secularization theory, religious ideas and practices shape national ideologies in subtle and creative ways.

The present volume builds on Van der Veer and Lehmann's collection by extending the analysis to regions not covered in their volume. But, more than broadening the geographical coverage, the essays in the second section ask somewhat more basic questions about the relation of religious reform to the construction of nationalism. Religions were always more, and less, than symbolic reservoirs for the nationalist imagination. In India, Japan, and the Ottoman Empire, nine-teenth-century nation builders had to purge religions of their divisive and het-erodox elements before they could serve as the practical basis uniting disparate peoples under national solidarities. The essays in the second section outline the dynamic, mutually creative relationship between nationalism and religious re-form. The reform of religion, they argue, was part and parcel of the process of nation building.

Sanjay Joshi's essay on Hinduism in colonial north India reconstructs the way middle-class intellectuals republicized religion, making Hinduism into a foundation of national citizenship. Criticizing Partha Chatterjee's influential the-sis on the relation of religion to colonialism, Joshi argues that Hinduism was never simply a spiritual sphere of sovereignty, autonomous from the British state.[24] Hinduism was, rather, an arena of debate and struggle, as middle-class activists worked to create a nonhierarchical, scientific Hinduism by suppress-ing religious itinerants and purging their religion of its irrational recrudescence. Liberated from its social contexts and made modern, this republicized Hindu-ism became a template for the Indian nation, even for secular nationalists such as Nehru. To understand Indian modernity, argues Joshi, scholars must see how religious reform laid the intellectual groundwork for the nationalist imagination of the middle class.

Sarah Thal's essay on the making of Shinto in late-nineteenth-century Ja-pan similarly demonstrates how religious and national identities were concur-rently crafted. Under the foreign rule of the Tokugawa shogunate, the Japanese gentry codified the diffuse and unsystematic "way of the ancestors," creating a systematic Shinto ideology by suppressing irrational lower-class practices and ideas. With the fall of the shogunate in the 1860s and the installation of the Meiji emperor, participation in these purified Shinto rituals became the basis of Japa-nese nationalism. Practicing Shinto, nationalists argued, was a way of venerating the emperor and fulfilling civic duty. As Shinto became public ritual, Buddhism and other non-Shinto practices were labeled religious and confined to the pri-vate, personal sphere. Religion, argued nationalists, was divisive and antinational. As public ritual, Shinto was "not a religion"; practicing Shinto was, rather, pa-triotic duty. Like the public Hinduism described by Joshi, Shinto rituals were for Japanese nationalists the index of national citizenship.

James Gelvin's essay extends this argument to the study of Middle East-ern nationalisms in the nineteenth century. The secularization thesis led earlier scholars of Islam to expect the gradual decline of religious values and ideas in the discourse of national states. The 1979 Iranian Revolution threw this schol-arly consensus into flux and demanded new ways to understand Islam's vitality. Gelvin suggests that the contemporary fluorescence of Islamic theopolitics has its origins in the political theories of legitimation propounded by the Ottoman emperors of the nineteenth century. Focusing on the modernizing reforms of Abdülhamid II, Gelvin shows how the imperial state set about standardizing Islamic belief in order to forward *Osmanlalik,* civic nationalism. By policing heterodox Sufi sects, by instituting a monopoly of religious publishing, and by incorporating orthodox clerics into state councils, the Ottoman regime converted Islam into a governing ideology. This standardization of Islamic practice, Gelvin suggests, was intimately tied to the making of a theory of national citizenship. It was also a means of suppressing dissent.

In each of these cases national elites had to fight internal battles against popular ideas and practices before their religions could be republicized and made into an intellectual basis for a national imagination. Taken together, the essays of the second section raise the question: what are the intersections between religious reform and the construction of nationhood? How do religious practices map out geographic and political entities that become national? Gyan Prakash has recently argued that a network of railroads, irrigation, mining, and agencies of administration configured India as a geographic and administrative entity.[25] The present collection suggests that religious reform similarly mapped out the geographic, political, and intellectual space of the nation in India as in Japan and the Ottoman Empire. Religion was never simply the predecessor to nationalism on a linear time scale. Instead, religious reform went hand in hand with the making of national politics.

Religious Displays

But what happens to religious ideas and objects when they become the province of the nation? Is it possible to locate points of resistance and contestation in the making of religion as a national project? The third set of essays asks these questions by exploring national museums and tourist venues as scenes of struggle over the interpretation of religious objects. As Timothy Mitchell has shown, exhibitions and museums constitute political and social realities.[26] Exploring nineteenth-century world exhibitions in Paris and elsewhere, Mitchell demonstrates how the Orient was displayed as an object, a picture to be viewed, gazed upon, and investigated by Europeans. The 1878 Paris World Exhibition, for example, placed the French exhibit at its center, with the exhibits of Europe's colonies radiating out from it. Mitchell argues that these symbolic representations of cultural and colonial order were the means of producing and constituting Europe's vision of the world. The exhibits rendered history, progress, culture, and empire itself in objective form. Representation thus created an image of the real; the empire was arrayed before the eyes of observing Europeans in the form of an exhibition.

If museums are a site at which history and the future are represented and concretized, then studying museums means studying the state's strategies of self-positioning. Wendy Shaw's essay in the present collection demonstrates how contemporary Turkish nation builders use exhibits to create and naturalize a national history. Turkish museums claim Islamic prayer rugs, Qurans, and Sufi clothing as national symbols, inspirational forebears to the secular Turkish nation. Disconnected from their ritual and religious uses, divested of their contextual significance, these objects are meant to invite aesthetic appreciation and invoke national pride—thus constituting a material dimension of the making of religion as a national ideology. By abstracting Islamic objects out of their local, ritual uses, secular nationalists lay claim to Islam itself, not as a vital force in the world but as a symbol of national unity. Religious displays thus give shape and historical depth to a secular Turkish nation, just as exhibiting the Orient helped nineteenth-century Europeans configure their empires.

But, unlike Mitchell, who regards exhibitions as an unambiguous expression of political power, Shaw argues that these displays are sites of struggle between authorized and unauthorized readings of religious objects. Secular museums housed in Sufi tombs have today become sites of religious pilgrimage. Tourists in Turkey's secular museums mingle with Islamic pilgrims, who pray at Sufi tombs, imbibe springwater reputed to have healing qualities, and venerate the mantle of the prophet Mohammed. Their creative acts of worship, argues Shaw, reanimate sterile exhibitions, turning secular museums into scenes of religious devotion.

Shaw's essay makes it possible to think of the nationalization of religion not simply as an unimpeded, coercive process of reform but also as a struggle over the meanings of ritual objects. Thinking of religion in this way directs attention away from politically authorized representations of religion and toward the lived experiences of individuals who interpret religious ideas and objects. Aaron Ketchell's essay on Ozark tourism shows how religious and secular categories are transgressed and remade every day in the experiences of tourists in Branson, Missouri. Modern scholarship has assumed that the market and faith are inimically opposed, that commodity capitalism would inevitably win out over the outmoded, local virtues of religious traditions. Against this notion, Ketchell shows how commodity marketing in the Ozarks refoundationalizes the virtues of God, family, and country. At the Precious Moments Chapel, in leisure resorts, and in other places of entertainment, tourists experience and imbibe Christian virtues through the mundane, by listening to music, dining, and shopping. This tourist culture of commodities, Ketchell suggests, is a domain of popular religion, one in which consumption, leisure, and worship mix in subtle and creative ways.

Both Ketchell and Shaw argue that tourist destinations are arenas of contention between authorized and popular readings of religious objects and materials. Shaw's pilgrims contest official Turkish history, thronging to secular museums in order to transact the very unsecular business of religious devotion. Ketchell's tourists turn shopping malls into grottoes and gift shops into churches. Both the Precious Moments Chapel and Turkish museums blur the lines between the secular and the religious, in large part because pilgrims and tourists continually reinterpret the material lessons offered in secular displays.

Seeing museums as arenas of struggle over the interpretation of religious objects links the study of Turkish museums and the Precious Moments Chapel to themes investigated elsewhere in the volume. This volume argues that the definition of religion as an apolitical and personal essence is a historical invention. Nationalists and colonial officials represented certain religions in this way in order to contain and control the political thought of their subjects. This model is today used in scholarship to truncate the meanings of religious actions and ideas. The present volume defines an alternative trajectory for religion scholarship. Instead of assuming that religion naturally amounts to an otherworldly belief system, these essays reconstruct how the powerful work to guarantee particular readings of religious rituals and practices. Some religious traditions—Buddhism, for example—were and are represented as otherworldly and timeless. Other religions—Hinduism, for example, or Shinto—were made public, purged of their divisive or idiosyncratic elements in order to serve as the foundation for national communities. Along the way pilgrims and inquirers poached from the ordered histories of the powerful, recombining secular and religious ideas in creative ways. Thinking of religion as a historical invention helps us see religion not as an a priori category organic to human existence nor as a past bound to be superseded by the secular future. Studying religion in its creation links the study of ontology and ritual to politics and helps trace out the struggles involved in the constitution of modernity.

The Political Stakes of Rethinking Religion

By treating the religious not as a passive repository of beliefs but as a contested social space constituted by power, this volume repositions religion in scholarship. Its agenda is to bring together philosophy and theology with history and politics, to show how struggles over theological categories authorize and undermine the configuration of nationalism and modernity. The volume's two concluding chapters develop these themes in markedly different directions. Enrique Dussel's chapter joins the study of history with the project of liberation theology. Like many of the other essayists, Dussel argues that secularism was a means of self-definition for modernizing Europe. Secularism arose not from an autochthonous development in European culture but, rather, from the management of the world system by the West. As a mark of superior development, secularism helped Europeans differentiate themselves from religious others in a world economic system in which Europe was increasingly the center.

Seeing secularism as an ideology that legitimated Europe's centrality within a world economic system allows Dussel to see religion not as an archaic, outdated belief system but as a resource for political critique. Here Dussel moves beyond historical description and toward political engagement. World religions, he argues, carry within them the ethical foundations for a project of liberation. Surveying the development of religious traditions from ancient Egypt to the present, Dussel finds ethical systems in the founding narratives of world religions. These ethical systems survive today in the popular religious traditions of ordinary people. Dussel's project is to connect these popular ethical systems with the revolutionary agenda of Marxism by foregrounding the liberatory and radical elements within popular religions. As a historian, therefore, Dussel argues that the opposition between secularism and religion is a Eurocentric myth, produced after the Enlightenment as a way of justifying colonial expansion. As a philosopher, Dussel argues that secular Marxism needs religious ethics, that critical religion and radical politics can be joined through a common project of liberation.

Like Dussel, Gauri Viswanathan describes an epistemological and critical function for religion in postsecular, postcolonial societies. For Viswanathan, however, the power of religion lies not in an ethical core or a liberating theology but, rather, in conversion. Contemporary Hindu nationalists define India as organically and naturally Hindu. In such a context secular pluralism offers little hope for real political communication between Hindu nationalists and political and cultural minorities. Pluralism undermines the totalistic values of religious absolutists but offers no means for negotiating among incommensurable worldviews. In Viswanathan's view conversion can fulfill this function. In its tendency to erase or remake markers of religious identity, Viswanathan argues, conversion can serve as a means of communication for postpluralist societies as well as a means also of criticizing ruling orthodoxies.

The differences between Viswanathan and Dussel help clarify the political stakes involved in rethinking religion. For, as the authors in this volume contend, defining religion has always been a political act, a means of claiming authority for nationalists, scholars, and missionaries alike. Thinking of religion not as an outdated belief system but as a way of doing things in the world is therefore an act of criticism. But on what grounds does rethinking religion entail political critique? To this question Viswanathan and Dussel give contending answers. Dussel looks for an ethical core in world religions, a platform from which liberating critiques of secularism and postcolonialism can adequately be mounted. Viswanathan, in contrast, argues that the power of conversion is precisely to upset given religious and political identities. Her interest is not in the theological content of religious traditions but in conversion as a critical praxis, as an act of resistance to positivism. At stake in their disagreement are critical questions for students of religion: what is the proper agenda for religious studies in a context in which the object of study, religion, has been invented or worked over by powerful economic, social, and political forces? Is it our task to reconstruct the ethical core of world religions, to recover their foundational dogmas in order to challenge the power of global economic and political elites? Or should scholars look for the fluidity of religious categories, highlighting how conversions destabilize nationalism's tendency to fix religious identities as invariant?

Rethinking religion also raises important questions about religious pluralism, which in the West has historically been linked to secularism, to the differentiation of the rational public sphere from the sphere of personal, apolitical religion. To return to McCutcheon's language, religious pluralism has depended upon a conception of religion as sui generis. In rejecting the a priori assumption that religion is sui generis, this volume criticizes the notion of pluralism. How does the ideal of pluralism play into the process of suppressing the political and social meanings of religious actions? Is the connection between toleration and sui generis religion simply historical, or is it a necessary one—that is, must religion be formulated in this way if disparate religious communities are to coexist peacefully?[27] Is it possible to reconceptualize pluralism, toleration, and freedom of conscience in ways that are not wedded to sui generis religion? To what degree, for example, is religious pluralism possible in places such as India, Japan, and Turkey, where public religions serve as templates for national identity? Current religious conflicts across the globe not only testify to the inadequacy of current approaches to religion, in both scholarship and politics; they also demonstrate the urgency of such questions.

Notes

1. Russell McCutcheon, *Manufacturing Religion: The Discourse on Sui Generis Religion and the Politics of Nostalgia* (New York: Oxford University Press, 1997).
2. McCutcheon, *Manufacturing Religion,* 38–41.
3. McCutcheon, *Manufacturing Religion,* 212.
4. Jonathon Z. Smith, "'Religion' and 'Religious Studies': No Difference at All," *Soundings* 71 (1988): 231–244.
5. David Chidester, *Savage Systems: Colonialism and Comparative Religion in Southern Africa* (Charlottesville: University Press of Virginia, 1996).
6. See Michel Foucault, "Governmentality," in *The Foucault Effect: Studies in Governmentality,* ed. Graham Burchell et al. (London: Harvester Wheatsheaf, 1991), 87–104.
7. John Locke, *A Letter Concerning Toleration,* ed. James H. Tully (Indianapolis: Hackett Publishing Co., 1983), 51.
8. Locke, *Letter,* 46.
9. Talal Asad, *Genealogies of Religion: Discipline and Reasons of Power in Christianity and Islam* (Baltimore: Johns Hopkins University Press, 1993), chap. 3.
10. For an overview of the broader trends of which Locke was a part, see J. B. Schneewind, *The Invention of Autonomy* (Cambridge, U.K.: Cambridge University Press, 1998).
11. E. B. Tylor, *Primitive Culture* (London: John Murray, 1871).
12. For an analysis of Tylor's thought, see G. Stocking, *Race, Culture and Evolution* (New York: Free Press, 1968).
13. E. E. Evans-Pritchard, *Nuer Religion* (Oxford: Clarendon Press, 1956), 322.
14. V. Turner, *The Forest of Symbols: Aspects of Ndembu Ritual* (Ithaca, N.Y.: Cornell University Press, 1967), 19.
15. Mahmood Mamdani, *Citizen and Subject: Contemporary Africa and the Legacy of Late Colonialism* (Princeton, N.J.: Princeton University Press, 1996).

16. Malcolm Ruel, *Belief, Ritual and the Securing of Life: Reflexive Essays on a Bantu Religion* (Leiden: Brill Academic Publishers, 1997).

17. Ruel, *Belief, Ritual,* 102.

18. An analytic agenda proposed by Talal Asad, "Interview: Modern Power and the Reconfiguration of Religious Traditions," *Stanford Electronic Humanities Review* 5, 27 February 1996, <http://www.stanford.edu/group/SHR/5–1/text/asad.html>.

19. On tradition, see Eric Hobsbawm and Terrence Ranger, *The Invention of Tradition* (New York: Cambridge University Press, 1983).

20. Eric Hobsbawm, *Nations and Nationalism since 1780: Programme, Myth, Reality* (New York: Cambridge University Press, 1990); Benedict Anderson, *Imagined Communities: Reflections on the Origins and Spread of Nationalism* (London: Verso, 1983).

21. Hobsbawm, *Nations and Nationalism,* 67–73.

22. Adrian Hastings, *The Construction of Nationhood: Ethnicity, Religion and Nationalism* (New York: Cambridge University Press, 1997).

23. Peter van der Veer and Hartmut Lehmann, eds., *Nation and Religion: Perspectives from Europe and Asia* (Princeton, N.J.: Princeton University Press, 1999). See also Peter van der Veer, *Imperial Encounters: Religion and Modernity in India and Britain* (Princeton, N.J.: Princeton University Press, 2001).

24. Partha Chatterjee, *The Nation and Its Fragments* (Princeton, N.J.: Princeton University Press, 1993).

25. Gyan Prakash, *Another Reason: Science and the Imagination of Modern India* (Princeton, N.J.: Princeton University Press, 1999).

26. Timothy Mitchell, *Colonising Egypt* (Berkeley: University of California Press, 1991).

27. Some contemporary liberal theorists argue that this is the case. Richard Rorty, for example, claims, "we shall not be able to keep a democratic political community going unless the religious believers remain willing to trade privatization for a guarantee of religious liberty" ("Religion as a Conversation Stopper," *Common Knowledge* 3, no. 1 [1994]: 3). Similarly, John Rawls has argued that liberal politics must be conducted in the terms of "public reason," thereby excluding public claims made on the basis of religious convictions. See *Political Liberalism* (New York: Columbia University Press, 1993), 243ff.

PART I

CHAPTER 2

Why Study
Indian Buddhism?

☙❦❧

RICHARD S. COHEN

*H*ow historical is the field known as history of religions? How historical can it be? Are religious phenomena susceptible to historical analysis? Is it possible to study religious phenomena without reproducing theological, or crypto-theological, assumptions? Can a scholar approach religion without representing god, salvation, ultimate truth, and other icons of transcendence as historical agents in their own right? Can one situate the disruptive irruptions of transcendence, characteristic of religious discourse, within a homogeneous and secular time? If transcendence is properly not a matter of history, then can a historian talk about transcendence but do so in a way that does not trivialize or wreak violence against religious mentalities?

This essay will look to the study of Indian Buddhism for one possible answer. Indian Buddhism differs from Islam, Judaism, Christianity, even Hinduism, in at least one fundamental way. Those religions possess multiple communities that have long sought to influence and direct scholarly representations of themselves. Accordingly, one might agree with Heinrich von Stietencron that "the term 'Hinduism' is a relatively recent one. Not only is the term modern . . . but also the whole concept of the oneness of Hindu religion was introduced by missionaries and scholars from the West."[1] But, even if Hinduism—term and concept—is acknowledged to be a nineteenth-century construction, Hinduism was nevertheless constructed at that time in a dialogue between British colonialists and Western Orientalists, on the one hand, and Indian nationalists and neo-Hindus, on the other. Indian Buddhism differs here in that there was no equivalent dialogue with Indian Buddhists, for there were none to talk to. By the time the word *Buddhism* first found its way into the title of an English-language monograph in 1829, Buddhism already had been dead in India for five centuries.[2]

Unlike Hinduism, therefore, Indian Buddhism was reconstituted in a monologue, scripted by scholars using manuscripts, inscriptions, artifacts, statues, and monuments—remains without a living community of interest. Six principles shaped this monologue. (1) Buddhism is a religion like other religions. (2) Buddhism is pan-Asian in scope. But (3) the sociocultural idiosyncracies found in the national Buddhisms of Japan and China, for instance, or Thailand and Tibet can be cleared away, leaving (4) a residue: Buddhism's transhistorical essence. Indeed, (5) the search for that residue places particular emphasis upon the study of Buddhism in India, the land of its origin, the only place where it would have escaped the taint of cultural and historical accretions. Thus, (6) by mastering authentic Indian Buddhism, a scholar masters Buddhism itself.[3] In this way ancient Indian Buddhism is a modern construct, a construction of modernity. This essay's title—"Why Study Indian Buddhism?"—questions the complexities of a past, wholly enveloped within the present, represented as transcending time. The contemporary scholar of Indian Buddhism would seem to be focused on nice matters of antiquarian curiosity. It is a dead religion. But, as such, it rises from the grave, unruly, straining against disciplinary strategies and intellectual boundaries.

In this essay I will tease out several implications of ancient Indian Buddhism's modernity in three steps. First, I will present scholarly stereotypes of Buddhism and Hinduism. Even more than the word *stereotype,* I prefer a notion of scholarly common sense, loosely borrowing Clifford Geertz's observation that common sense "is what the mind filled with presuppositions . . . concludes."[4] Common sense is that which seems to require the least probing and therefore (of course) requires the most. Buddhism and Hinduism have been common sensically modeled by scholars as two essentially separate socioreligious systems that are almost complete inversions of each other.

Next, I will assess certain ramifications of this categorical system, which relegates Buddhism to the margins of South Asian religiosity. I will explore how this opposition enters into contemporary discourse on the religions of ancient India by referencing a speech given by L. K. Advani, the Bharatiya Janata Party's (BJP) minister for home affairs. Advani's characterizations of Buddhism rely upon a post-Reformation definition of religion which equates the practice of religion with the profession of belief.

In the final section I turn to my research on the history of Buddhism in ancient India. If Buddhism is an ancient Indian cultural form and the category *religion* has a modern provenance, how does one mediate this disjunction? To get at an answer, I explore a single example from the Ajanta caves, the fifth-century C.E. Buddhist monastic complex that has served as the empirical focus for my research. Buddhism at Ajanta was constituted through an engagement with manifold discursive centers. For Ajanta's Buddhists religion was a matter of politics as much as of liberation, as much a matter of instrumental power as of transcendent truth. To comprehend Buddhism in ancient India, one needs a more nuanced notion of religion than that provided by the equation of religion with belief, or else one needs to find a term other than *religion* altogether.

Material Hinduism and Spiritual Buddhism

Let us enter into the imaginal world of contemporary Indology with the paraphrase of a Buddhist text that purports to record a dialogue between Śākyamuni buddha and Kāśyapa, one of his advanced disciples. Śākyamuni is the name of the historical buddha, born circa 488 B.C.E. This dialogue, entitled *Kāśyapaparivarta sūtra* (The Kāśyapa Chapter), was composed some time around the first century C.E., a half-millennium after Śākyamuni's death. *The Kāśyapa Chapter* is highly polemical, exposing deep animosities that divided Buddhist groups of its day. This text's polemic, however, is not apposite to my current discussion. I will return to the polemic in the essay's final section. In this first instance, let me translate two brief passages from *The Kāśyapa Chapter,* leaving aside the Buddhist shibboleths.

> [The buddha said:] "Imagine, Kāśyapa, that the chief queen of the anointed king, a *kṣatriya*, commits adultery with a beggar. Imagine that his son is born from that [union]. What's your opinion, Kāśyapa? Should that boy be called the king's son?"
>
> [Kāśyapa] replied, "Certainly not, blessed lord." . . . On that [same subject] it was said:
>
> Suppose that a king's enticing queen has sex with a beggar.
>
> Her son born from that [union] is not a prince, and will not become king.
>
> "[Now] imagine, Kāśyapa, that the anointed king, a kṣatriya, consorts with a low-caste servant. Imagine that his son is born from that [union]. Kāśyapa, although that boy is born from the womb of a low-caste servant, shouldn't he nevertheless be called the king's son?" . . . On that [same subject] it was said:
>
> Suppose an emperor has sex with a servant, and sires a son.
>
> Though the boy is born of a servant's womb, in the world he is spoken of as the king's son.[5]

Let us now consider. The given data includes a time, approximately the first century C.E., and place, India. From that starting point we see that each boy is destined for a vastly different life, yet the principle determining each boy's fate is the same. In both cases the precise placement of the father within a fixed social hierarchy determines the son's legitimacy and acceptability. The son of a king enters public discourse as a prince; he can become a king, regardless of his mother's lowly status. The son of a beggar has no claim on royal power, however highborn his mother. Although these vignettes are taken from a Buddhist text, when they are presented like this, stripped of overtly Buddhist terminology, we find them to be an odd hybrid. For clearly there is a social logic at work in these two descriptions. But one could read the corpus of Indian Buddhist legal writings and not find an explanation of, or justification for, that social logic. In fact, as I will show, this logic violates presumptive principles of Buddhist law. To understand what is going on here, one must crack books of Hindu law, the *dharmaśāstras*.

The Kāśyapa Chapter, a Buddhist text with a long and important history in India, presents the society of its day as operating according to norms whose explicit articulation can now only be found in the codes of Hindu, *dharmaśāstric,* law. While it is noteworthy that *The Kāśyapa Chapter* presupposes *dharmaśāstric* norms, it is even more interesting that this text appropriates those norms to articulate a sectarian Buddhist polemic. Again, I will defer my discussion of this point until later. If nothing else, these vignettes make clear that a consideration of common sense about Indian Buddhism cannot be separated from the broader consideration of the social hierarchies explained and legitimated in ostensibly Hindu texts.[6] So, let me set *The Kāśyapa Chapter* aside and turn now to scholarly representations of Hindu society. This Indological material provides a necessary foundation for my critical analysis of scholarship on Indian Buddhism. To lay this foundation, I will use Ronald Inden's 1992 work *Imaging India,* a cogent and sophisticated analysis of Indological common sense. Inden himself seeks to unpack the Orientalist and imperialist interests inscribed in Indology's categories. I must choose my battles strategically. So, although I borrow Inden's descriptions, I leave his critiques to the side. Inden's caricatures, in their capacity as stereotypes and points of common sense, provide a stable field within which to address my broader concerns about Buddhism and religion.

In a nutshell Inden draws attention to a fundamental chain of associations mobilizing traditional Indology and determining its discourse. "Caste" is called the "main 'pillar' of Indological constructs."[7] Around caste cluster several other constructs, including the idea of "India," geographically unified as the land of caste, and "Hinduism," as the religion of caste. The word *caste* is of Portuguese origin. The Sanskrit equivalent, *jāti,* literally "birth," says it all: birth alone determines an individual's location within a system of social classifications, graded hierarchically according to purity, prestige, and power. One can critique the naturalization of caste as a totalizing construct; caste certainly does belong to a repertoire of colonial strategies for derationalizing and mechanizing South Asian subjects. Nevertheless, one also cannot deny that *The Kāśyapa Chapter*'s own common sense about parentage and social role relies upon a discourse of *jāti.* *The Kāśyapa Chapter* presupposes the seminal importance of paternal status for fixing a hierarchical social matrix. Thus, this Buddhist sutra seems to lend credence to a common Indological stereotype—that is, that caste is India's essential feature and the irreducible basis for India's uniqueness as a civilization. In

Inden's words, caste is "displaced . . . on to every area of Indian life; it is associated with race and occupation, religion and status, land control, and psychic security, with birth and death, marriage and education."[8]

Caste fills the mind as well, since Indological common sense, which posits caste as Indian civilization's pillar, posits Hinduism as the eternal concomitant of caste. For Indologists, the nexus of caste and Hinduism is a virtually closed system and as a unit defines what is most proper to South Asia. According to Inden, "Historians of religion and Indologists have not only taken their Hinduism to be the essential religion of India; they have viewed it as the exemplification of the mind of India, the mentality that accompanies caste."[9] To show what is at stake here, let me rephrase two of these statements, replacing *caste* with *jāti*'s literal translation, *birth:* Hinduism is the eternal concomitant of birth; Hinduism is the mentality that accompanies birth. Translated this way, it is clear just how potent these claims really are.[10]

Here a deterministic materialism undergirds the caste/Hinduism nexus: social form determines belief system. And, just as births are deployed in a fixed hierarchy, so the religious superstructure, Hinduism, legitimates that hierarchy. That is to say, all Hindus are not created equal. Brahmin priests stand atop the system. The *dharmaśāstras* characterize brahmins as "masters of the universe," "lords over all creatures," and "the eternal embodiment of truth."[11] This wisdom has been received by Indologists as betokening, in the 1919 words of Vincent Smith, that "essentially Hindu" India is "the land of the Brahmans."[12] Nor is this equation a mere relic of the colonial past. Contemporary scholars still equate Hindu orthodoxy with the acceptance of the brahmins' hegemony, though they do not use that precise phraseology. Instead, the rhetorical burden is placed upon a literary genre, the Vedas, the most ancient of Hindu texts. As one recent textbook put it, "The acceptance of Vedic authority is perhaps the sole formal test of orthodoxy in Hinduism."[13] But this is no different than defining Hinduism through the acceptance of the brahmins' preeminence, for the Vedas are brahmin texts par excellence. It is precisely because brahmins "preserve the Veda" that they are acclaimed "masters of the universe."[14] The Vedas are a keystone in this complex edifice. On the one hand, the Vedas describe a fourfold social order and privilege brahmins within that order. On the other hand, acceptance of Vedic literature as sacred and authoritative is the single thing that all proper Hindus are expected to have in common.

At this point we can readily make the transition to Buddhism. For, if scholarly common sense posits acceptance of Vedic authority as the baseline of Hindu orthodoxy, then Śākyamuni, the historical buddha, cannot have been Hindu. One uncontested fact—there are not many—is that Śākyamuni rejected all claims of Vedic authority. Thus, Śākyamuni is heterodox. Moreover, this differential logic defines Śākyamuni as heteroprax. By rejecting Vedic authority, Śākyamuni must, according to the binary logic in play, refuse to participate in the system of birth-based legitimation, which has no ideological justification outside the Vedas. Thus, for instance, one finds the following simile attributed to Śākyamuni: "As great rivers . . . on reaching the great ocean, lose their former names and identities and are reckoned simply as the great ocean, even so, monks, (members of) the four castes . . . having gone forth from home into homelessness . . . lose their former names and clans and are reckoned simply as recluses."[15] Brahmin claims to social and spiritual supremacy based upon their *jāti* are sucked into an eddy of this hydrological imagery and are washed way. In short, insofar as the caste/ Hindu nexus is deemed the essence of South Asian religiosity, Buddhism must be relegated to the status of an internal other.

This differential determination of Buddhism's place within the South Asian religious scene is complemented by positive representations of Buddhism's doctrines and practices. Imagery such as that of the rivers becoming one as they flow into the ocean inspired the leader of the Mahar untouchables, Dr. Babasaheb Ambedkar, to convert to Buddhism in 1956, rejecting Hinduism as a system of institutionalized inequality. But Ambedkar did not turn to Buddhism merely because he believed that it rejected inequalities. More important, he looked upon Buddhism as affirming the essential equality of all beings: all have an equal capacity to realize ultimate truth. This truth—called *Dharma* in Sanskrit—is uniform for all, applicable to all, and accessible to all. Highborn and lowborn, male and female, brahmin and outcaste, all beings are stuck in a realm of suffering, called samsara. Beings are born again and again because they have not realized the highest truth. Beings do not know truth because they are blinded by passions and are blinded by passions because they do not know truth. By controlling passions and realizing truth, one escapes suffering, ends rebirth, gains nirvana.

One's ability to pursue this course has nothing to do with the identity of one's father and everything to do with individual effort. As a well-known verse goes: "Monks, be islands unto yourselves, be a refuge unto yourselves, with no other refuge. Let the Dharma be your island, let the Dharma be your refuge, with no other refuge."[16] One must be self-reliant as an *individual*. Characterizations of Buddhism as a form of religious individualism often portray Śākyamuni himself as an empiricist, as a pragmatist, even as a scientist, guided by practical reason. Thus, Hermann Kulke and Dietmar Rothermund's popular *History of India* charts the development of religiosity in fifth-century B.C.E. India as "a transition from the magic thought of the *Vedas* and the mystical speculations of the *Upaniṣads* to a new type of rationality . . . the rationally enlightened experience" of Śākyamuni buddha.[17] Buddhism, thus stereotyped, is a religion that even Kant could love.

I think it is worth noting a certain discontinuity between the representations of Buddhism and Hinduism. Scholarly common sense on Hinduism has *materialist* assumptions: a social system determines doctrinal legitimations thereof. By contrast, common sense on Buddhism is fundamentally *idealist:* a universal truth, equal for all, locates meaningful agency in the individual; social status is a purely contingent factor. Thus, Richard Gombrich has character-ized "the Buddha's message as a pure soteriology,"[18] signifying in his own words that, "for Buddhists, religion is purely a matter of understanding and practicing the Dharma," the truth.[19] Edward Conze makes this point still more forcefully, using terms that will become more meaningful later in this essay. According to Conze, "There is nothing, or almost nothing, in the Buddhist interpretation of spiritual truth which ties it to any soil or any climate, to any race or tribe."[20] By contrast, Hinduism "is full of tribal taboos,"[21] for Hinduism is fundamentally a matter of a specific culture tied to a specific place; Hinduism's concern for spiri-tual truth is ever only secondary.

Moreover, scholars have displaced this predication of pure Buddhism into representations of the Buddhist social sphere. Their frame is binary: some fol-lowers of buddha devote themselves to "pure soteriology," and some do not. In this view only the former properly deserve to be called "Buddhists." Earlier I noted that, for caste to work as a system, it is necessary to accept the principle that all Hindus are not created equal. By contrast, for Buddhism we find the common sense on social hierarchy echoed in the writings of George Orwell: all Buddhists are equal, but some Buddhists are more equal than others. Here the social division between lay and monastic is determinative, and the "more equal" Buddhists are the monks. Accordingly, Conze proposes that "in its essence and inner core, Buddhism was and is a movement of monastic ascetics,"[22] and that monks "are the only Buddhists in the proper sense of the word."[23] Monks are more equal than other, lay Buddhists because, freed from the concerns of home and family, they alone are able to devote themselves as individuals to pure soteriology purely.

Advani and the BJP

It is now time to move on to a critique of this scholarly characterization of Buddhism as individualist, rationalist, idealist, antisocial, and purely oriented toward nirvana in its essence. This critique stands at the base of my own attempts to reconceive Buddhism's place within the landscape of South Asian religiosity. The most obvious tactic here is to begin by marshaling contradictory evidence from Indian Buddhist history, evidence that shows Buddhists were not individu-alists, rationalists, idealists, antisocial, or purely oriented toward nirvana in their religion. Certainly, I will present such evidence, albeit a little later. Rather than turn immediately to ancient data, I think it crucial to begin with a pragmatic critique. That is to say, before I show how this stereotype is inaccurate as a his-torical reconstruction, I will first explore how it is problematic as a modern con-struction. Remember, I have been discussing common sense—what the mind filled with presuppositions concludes. So, I want to get at the presuppositions around which Indian history has been constructed before offering my own alternatives.

Let me enter into this pragmatic critique with a practical example. On 6 November 1998 the BJP, the political party then running India's central government, sponsored a seminar called "World Unity in the Buddha's Trinity," in Sarnath, the village in which Śākyamuni buddha is said to have given his first religious discourse nearly twenty-five centuries ago. L. K. Advani, the minister for home affairs, second only to the prime minister in power, opened the seminar with a speech. Advani is an ideologue and master of political theater—I know about this conference because Reuters picked up the story. For its part Reuters deemed this little meeting newsworthy because Advani caused an uproar when he said: "The Buddha did not announce any new religion. He was only restating with a new emphasis the ancient ideals of the Indo-Aryan civilisation."[24] Here is a quick and dirty translation: Buddhism is a skewed derivative of Hinduism.

This line from Advani's speech resonates with the binary oppositions I just outlined, which it both appropriates and violates. Advani has been a longtime proponent and theorist of Hindutva, the BJP's regnant ideology. The term *Hindutva* translates literally as "Hinduness." For Advani, Hinduness—what he called in Sarnath, "the ancient ideals of the Indo-Aryan civilisation"—is a given fundamental fact. Thus, for Advani, Buddhism in India has always been encompassed within the Hindu fold. This is not because he holds Hinduism to be necessarily more valid than Buddhism from a spiritual perspective (though, doubtless, he does). Rather, it is because for Advani the Indian subcontinent is an *essentially* Hindu land. For the radical Hindutva all cultural formations on the subcontinent must necessarily be acknowledged as forms of Hinduism, or they must be eliminated. The 1999 murder of Stewart Staines and his two sons in Bhubaneswar—incinerated while sleeping in their jeep; guilty in their murderers' minds of proselytizing Christianity—and other incidents like it are terrifying expressions of this principle. Less physical, less desperate, but no less problematic is a statement Advani made in 1993 to the effect that "Muslims, Christians, and Sikhs living in India should be referred to as 'Mohammadi Hindus,' 'Christian Hindus,' and 'Sikh Hindus.' "[25]

For Advani, Hinduness is far more than a matter of religion, if by *religion* we mean what Gombrich meant when he described Buddhism as "pure soteriology." In the words of another Hindu nationalist author, the religious dimension of Hinduism "is only a derivative, a fraction, a part of Hindutva," of what it means to be Hindu.[26] Indeed, the BJP's official website glosses the term *Hindutva* as "cultural nationalism." This website informs us that "Hindutva is a nationalist, and not a religious or theocratic, concept."[27] By contrast, for the proponents of Hindutva, Buddhism is definitively and solely religious in nature. Another Hindutva publication chides India's Buddhists by claiming that Buddhism and Jainism "never made any contribution to social and political thought as such. We have not inherited any arthashastras (politics and economics) or dharmashastras (social laws) from them." With a dismissive sweep of the hand, this author continues: "All we have from them are various moksha-shastras pertaining to the supreme salvation of the individual soul."[28]

What is surprising and ultimately troubling is that this phrase *the supreme salvation of the individual soul* sounds a great deal like Gombrich's phrase *pure soteriology.* It seems that the proponents of Hindutva have learned their lessons well from traditional Buddhology. They have learned that Buddhism is individualist, rationalist, idealist, antisocial, and purely oriented toward nirvana in its essence. Even criticisms levied against Advani by his audience in Sarnath only serve to confirm the Hindutva position. The director of a Buddhist university reacted to Advani by saying, "He is making a political statement that is 100 percent wrong, I may call it 101 percent wrong." By castigating Advani's words as "political," this scholar reserves the highroad of the nonpolitical, and nonsocial, for Buddhists' own self-representations. A second member of the audience, a teacher of Buddhist meditation, disputed Advani's specific association of Buddhism with Indo-Aryan civilization by insisting that "the original teachings of the Buddha are totally universal and nonsectarian." But this criticism recapitulates the very same common sense that the Hindutva plays upon. Again to cite Gombrich, "Buddhism was attached neither to community nor to locality, neither to shrine nor to hearth, but resided in the hearts of its adherents."[29] The proponents of Hindutva turn this logic on its head. If Buddhism really is just a matter of religious truth, then because the buddha's beating heart was located in India, and because all discourses on truth articulated within India are definitively Hindu, Buddhism is just one path to truth among Hinduism's many paths to truth.

Here, then, we reach the crux of the matter. These two groups agree over where to locate the essence of Buddhism. And at the heart of that agreement there is a shared understanding of the term *religion.* For both, Buddhism is a religion in the contemporary sense of this word, where *religion* is interchangeable with other terms, such as *faith* and *belief.* It is a matter of the heart. This, of course, is not all that surprising, since in modern usage "*belief* is the defining characteristic of religion,"[30] not ritual practice, not social organization or political advocacy. Here I concur with claims that Talal Asad makes in his *Genealogies of Religion,* echoed in a more recent interview, in which he says: "Belief has now become a purely inner, private state of mind, a particular state of mind detached from everyday practices. But, although it is in this sense 'internal,' belief has also become the object of systematic discourse, such that the system of statements about belief is now held to constitute the essence of 'religion.' "[31]

The proponents of Hindutva refuse to call Hinduism a religion precisely because they want to emphasize that Hinduism is more than mere internalized beliefs. It is social, political, economic, and familial in nature. Only thus can India the secular state become interchangeable with India the Hindu homeland. Similarly, as I noted earlier, we find scholarship on Buddhism stating that political, economic, and familial considerations are not essential to Buddhism. They are "mere tribal taboos," in Conze's words. Insofar as these social formations affect the religion, they come from outside Buddhism proper; their importance can be dismissed through a rhetoric of contagion and influence. It would seem that when the scholars say that "for Buddhists, religion is purely a matter of understanding and practicing religious truths," they may be taking their own presuppositions as conclusions and articulating a tautology as a truth.

As a scholar whose research focuses upon Buddhism in ancient India, I find this complex of ideas, beginning with the fundamental equation between religion and belief, vexing and confused. First, at a broad level it threatens to make the study of religion irrelevant. If religion is held really to be a matter of beliefs and essences—in a word, of the sacred—then the scholar of religion has little of value to contribute to the broader scholarly conversation on profane matters of politics, economics, and families.

More problematic, if religious action is "the execution of a 'script' of doctrines, beliefs, and traditions,"[32] then the historian of religion takes on the mantle of a conservator of religious normativity and a judge of religious action. He looks down from on high: do these religious actors obey their divine script, or are they guilty of transgressive improvisation? Thus, Ashis Nandy suggests that religion can be "misused"[33]—for instance, when a secular grab for power is cloaked strategically in religious garb. The BJP comes to mind, of course. (In fact, Nandy calls the BJP one of "the most secular parties in India," because he sees its "use" of religion as wholly instrumental.) But George W. Bush comes to mind as well. Asked to name his favorite "political philosopher or thinker" while campaigning for the Republican nomination in late 1999, Bush named Jesus Christ, saying that Jesus was his choice, "because he changed my heart." Was Bush misusing religion when he gave this answer? Or was Bush, by giving an answer with his heart when asked for an answer with his head, letting us in on an open secret: a man running for president of the United States cannot afford to know the difference between a political philosopher and a religious teacher? Did Henry Hyde, chair of the House Judiciary Committee during the Clinton impeachment debacle, misuse religion when, in answer to criticism over his unpopular course of action, he quipped, "If Jesus Christ had taken a poll, he never would have preached the Gospel"? Although I would say that there is something "religious" here, I certainly do not mean to imply that Hyde has privileged access to a sacred sphere. Rather, there is some factor in Hyde's expression of his convictions which violates the ideally uniform rationality of the secular sphere, which interrupts it, resists it, transcends it, and yet is fully at home within it. (Writing these words, I recognize that there is something deeply troubling about any suggestion that George W. Bush and Henry Hyde could be looked upon as figures of resistance. But, for me to be able to articulate why this is so troubling, I must be willing to investigate why it even seems possible. And I cannot do that until

I forgo the reduction of religion to belief, and belief to mere ideology or false consciousness.)

Here is the proper province for religious studies: this point of contact between transcendence perceived and worldliness perceived; this rupture, in which worldly order opens onto cosmic order. We cannot grasp Henry Hyde's politics without getting at this religious element. And we cannot grasp George W. Bush's religion if our focus rests solely upon the deep core and kernel of his beliefs, if religion is held to be a matter of essences.

Religion at Ajanta

This then brings me to my own historical work on Buddhism in ancient India. For in that work I have sought to retheorize Buddhism as a religion by looking beyond enlightenment to the activities of Buddhists as worldly/religious performances. Rather than treating religious identity as the personal expression of translocal, transhistorical doctrinal truths, I attempt to explore how mundane activities create culture, authority, and transcendence. Naturally, such performances invoke and play off an inherited corpus of terms, values, and rituals. But the point is, the significance of religious performance cannot be reduced to that corpus of terms, values, and rituals. Religious identity is constructed in a dynamic process that includes so-called religious belief but which also includes familial micropolitics, storms, crops, babies, and kings as well as sprites and demons seemingly without number. In this way religion percolates upwards from all realms of human existence.

Let me now turn to my research. In particular, I want to focus upon one detail from my study of the Ajanta caves, a set of Buddhist caves—monasteries and shrines—carved into a sheer 250-foot-high wall of rock about two hundred miles east of Bombay. Ajanta is a rich source for archaeological evidence, including epigraphs, architectural programs, paintings, and sculptures. But Ajanta's true wealth does not lie in its material artifacts alone. Rather, this site is unparalleled as a source for Indian Buddhist social history because we can contextualize its materials with remarkable precision. Indeed, one of the most intractable problems confronting every scholar of Indian Buddhism is the lack of adequate sources through which to reconstruct the religious lives of Buddhists as members of an actual, historical community. I cannot overemphasize how little good, localizable evidence exists for ancient India. Ajanta is an exception. One of the reasons for Ajanta's singularity is that the majority of the site's artifacts can be dated with close precision to between approximately 460 and 480 C.E., the major patrons from this century all owing allegiance to the court of a single king, the Vākāṭaka overlord Hariṣeṇa. This grand project was closely associated with Hariṣeṇa's reign. It was begun soon after Hariṣeṇa's ascension, a public display of the Vākāṭakas' power, wealth, and piety (the monasteries also likely served as military garrisons and way stations for merchants and pilgrims). But Hariṣeṇa's family fell from power before the site was finished. Ajanta's caves were swiftly abandoned by artisans and monks alike, resulting in their singular state of preservation.

Ajanta is of interest not because it represents a singularly authentic form of Buddhism but because its particularly rich data allows for the writing of a micro-history, with all the specificity and antinormativity that term can evoke. Micro-studies and micro-histories provide localized and richly contextual representations of historical moments, revealing the on-the-ground complexities of religion as lived by real people. They furnish evidence for what Eduardo Grendi has called "normal exceptions."[34] That is to say, micro-histories provide a check against the ideological representations of elite texts; they support the investigation of hegemonic structures; they draw the scholar's attention to the possibility of generalized alternatives to accepted master narratives. So, it is not my claim that ancient India never was graced by the feet of individual Buddhists who dedicated their bodies and minds to realizing the injunction "Be islands unto yourselves, be a refuge unto yourselves, with no other refuge," in accord with nomological texts. Rather, my aim is to destabilize claims that such people were more properly "buddhist" than other Buddhists. Historians of religion have no business placing adjectives such as *essential* or *authentic* or *real* or *proper* or *genuine* in front of the noun *Buddhist.* Accordingly, I am also not making a counterclaim that Ajanta's Buddhism should somehow be viewed as normative or essential. Ajanta is a "normal exception." In India Buddhism possessed myriad strands, none of which possesses an intrinsic claim to the historian's attention. Buddhism as it was practiced at Ajanta represents one of those strands.

I chose to study Ajanta in part in order to discover which categories, precepts, images, and stories were important to Indian Buddhists, outside the academy as it were. One of the facts I discovered was that this Vākāṭaka monastic site was peopled with self-described Śākyabhikṣus. This epithet *Śākyabhikṣu* has two components: *Śākya* is the name of the buddha's family (*Śākyamuni* is a "sage of the Śākya clan"), and *bhikṣu* is Sanskrit for "monk." *Śākyabhikṣu* is a title, not a proper name. It describes a formal religious identity, but, unfortunately, there are no independent literary records to tell us which doctrines were held by Ajanta's Śākyabhikṣus or where they fit within the broadloom of Indian Buddhist institutions. Nevertheless, a thick, site-specific analysis of Ajanta's Śākyabhikṣus suggests that this epithet encapsulates a complex strategy for manufacturing a Buddhist identity that is also a local Vākāṭaka identity. The epithet patently emphasizes a monk's identification with the family of Śākyamuni buddha, the Śākya family. This is not to say that Ajanta's Śākyabhikṣus were Śākyamuni buddha's blood descendants. We have no evidence of that. Rather, this epithet brings together an index of spiritual status with a declaration of familial affiliation. It is a representation of religious kinship articulated in the language of blood kinship. When a monk at Ajanta called himself a Śākyabhikṣu, he was telling the world, in effect, that it should know him to belong to a superior spiritual lineage because he could claim affiliation with a superior blood lineage.

While one level of Buddhist doctrine proposes that the successful pursuit of Dharma has nothing to do with the identity of one's father and everything to do with individual effort, at Ajanta, it would seem, individual effort was best expended toward having the correct father.

For a Śākyabhikṣu at Ajanta the spiritual was not to be disentangled from the social as determined by family and lineage; social worth was always already at stake in claims of spiritual supremacy. And social worth here was gauged by how well a Buddhist fulfilled duties and responsibilities imposed by birth. A monk who publicly represented himself as a Śākya, in other words, was signaling that he would willingly accept the concrete duties associated with membership in the Śākya family. The Śākyas were an ancient warrior clan, with a proud noble history. As the family's head, Śākyamuni was imagined regally, as the king of Dharma, the *Dharmarāja;* monks who were his kinfolk were represented suitably through martial imagery as well, as the Dharmarāja's army. These characterizations were not mere metaphors, or the reduction of transcendental realities to worldly tropes. At Ajanta, Śākyabhikṣus acted as warriors—not by taking up arms (thus "peacekeepers" might be the better characterization) but, rather, by forming an alliance with the Vākāṭaka lord, Hariṣeṇa. Through their presence and through their rituals Ajanta's Śākyabhikṣus protected a strategic mountain pass from enemies, both human and inhuman. They played a vital role in the Vākāṭaka's political order, a role directly imbricated with their adopted family name. Status as a Śākyabhikṣu was as much a political identity as it was a religious identity. As a political identity, it did not violate local Buddhist principles; it expressed them.

There is no way to understand Ajanta's Śākyabhikṣus as Buddhists unless one also concretely approaches Ajanta's Śākyabhikṣus as Vākāṭaka subjects. And there is no way to approach them as Vākāṭaka subjects as long as one equates religion with belief or considers practice to be the execution of a script of mystical doctrines and antisocial traditions. This, finally, leads us back to the two vignettes from the Buddhist text *The Kāśyapa Chapter.* That text asks us to imagine a queen and a king, both of whom conceive sons with lowborn partners. In the case of the queen the resulting issue is an outcaste pariah. In the case of the king, his liaison with a servant produces a prince in line for the throne. Earlier, when I presented these vignettes, I left out the explicitly Buddhist content. Let us now see how well these two sons fit into the common sense on Buddhism. Think of this as a freeze-dried meal, here to be reconstituted with the boiling water of religious polemic.

> Suppose that a king's enticing queen has sex with a beggar.
> Her son born from that [union] is not a prince, and will not become king.

Similarly, disciples [*śrāvaka*], free of passion, should never be legiti-
mated as my sons.
For, [*śrāvakas*] focus on their own welfare,
[While] the buddha's sons work to benefit others as well as themselves.

Suppose an emperor has sex with a servant and sires a son.
Though the [boy] is born of a servant's womb, in the world he is spo-
ken of as the king's son.
Similarly a bodhisattva, who has just set out toward buddhahood, is
powerless.
[But] because of his generosity and clever ploys to discipline beings
who wander through the three realms,
He is spoken of as the buddha's son. He is a holy person.[35]

In the full telling of *The Kāśyapa Chapter* the outcaste son of the adulterous
queen is equated with what Buddhists call a *śrāvaka*, literally an auditor or disciple. The significance of this term is highly contested within Buddhist traditions—that, after all, is the point of polemic. But within *The Kāśyapa Chapter*'s
lexicon, a *śrāvaka* is individualist, antisocial, and purely oriented toward his own
nirvana. And that's bad. In other words, *The Kāśyapa Chapter* describes an ille-
gitimate bastard, a Buddhist failure, a follower of buddha who does not deserve
the name "son of buddha," by deploying the same set of predicates that scholars have commonly used to stereotype normative, good Buddhism.

The values, practices, and aspirations associated with the king's princely
son, by contrast, come very close to those articulated and participated in by
Ajanta's Śākyabhikṣus. *The Kāśyapa Chapter,* however, does not use the particular
term *Śākyabhikṣu*. Rather, this text calls the king's son a bodhisattva, literally
someone who is *sakta,* attached, to *bodhi,* awakening. The term *bodhisattva* is
used for someone who vows to become a buddha and who practices rituals of
generosity, worship, and meditation toward that end. *The Kāśyapa Chapter* asserts that *śrāvakas* "focus on their own welfare, [while bodhisattvas,] the buddha's
sons, work to benefit others as well as themselves." Similarly, another text,
Gaṇḍavyuha sutra (The Amazing Revelation), claims that bodhisattvas, no matter
how callow, no matter how inexperienced, are always superior to *śrāvakas,* no
matter how advanced, no matter how wise.[36] Like *The Kāśyapa Chapter,* like
the epithet *Śākyabhikṣu,* this latter text invokes images of kinship. According to
The Amazing Revelation, bodhisattvas surpass *śrāvakas* because bodhisattvas are
the buddha's sons. In fact, *The Amazing Revelation* is even more explicit. A
bodhisattva is a bodhisattva because he has been born into the buddha's family;
a bodhisattva is spiritually superior to the *śrāvaka* because of his superior *jāti,*
his birth.

Indological common sense holds that Hinduism is the concomitant of *jāti*
in India; Hinduism is the mentality that accompanies birth in India. Yet here *The
Kāśyapa Chapter* and *The Amazing Revelation*—texts attributed by some Bud-

dhists to the buddha himself—both endorse hierarchical kinship structures. Both texts play upon the discourse of royal genealogy, familial prerogative, and social ascendancy in order to represent bodhisattvas' superiority over *śrāvakas*. Both texts emphasize the bodhisattva as a beneficial social figure. Both texts find confirmation of the bodhisattva's superiority within the common fund of Indian social values—social values whose explanation requires a scholar to read Hindu law books. Thus, I have argued in a recent article that, at Ajanta, the epithet *Śākyabhikṣu* is a complex synonym for *bodhisattva*.[37] This epithet is a critical datum for reconstructing Indian Buddhism's social history because it shows that, when Indian bodhisattvas sought to present themselves publicly as bodhisattvas, they articulated their status as such, not by taking recourse to an abstract language of the interior heart but by infusing characteristically Buddhist terms with characteristically Indian meanings.

Conclusion

In conclusion I wish to return to the question "Why study Indian Buddhism?" Earlier I demonstrated how scholarly common sense has constructed Buddhism and Hinduism as rough, binary opposites. I then offered a practical example for how this opposition enters into contemporary discourse on the religions of ancient India, by reference to a speech that L. K. Advani gave in Sarnath. As a figment of the Hindutva imagination, Buddhism is an Indian religion that focuses exclusively on absolute truths and thus is contained within the broader sociocultural ambit of Hinduness. Advani's audience in Sarnath disputed his characterization of history. But the criticisms levied by this audience merely recapitulate the same common sense that the Hindutva plays upon: Buddhism is totally universal; it is not a matter of politics or sectarian institutions but of the heart. I then came to the fulcrum of my argument—namely, that such stereotypes of Buddhism presuppose a modern discourse in which systematic statements about belief are held to constitute the essence of religion. The obvious question, therefore, is whether religion thus constituted is an adequate category through which to reconstruct ancient Indian Buddhism. I suggested that it is not, referring to my own work on the Śākyabhikṣus at Ajanta. To summarize: stereotypes of Indian Buddhism represent Dharma as an abstract truth equally accessible to all, regardless of parentage. But evidence from Ajanta demonstrates that some fifth-century Buddhist monks were very concerned to let people know the identity of their "father." Ajanta's Śākyabhikṣus perceived their association with the Śākya family as giving them a privileged relationship to Dharma at the same time that it gave them specific social obligations. Members of Ajanta's community conceived of their identities as Buddhists in filial terms and performed their roles as sons in a complex manner that relied as much upon Hindu as on Buddhist norms. Ajanta's data allows the historian of religion to complicate the simplistic claim that the pursuit of supermundane liberation was, and is, singularly essential to Buddhism. But Ajanta is a normal exception; the Buddhism found there should also not be regarded as essential or normative.

An interesting enough point, perhaps, but why study Indian Buddhism? In a word, borrowed from Jacob Neusner, "modulation." The study of ancient Indian Buddhism provides a platform through which to modulate the category "religion," to alter it, expand it, problematize it, historicize it. Buddhism, especially Indian Buddhism, was practically unknown before the nineteenth century. As a figure in the scholarly imagination, Buddhism has never not been gazed upon by eyes that also looked upon religion in the guise of belief. There are no Indian Buddhists claiming to preserve an unbroken tradition from Śākyamuni's own time; scholars have met little or no native resistance as they have reconstructed the details of Indian Buddhism in their own image, upon a framework of religion as belief. And so Buddhism has become a religion par excellence. The study of religion is less than central to the modern academy, in part because we lack an adequate vocabulary through which to articulate religion's worldliness and therefore to represent it as a vital, integral factor in the secular, profane sphere. By recovering the history of Buddhist practice, we might develop a conceptual vocabulary through which to represent religion as a mundane phenomenon, without essentializing it or reducing it.

We also lack a vocabulary adequate enough to articulate the contemporary world's religiosity. Gauri Viswanathan has spoken of religious belief as modernity's "estranged self."[38] Insofar as Buddhism is construed as pure religion or pure soteriology, Buddhism becomes a receptacle for everything not modern. Buddhism becomes a natural refuge for those moderns who find themselves estranged; those moderns who, alienated from their own time, seek a truth beyond time. In this way the study of ancient Indian Buddhism can become a field within which to explore constructions of modernity. How do scholars and religious seekers alike work to bridge the gap between ancient India, suffused with religion, and the modern secular world? How do they appropriate ancient Buddhism and through that gesture serve the construction of modernity? How does this appropriation simultaneously expose and conceal modernity's own religiosity, its estranged self? Indeed, by addressing such questions, the scholar of Indian Buddhism can add his voice to all those that would sully, smear, confound, and disrupt all pretensions to purity. Whether it is sacred purity or secular purity, the leviathan of pure Hindutva or the essenceless essence of pure Buddhism: it is purity that is the danger.

Notes

1. Heinrich von Stietencron, "Religious Configurations of Pre-Muslim India and the Modern Concept of Hinduism," in *Representing Hinduism: The Construction of Religious Traditions and National Identity,* ed. Vasudha Dalmia and Heinrich von Stietencron (New Delhi, India: Sage Publications, 1995), 51.
2. In *The British Discovery of Buddhism* (Cambridge, U.K.: Cambridge University Press,

1988) Philip Almond claims that "the first book in English to include the world 'Buddhism' in its title" was Edward Upham's *The History and Doctrine of Buddhism* (London: R. Ackermann, 1829). See Almond's work for an extended discussion of the early history of Buddhism as a figment of the modern imagination.

3. This chain of associations is inspired by the argument in Donald S. Lopez, ed., *Curators of the Buddha: The Study of Buddhism under Colonialism* (Chicago: University of Chicago Press, 1995), 7–8.

4. Clifford Geertz, "Common Sense as a Cultural System," *Antioch Review* 33 (1975): 16–17.

5. Baron A. von Staël-Holstein, ed., *The Kāśyapa parivarta: A Mahāyānasūtra of the Ratnakūṭa Class* (Shanghai: Commercial Press, 1926), 116–118.

6. I have rushed through this point. To find cogent arguments for why Buddhism cannot be considered apart from a brahmanical milieu, see Paul Mus, *Barabudur: Sketch of a History of Buddhism Based on Archaeological Criticism of the Texts* (New Delhi, India: Sterling Publishers, 1998); and Peter Masefield, *Divine Revelation in Pali Buddhism* (Colombo: Sri Lanka Institute of Traditional Studies, 1986).

7. Ronald B. Inden, *Imagining India* (Cambridge, Mass.: Basil Blackwell, 1992), 4.

8. Inden, *Imagining India,* 83.

9. Inden, *Imagining India,* 4.

10. Kancha Ilaiah confirms the on-the-ground reality of this Indological equation at the same time that he puts an ironic twist on it, in his book *Why I Am Not a Hindu: A Sudra Critique of Hindutva Philosophy, Culture, and Political Economy* (Calcutta, India: Samya, 1996). Ilaiah identifies the all-enveloping nature of caste identity as the reason for his *not* being a Hindu: "I was not born a Hindu for the simple reason that my parents did not know that they were Hindus. . . . My parents had only one identity and that was their caste" (1).

11. *Manusmṛti,* vv. 1.93, 1.99, 1.98. My translations are based upon the electronic edition: Jost Gippert, "TITUS Texts: Manu Smrti," 1 June 2000 <http://titus.uni-frankfurt.de/texte/etcs/ind/aind/ved/postved/dhs/manu/manu.htm> (19 May 2001).

12. Cited in Inden, *Imagining India,* 86.

13. Arvind Sharma, *Our Religions* (San Francisco: HarperSanFrancisco, 1995), 5.

14. *Manusmṛti,* v. 1.93.

15. I. B. Horner, trans., *The Book of Discipline,* vol. 5: *Cullavagga* (Oxford, U.K.: Pali Text Society, 1988), 334.

16. Maurice Walshe, trans., *The Long Discourses of the Buddha: A Translation of the Dīgha Nikāya* (Boston: Wisdom Publications, 1995), 395.

17. Hermann Kulke and Dietmar Rothermund, *A History of India* (London: Croom Helm, · 1986), 54.

18. Richard Gombrich, *Theravāda Buddhism: A Social History from Ancient Benares to Modern Colombo* (London: Routledge and Kegan Paul, 1988), 29.

19. Gombrich, *Theravāda Buddhism,* 24.

20. Edward Conze, *Buddhism: Its Essence and Development* (New York: Harper and Row, 1975), 76–77.

21. Conze, *Buddhism,* 77.

22. Conze, *Buddhism,* 70.

23. Conze, *Buddhism,* 53.

24. In November 1998 I found a report on Advani's speech from the Reuters News Service

on the Internet at <http://www.infobeat.com/stories/cgi/story.cgi?id=2556965151-bd6>. Unfortunately, this URL has become inactive. Advani's remarks can now be found in Praful Bidwai, "Hindutva's Fallacies and Fantasies," *Frontline,* 21 November 1998, <http://www.frontlineonline.com/fl1524/15241040.htm> (19 May 2001). In making this claim, Advani was borrowing the words of India's past president Sarvepalli Radhakrishnan, who wrote: "The Buddha did not feel that he was announcing a new religion. He was born, grew up, and died a Hindu. He was restating with a new emphasis the ancient ideals of the Indo-Aryan civilization" ("Foreword," in *2500 Years of Buddhism,* ed. P. V. Bapat [Delhi: Publications Division, Ministry of Information and Broadcasting, Government of India, 1971], ix).

25. "Identify with Hindutva: Advani," *Times of India,* 30 January 1993.

26. V. D. Savarkar, *Hindutva* (Poona City, India: S. R. Date, 1942), 3.

27. "BJP Philosophy," <http://www.bjp.org/philo.htm> (21 May 2001). To reach this quote, click on the icon for "Hindutva."

28. *Organiser,* 10 June 1963. Cited in Partha Banerjee, *In the Belly of the Beast: The Hindu Supremacist RSS and BJP of India, an Insider's Story* (Delhi, India: Ajanta Press, 1998), 140.

29. Gombrich, *Theravāda Buddhism,* 77.

30. Jonathan Z. Smith, "Religion, Religions, Religious," in *Critical Terms for Religious Studies,* ed. Mark C. Taylor (Chicago: University of Chicago Press, 1998), 271.

31. Talal Asad, "Interview: Modern Power and the Reconfiguration of Religious Traditions," *Stanford Electronic Humanities Review* 5, 27 February 1996, <http://www.stanford.edu/group/SHR/5–1/text/asad.html> (19 May 2001).

32. Catherine Bell, "Performance," in *Critical Terms for Religious Studies,* ed. Mark C. Taylor (Chicago: University of Chicago Press, 1998), 207.

33. Ashis Nandy, "The Twilight of Certitudes: Secularism, Hindu Nationalism, and Other Masks of Deculturation," *Alternatives* 22 (1997): 159.

34. Eduardo Grendi is cited in Edward Muir, "Introduction: Observing Trifles," in *Micro History and the Lost Peoples of Europe,* ed. Edward Muir and Guido Ruggiero (Baltimore: Johns Hopkins University Press, 1991), xiv.

35. Von Staël-Holstein, *The Kāśyapa parivarta,* 116–118.

36. "It is like this: a newborn prince surpasses all senior ministers at the pinnacle [of their careers] through the power of [his] birth into the [royal] family. Similarly, a novice bodhisattva, who has just conceived the aspiration for awakening, is reborn into the family of the tathāgata, the Dharma king. Through the power [of his] aspiration for awakening and great compassion, this [bodhisattva] surpasses advanced śrāvakas who have followed the religious life for a long time" (Daisetz Teitaro Suzuki and Hokei Idzumi, eds., *The Gaṇḍavyūha Sūtra* [Kyoto: Sanskrit Buddhist Texts Publishing Society, 1936], 506).

37. Richard S. Cohen, "Kinsmen of the Son: Śākyabhikṣus and the Institutionalization of the Bodhisattva Ideal," *History of Religions* 40 (August 2000): 1–31.

38. Gauri Viswanathan, *Outside the Fold: Conversion, Modernity, and Belief* (Princeton, N.J.: Princeton University Press, 1998), xiv.

CHAPTER 3

Gambling with God

RETHINKING RELIGION IN COLONIAL CENTRAL KENYA

DEREK R. PETERSON

One Sunday evening in 1909, the Presbyterian missionary Arthur Barlow conducted a service for Gikuyu villagers near the Tumutumu mission station in northern central Kenya. The service went as follows: "Mr. Barlow began the service by making the people repeat the words to the hymn 'Stand up, Stand up for Jesus.' This caused great amusement among the people, and especially among the girls. The idea of their repeating words was wholly new to them, and at first they looked upon it as a great joke. . . . When they were asked to shut their eyes in order to join in prayer, they again found it difficult to restrain themselves, the closing of their eyes being so novel a proceeding."[1]

People around Tumutumu were rarely interested in sermons. Many dozed off during the evening services held in the homesteads surrounding the mission.[2] Others ran and hid when missionaries appeared. When they did listen, most were indifferent to the message that missionaries sought to convey. Barlow reported in 1908 that eight young men had asked him why he sang hymns so frequently. He replied, "Because there is joy in my heart when I think of God's goodness." When the young men convulsed with laughter during prayers, they explained that it was because of the joy in their hearts.[3] A slide show depicting the Crucifixion of Christ in 1914 was nearly ruined when villagers invaded the church and laughed uproariously at the pictures.[4] Missionaries lectured them sternly about how their sins had killed Christ, but privately they lamented that the Gospel seemed like a "kind of diversion, and not a matter needing serious attention" to most of their listeners.[5]

What did this hilarity mean? Missionaries thought it was caused by the strangeness of the new Christian words and ideas. But there was something more than naive incomprehension in hearers' laughter. At stake in this hilarity was the possibility of meaningful religious dialogue. Missionaries hoped to draw their listeners into a serious, purposeful dialogue comparing the propositions of African and Christian religion. They sought to make converts. But, instead of engaging in the religious debate that missionaries desired, early hearers laughed. In their refusal to offer an antithesis—a traditional religion—to answer the claims of missionary Christianity, early Gikuyu hearers disrupted the religious dialectic on which missionary evangelism was founded.

It is commonplace to think of African colonial history as a confrontation between European modernity and African tradition. This approach is reproduced in comparative studies of Christianity and African Traditional Religion (ATR). John Mbiti's *African Religions and Philosophies* pioneered the scholarly study of African religions in 1969.[6] Mbiti argued that African religions all over the continent share with "world religions" certain core concepts: among them, an idea of God, formulas for worship and sacrifice, veneration for spiritual beings, an account of creation, and a concept of the hereafter. Later historians accepted this basic account of African religion. Many were pointedly critical of the missionaries for their failure to be sufficiently liberal, for the cultural chauvinism that prevented them from fully appreciating the principles of African religion. But with Mbiti, they argued that religion—conceived as a system of rituals and beliefs oriented toward the sacred—was as intrinsic to Africa as to Europe.[7]

This essay looks for new ways to explore Africa's history of religion. Instead of examining colonial evangelism as a dialectical contest between two fully formed systems of religion, I treat ATR and Christianity in Kenya as conjoined aspects of historicity. Following Talal Asad, I am interested in how it became possible to think of African social practices as "religious" in the sense described by Mbiti and others. Asad traces how religion shifted from a knowledge-producing, creative way of being in the world to an otherworldly, passive repository of belief.[8] Searching for common denominators basic to all human cultures in an era of colonial expansion, Enlightenment intellectuals invented the notion of "Natural Religion." This universal definition, Asad shows, distinguished religion from the domain of politics, economics, and social relations: religion was supposed to be an otherworldly belief system, a contract agreed upon by God and believer. This disembodied, propositional definition of religion was the template that allowed European intellectuals to make sense of the ideas of colonized subjects. By reducing difference to sameness, by disembodying subjects' ideas and practices, comparative religion functioned as a strategy of intellectual and political control.[9]

This essay will illuminate how the notion of religion was crafted and contested in the earliest years of evangelical labor in colonial Gikuyuland. Protestant evangelism among Gikuyu people, I argue, played out not as a dialectic between two counterpoised religions but as a struggle precisely over modern religion. Missionaries were practitioners of comparative religion; they hoped to induct their Gikuyu listeners into an abstract conversation about contending dogmas and beliefs. To elicit these conversations, they asked inquirers to speak as subjects, as holders of certain beliefs about God. What came to be called traditional religion began as a Christian evangelistic strategy, a means by which missionaries roped Gikuyu into conversations about the divine.

But the first Gikuyu listeners refused to be drawn into conversation about contending beliefs and propositions. Their political thought did not make strong divisions between subjects and objects; the world was too fluid, too dangerous, to be thought of in such dualistic terms. Pragmatic clearers of the forest that had carpeted central Kenya in the nineteenth century, Gikuyu had long experimented with a variety of physical techniques to guard human civilization from danger. Missionaries' medicine, writing, and material culture became for them an experimental, embodied grammar with which to diagnose the politics of colonialism. Gikuyu did not engage with missionaries as spokesmen of a propositional religion but as gamblers, speculating about political and cultural change using missionary medicine, clothing, and writing.

A history of "religion" in colonial Gikuyuland is thus a history of struggle over the terms on which humans engaged with and lived in the world—a struggle, that is, over the hierarchies of truth created by colonial power.

Gikuyu Gambles

This section briefly examines two practices, *tahikio* and *magongona,* to sketch out how nineteenth-century Gikuyu engaged with the world. They learned their most important political and moral lessons from their history of forest clearing. Gikuyu knew that human civilization needed protection against an encroaching wilderness. At the bottom of Gikuyu social thought were oppositions between civilization and the wild. The forest was "hot," wild, and uncontrollable. Dying men and women were taken from their homes and left in the forest by their relatives, who feared that death would extend its reach on the living. Certain types of plants connoted heat and danger. The *mugaa* tree, for instance, was thorny and useless as firewood. It was used in dangerous oaths that called down death on the partaker.[10] Homesteads, in contrast, were "cool," fertile realms of civilization and reproduction. They were protected with thick fences walling out the wild and ensuring the family's prosperity. The verb *gita* linked domestic order to wealth: it connoted both "to grow too thick to be seen through (as in a hedge)" and "to flourish, prosper."[11] The wealthy constantly swept their homesteads, carefully keeping dangerous leaves and dirt away from children. Wealthy families planted sweet-smelling *mukenia* trees in their courtyards, flowering shrubs that had important medicinal uses. Senior elders carried staffs of flowers.[12] Human fertility was an achievement, accomplished through the hard work of clearing the forest and protecting children from danger.

Thahu, ritual pollution, was the most immediate skirmish in the continual battle between civilization and the wilderness. Menstruating women visited pollution on their households when they handled sugarcane or cooked food. Eaters of wild animals were polluted; wild meat was dangerously uncivil.[13] Thahu was not so much a condition as an imbalance, a juxtaposition of wild, dangerous things with human life. Gikuyu afflicted with thahu looked to *ago*, wise men, to purge them of the substances that polluted them. This process was called *tahikio*, "vomiting."[14] Wise men induced this restorative vomiting by holding the hoof of a goat up the lips of the victim, enjoining him or her to vomit out the thahu. The wise man then brushed the sufferer with the leaves of the sweet mukenia tree, dipped in a collection of powders. *Ngondu*, one of the powders wise men used in this process, was derived from the stomach contents of the tree hyrax, sugarcane, sweet potatoes, the stomach contents of a ram, and fig tree leaves.[15] Each of these substances was in some way "cool"—the ram, for instance, ate only the soft leaves of non-thorny plants. The contents of its stomach, which distilled the cooling leaves, were useful in cleansing sufferers of heated contaminants.

Missionaries and anthropologists called tahikio "magic" and dismissed ngondu as a "potion," an accessory to the "spells" that wise men levied on their "patients." It is important to recognize precisely how this characterization misconstrued Gikuyu healing practice. The leaves and powders that wise men used to restore bodily health and coolness were not props in a play scripted by cunning magicians. The cooling feel of digested leaves and the sweet smell of flowering bushes acted in real ways to dispel dangerous heat with sociable coolness. Leaves and powders directly engaged sufferers with desirable natural qualities. The values of these substances are not always clear to historians. We do not know precisely how ngondu worked to restore health in sufferers. Some plants, like the sweet mukenia shrub, were used in healing in part because their names evoked positive conditions—*mukenia* comes from the verb -*kena*, "to be happy." Other substances were taken from plants that embodied admirable qualities. A deep-rooted and productive yam plant, for instance, was often used to heal infertile women. These substances were never simply symbols, standing in a fixed relationship to the heat of thahu. They were unstable, unpredictable, probably dangerous substances whose effects were not mechanically determined.

Tahikio was an experimental, metonymic means of addressing bodily pollution, part of a larger balancing act by which Gikuyu protected human life from the dangers of the wilderness. *Magongona*, the second practice I mentioned earlier, similarly guarded human civilization from danger. Magongona were elders' effort to mark off spaces for human habitation from the uncontrollable dead. Gikuyu afterlife was a local problem. All ancestors were chronically unpredictable, sometimes causing sickness or dementia among relatives who ignored them.[16] When faced with an inexplicable disease in their family or when worried over the failure of their crops to bear fruit, elders slaughtered a specially fattened ram at a fragrant tree located on clan land.[17] They poured the fat at the base of the tree, ate some of its roasted meat, and left the remainder to be consumed by the ancestors. These "sacrifices" to familial ancestors were called *kuhaka magongona*. One meaning of the verb *kuhaka* was to "draw boundaries," to "separate." The boundary between two different clans was called a *muhaka;* to castrate a goat was to *hakura* it. Kuhaka magongona used animal fat, a mark of domestic wealth and productivity, to cordon off a space that excluded troublesome ancestors and ensured peaceful human reproduction.

Magongona were householders' effort to protect the living from the uncharitable dead. But some problems transcended the pressingly domestic diet of ancestors, necessitating more general answers. When rain failed to fall or when plague killed people without discrimination, elders from around a given region banded together to slaughter a ram for *Ngai,* "God." Such magongona seem to have been speculative gambles meant to contain an unfamiliar deity. Etymologically, *Ngai* was adopted from the Masai language, a Gikuyuized version of the singular *En-kai* of the pastoralists.[18] An adoption from a foreign language, *Ngai* had little vernacular resonance: it belonged to the class of nouns associated with inanimate objects.[19] Gikuyu had few words to say about Ngai: the earliest collection of proverbs, recorded by a Catholic missionary who would have listened for God talk, listed only four that referenced the Deity by name.[20] Only one mentioned some positive quality about Ngai. Missionaries lamented the absence of Gikuyu talk about Ngai. Missionary Marion Stevenson, for instance, could only list two proverbs referencing Ngai, and even these she apparently misheard.[21] "Sacrifices" to Ngai were infrequent, offered by elders only during times of calamity.[22] Their prayers, *thaithano,* asked for rain and domestic productivity. *Thaithano* was the same noun applied to the funny songs and dancing that youths used to beg food from reluctant mothers.[23] Prayer, like magongona, was less a scripted "ceremony" than a creative performance with uncertain rewards.

It is impossible to know what nineteenth-century Gikuyu actually thought about God. What is clear is that the relationship between Gikuyu and Ngai, mediated in magongona, was not ritualistic worship enacted between created and Creator. Ngai did not stand behind magongona, receiving Gikuyu worship. Instead, magongona look like gambles, tentative attempts to protect human life from the unfamiliar. This is not to suggest that Gikuyu were atheists. But the absence of abstract Gikuyu theological discourse about God, and the exceedingly temporal economies of consumption which it inhabited, underscores the material, highly experimental nature of Gikuyu religious thought. Gikuyu religion dealt with God, and the ancestors, by marking out boundaries intended to protect the living from the incursions of the uncontrollable. This boundary making was never a mechanical, rehearsed "ritual" commemorating humanity's subordination to the divine. Magongona and tahikio were speculative, undetermined, temporally bound efforts by elders to guard humanity from unknown dangers.

Missionary evangelism worked by inducting Ngai, and magongona, into a natural religion. By translating Gikuyu practice into the atemporal categories of post-Enlightenment European thought, missionaries sought to create a world of rituals and propositions, a religious world to be converted through sermons about belief and governed in law.

World into Word?

Protestant evangelism had two, intimately joined faces: the material and the theological. Materially, missionaries worked to create a social space for the believing subject by restructuring the world in which their adherents lived. Using fences, clocks, and square-cornered houses, missionaries divided the world into a binary order: individuals and their meaning-making activities, on the one hand, and an inert structure that existed apart from human beings and framed their lives, on the other. Structuring the mundane in time and space thus helped define the subjective, personal space of belief. It was here that the material dimension of Protestant evangelism joined with the theological agenda of conversion. For, by calling the individual subject into existence through their material routines and building plans, Protestants also laid the groundwork for comparative, evangelizing conversations about personal religious beliefs. Distinguishing individual believers from their human and natural world made disembodied religious conversations possible.

I have space to sketch only the broadest outlines of this process here, focusing on the early history of the Scots Presbyterian mission at Tumutumu, some one hundred miles north of contemporary Kenya's capital city of Nairobi. Missionaries settled at Tumutumu in the wake of the sporadic punitive expeditions that amounted to British conquest of the central highlands. The first missionary, Arthur Barlow, carried two clocks with him when he arrived at Tumutumu in 1909 and requested another soon afterward.[24] Soon after his arrival he began sounding a bugle at nine o'clock in the morning, the time when workers and students were to arrive at the mission.[25] He divided the school day into a timetable, partitioning activities—reading, work, washing, sleep—into allotted periods. Passing in mechanical clocks, time was supposed to be a structure, an implacably inanimate framework, which lay behind activities at the mission. Clocks regulated human life. Students went to class for two and a half hours per day in 1909 and 1910. They paid a half-rupee per month. Workers were paid monthly wages for their labor in bush clearing. Time could be bought and sold, used productively in bush clearing at the mission or (missionaries lamented) wasted in dancing.

Just as time was made into a structure standing behind human activity, so was space supposed to map out and divide up human life. Barlow's first public activity on arriving at Tumutumu Hill was to mark the boundaries of the mission station with beacons provided by government.[26] His next activity was to lay out paths and gardens and plant flowers and trees.[27] Footpaths and carefully tended fences assigned a distinct function to spaces, dividing and containing territory according to its instrumental use. The hospital, which in its first four years amounted to a single mud and wattle hut, was carefully fenced off from the rest of the mission.[28] Its fence contained disease and protected schoolgoers from unpleasant sights and smells. Just as clocks rendered human activities down to minutes and hours, fences divided up the landscape, assigning functions to spaces.[29]

Presbyterian missionaries introduced more than a new religion at Tumutumu. In these early formative exchanges they sought to establish a different means of conceiving of the link between self and world. Clocks and fences were a means by which Tumutumu missionaries sought to divide up human life with mechanical units of measure—minutes, rooms, yards. The effect of this mapping of terrain and time was to make the world inert, manageable, and objective. Gikuyu were invited to confront this objective world as subjects, mastering it though words. Naming and mastering were, in Protestant thought, intimately related. Every convert at Tumutumu was encouraged to reenact the story of Adam, when animate objects were identified in the hierarchy of Creation. Reading lessons were the schoolhouse of Christian mastery. Missionaries taught their charges to read by connecting discrete letters and phrases with particular objects. Barlow sometimes carried flashcards to young men's dances, calling out syllables while jumping in time with music.[30] The cards were his favored method of teaching reading.[31] Charles Muhoro, who began schooling at Tumutumu around 1910, described his reading lessons: "There were some printed papers which were pasted onto two very broad boards. . . . On the first one was written: i n a b, then the capital letters would be written like this: I N A B. . . . Then: *bi-bi* [morsel], *ba-ba* [father], *ma-ma* [uncle], *i-na* [sing]. . . . As one continued to study, they would be taught: 'God has given the Kikuyu people a nice country, which lacks neither food nor water or forests, it is therefore good for the Kikuyu people to be praising God because it has been so generous to them.'"[32] Writing parsed out social relationships, catching fathers, uncles, and morsels in script. As students learned to read, they progressively mastered the world: by the end of their instruction they came to Genesis, the moment at which God gave the world to humanity.

In reading lessons, through labor regimes, clocks, and fences, missionaries encouraged converts to take up a deliberate posture toward the world. The world was supposed to be objective, real, something to be named and acted upon. This division between self and world went to the heart of missionaries' assumptions about belief. Religion, missionaries thought, was a socially and politically autonomous system, a matter to be believed in by an internal act of will and articulated though faith statements. Missionaries asked pagans and Christians alike to give voice to their belief systems, to talk about their theology. In evoking such faith statements, missionaries sought to engage Gikuyu in a battle of words, a battle of theologies. The invention of Gikuyu religion and the making of modern subjectivity were intimately joined.

Missionaries' theological argument began by analogy, making magongona into the ritualistic stuff of a religion. The sacrifices that elders periodically offered at fig trees, missionaries argued, were Levitical forebears of the "Great Sacrifice" of Christ. In their scripted predictability they mirrored the Christian practice of Communion. One Gikuyu-language catechism made the comparison in this way:

> Sacrificing for God under a fig tree can be equated to some of the Israelites' practices and of Christianity. . . . The lamb that was used for sacrifice under a fig tree was to be unblemished. The same was done by the Israelites. Jesus Christ was the unblemished lamb (I Peter 1.19); (John 1.29). Also under the fig tree Ngai was worshipped in words and songs. Also some meat was left for Ngai in the altar and the rest was divided amongst the elders. This is comparable with the holy communion among Christians.[33]

Missionaries thought Gikuyu engaged in the same variety of religious practices as they themselves, without the light of the truth. Later ethnographers would describe the elders as "priests" and their eating at the fig tree as a "ceremonial meal."[34] By representing magongona in this way, missionaries made it possible to think of Gikuyu practices as timeless, placeless ceremonies. In missionary thought magongona were formulaic rituals, not creative actions. Elders were priests playing prescribed roles, not experimental practitioners. And the slain lamb was a symbol for Jesus Christ, not a barrier speculatively drawn between humans and the unknown. Missionaries did not simply misrecognize the real meanings of Gikuyu religion in their sermons equating Christian and Gikuyu disciplines. By inducting magongona and other practices into the lexicon of modern religion, they worked to standardize Gikuyu thought, to fix its meanings, so as better to compare it with the tenets of their own faith.

The first object of missionary evangelism was, therefore, to turn Gikuyu gambles into a religion, governed by timeless laws and oriented toward an all powerful God. Where such laws seemed to be absent, missionaries created them. Early missionaries, for example, were haunted by the question of how to translate the term *sin. Thahu,* the pollution that afflicted Gikuyu homesteads, was one likely choice. But thahu seemed to depend on no law, no set of commandments which sinners transgressed. Barlow framed the problem: "What of sins against God? Here a vital difference is seen between our idea of sin and that of the Kikuyu. We regard all sin as committed against God, the Supreme Judge; we are responsible to Him in all our acts, even offences against the community involve sin against God. But with the Kikuyu God does not seem to fill the place of Judge, and they do not feel responsible to him for their actions. . . . It may be doubted whether he possesses a moral conscience: he is afraid of being found out and punished, but excepting this he is quite comfortable in his mind."[35]

Ngai gave no commandments with which to judge human actions. Early translations of Christian texts highlight how hard missionaries had to work to preach the law to Gikuyu. Missionaries first used *riathani* for law. Riathani was an oral verdict given by an elderly, wealthy man, not an unchanging rule.[36] Later, translators proposed *marua*,[37] which linked law specifically with textuality: marua were "letters," written by teachers in missionary schools. By 1913 translators had finally settled on *watho* for "law."[38] Like a riathani, a watho was a verdict delivered orally on a case.

Missionaries' dilemmas over *sin* and *law* were generated by their search for a suitably textualized social code around which to structure the Christian story of fall and redemption. Despairing of ever finding fixed norms with which to judge Gikuyu conduct, Barlow and other translators were forced to invent a new term, *mehia,* to stand in for *sin* in Christian lexicon. The word connoted whispers or lies, not infractions against an unchanging moral code. Mehia had to be taught to blithely innocent Gikuyu. As Marion Stevenson put it in 1913: "The Law was our schoolmaster to bring us to Christ. The average Kikuyu is probably perfectly sinless according to his own standard. He has no knowledge of the great thahu, and no sense of the need of a Savior. This has to be aroused. He requires to be taught the commandments, to have impressed on him that they are not for the white man or Mission people only, but for all man of all races."[39]

Confounded by the lack of law about which to preach about sin and repentance, missionaries set about teaching Gikuyu to believe in absolute truths. Early catechisms invariably began by teaching readers about the fall of man. One syllabus, for example, began with creation, moved to the "story of two trees, temptation and fall," on to "the curse and flaming sword," to the "development of evil," and from thence to the Ten Commandments.[40] The powerful pull of the law, missionaries hoped, would arouse sleeping Gikuyu consciences and bring them to repentance and from there to salvation. The word *forgive* they translated as *rekia,* to "release" or "untie."[41] The law bound Gikuyu into a Christian story climaxing in the release of salvation.

It is important to recognize that this reduction of a fluid social world into a matter of truth and law was not simply an innocent mistake. It was in the area between gambles and religion that colonialism worked. Gikuyu knew the world as a process, a kinetic bargain with a threatening wilderness. Missionaries sought to turn Gikuyu social praxis toward the atemporal categories of ritual and religion. By representing creative, dangerous practices as timeless ceremonies, by dividing up human activities with clocks and fences, by judging human actions with immutable laws, missionaries worked to create a mechanical world, a society governed by rules. Over time these rules would be elaborated, codified, and made into customary law, the guidebook for indirect rule in Kenya as elsewhere in colonial Africa.[42] The textualization of social life, the rendering of process into religious ritual and law, was as much a colonization of Gikuyu society as were the great moments of military conquest.

Soon after Arthur Barlow's arrival at Tumutumu, a group of elders visited him to request that a grassy path be left through the missionary compound to the top of Tumutumu Hill. There, three hundred yards above the mission station, was a fig tree, long used for elders' magongona. Barlow agreed to their request, and until 1930 a grassy path wound up to the top of the hill through the midst of the mission station. Missionaries saw nothing incongruous about the tree's existence; indeed, Barlow and others studied elders' sacrifices at the tree in order to better understand the old religion.[43] The fig tree at the top of Tumutumu Hill was for missionaries the visible testing ground of Christian evangelism, evidence of the religious world to be superseded by Christian truth. In 1930 the fig tree was toppled by a storm.[44] Missionaries hastened to send the trunk to Scotland to have a cross made of it. It was marked with a plaque and displayed prominently in the church. The fig tree / cross was proof that Gikuyu religion could take the shape of Christian faith, that missionary liberals could hew the truth out of the base wood of Gikuyu religion.

Sometime soon after the new cross was put on display at Tumutumu, a woman broke into the church building and made off with it.[45] Missionaries thought her mad. We know nothing about the fate of the cross, nor about the uses to which it was put. But by her strange action, the thief pointed toward the possibility that missionaries' symbols might be susceptible to insurgent acts of cultural theft. The woman's appropriation of the fig tree / cross suggests that there were other, only partially visible worlds of meaning in which loaded missionary symbols might take up residence. It is to these other worlds that we now turn.

Gambling with God

Missionaries hoped that, by preaching about God, Gikuyu would be drawn into a sustained, worshipful dependence on their Creator. But Ngai was in Gikuyu thought a gamble, less the absolute deity of a systematic theology and more a tentative, mutable way of thinking about the unknown. Missionary preaching made hearers nervous. Marion Stevenson reported on one evangelistic conversation in 1912:

> We talked of various things, and then I told them I had come to ask people to go to Ngware's on Sunday evening to hear God's word. Waweru, the leader, said they did not wish to hear, as it would make them feel sorrow in their hearts. I said he was mistaken—it made men's hearts rejoice. "Ah, no," he said, "when people are in sorrow or in pain, or when the rains fall, our hearts are sad, and we call on God." I knew that, I said, but it was God, our Father, who gave us life and food, the sun, the rain, and everything beautiful, and we should think of Him and His Word at all times—not only in sorrow; and we should talk to him often, and our hearts would become pure and bright and glad like His.

They did not know this, they said. They thought that if they sat round listening, God would surely come and kill one of them.[46]

Christian prayer brought the unknown close to home. As late as 1919, a Presbyterian catechism found it necessary to reassure readers that, if Ngai were to come into a man's village, he and his goats would not die.[47] The immanence of Christian preaching upset Gikuyu worried about drawing boundaries around Ngai. Hearers responded to missionary preaching about Ngai by trying to end the conversation. H. E. Scott lamented their ingenuity in 1912: "It is most difficult to obtain a definite opinion about what their god called Ngai is to them. As soon as you begin to cross examine them they seek umbrage under the customary reply, 'We don't know.' "[48] Hearers' avowals of ignorance turned aside missionaries' dangerous God talk. Other listeners sought different means to thwart missionaries' effort to pin down Ngai. Some elders staved off missionaries' words by arguing that there were two Gods, one the God of heaven, the other the God of earth.[49] It made more sense, they argued, to worship the God of earth than the Christian God of heaven. Other elders simply dismissed the Christian God as the "God of children."[50] Missionary religion was child's play. This was a telling depiction of Tumutumu's catechumens, all of whom were propertyless young men. But, moreover, the critique of childlike Christianity measured the wisdom of elders against the ill-considered, juvenile preaching of missionaries. Ngai, elders knew, was too capricious to capture with words.

Asked to speak as religious subjects about their beliefs, Gikuyu refused to talk. There were few dialogues over the nature of God on this colonial frontier, few theological battles to fight. Gikuyu did not confront missionaries as spokesmen for a traditional religion. Instead, they seem to have used Ngai as a way to think about missionaries and their material culture. At least one hospital patient, in 1913, wondered if Dr. Philp himself was Ngai.[51] He drew a sharp rebuke: "The doctor is only a man, and God is a Spirit," sermonized a hospital attendant. That Gikuyu be made to recognize the immaterial transcendence of God was a central concern of Christian preaching. But evangelistic sermons inspired Gikuyu to speculate on missionary materials, not abstract divinity. Some elders at Kimaro's, near the mission, thought they had seen all of Ngai when shown a picture of him.[52] They asked the evangelists to move on, reasoning that they had already known God. Missionaries lamented that hearers frequently labeled toys, cups, and other household utensils "God."[53] Some schoolgoers whispered that silver Communion vessels were made in "God's place."[54] Missionaries thought them dumbfounded at the new manufactured commodities. But the richness of Gikuyu material speculation on Ngai highlights their creativity, not their naïveté.

In response to the missionary demand that they speak the modern, disembodied language of religious belief, Gikuyu replied with disruptively embodied readings of European substances and theologies. This struggle over technique was precisely over the possibility of religion. By making European theology real, visible, corporeal, the vital object of an experimental vernacular discourse, Gikuyu hearers upset the careful hierarchies of reality and religion, object and subject, crafted by missionaries. The physicality of their speculation on the stuff of missionary culture, in other words, resisted missionary efforts to elicit comparative religious conversations. Theirs was a form of resistance, a profoundly creative deconstruction of the hierarchies of truth along which missionary evangelism worked.

We can glimpse how Gikuyu thought through missionary culture in the seemingly prosaic character of early inquirers' engagements with writing. Protestant texts were supposed to lead readers to the Word: reading and writing were avenues directing inquirers toward the meaning behind texts. But Gikuyu were more inclined to think with the physical apparatus of writing, as the missionary Marion Stevenson discovered in 1909.

> A short time ago one of the teachers who carries on an outschool came to the Mission Station and said, "Bibi, Wamagara says you must come and take the teaching box with the books and slates in it away from his village." But why? "He says his sheep and goats are dying of sickness, and that the wise man says it is because of the white man's box in the village." . . . "Well, you go and tell Wamagara that there is also much sickness amongst the sheep and goats in other villages where there are no boxes, so it cannot be caused by the box! . . . This talk of the wise man is foolishness. Do not let them think you take him seriously. The box remains where it is!" And there the box remained![55]

The mission box was good to think with. What this incident suggests is that early Gikuyu hearers understood and criticized Christian religion by speculating on the material culture and techniques of the mission. The physicality of early Gikuyu evaluations of mission schooling points toward the different kind of readings that seem to have been common on this colonial frontier. The earliest dictionaries attest that the first, speculative word that Gikuyu put for "to write" was *gutema*.[56] The term evoked the hard work of "chopping" trees; it also evoked the process of tattooing, marking the body at circumcision and other ceremonies of aging. The "letters" of the alphabet Gikuyu named *retemuo*, "cuts," *ruoora*, "branded mark, stripe," or *ndemwa*, "tattoos."[57] Writing was in some way a bodily discipline, an action that in a very direct way was involved with the body. Thinking of writing as tattooing made the act of writing visible: it emphasized the technique, the process of forming letters, over and above the meaning of words. In 1908 Marion Stevenson was disconcerted when she entered the hut of Wanjiko, a former laundry worker, and found incomprehensible letters chalked on the wall. They were Wanjiko's signature, she was told. Stevenson thought them a "rather pathetic effort to remember something she had learned at school."[58] But Wanjiko's writing marked something different than a halfhearted memory exercise. In response to the missionary demand that she name herself, clearly positioning herself in relation to an inert world, Wanjiko replied by working on her technique. Her writing had an (unknowable) purpose of its own, a purpose divorced from the lessons that missionaries taught about writing, communication, and mastering.

It is impossible to know what Wanjiko meant by her writing. She may not have meant to mean anything. What is clear is that Wanjiko's signature made visible a Gikuyu strategy of resistance. Her incomprehensible letters made writing into performance, a technique to be mastered, not a communicative medium to be understood. It was as if words spoke to and among themselves, losing their references to objects. Missionaries worried that schoolchildren memorized their reading texts and failed to dwell on the meanings of the words they spoke. Scott noted the problem in 1910: "The power of the school children to memorize their lessons is notorious. They commit to memory a whole page of their reading book and it is only when you ask them to begin to read in the middle of a sentence that you discover that what you took to be beautiful reading was only wonderful memorizing. . . . To teach the pupils how to think rather than memorizing becomes one of the first problems in our school work."[59]

That words be alienated from memory and made to lead readers to the Word was the central concern of missionary pedagogy. But Gikuyu consistently broke down the hierarchy of words and Word, making Christian words into a patter to be learned. The first adherents at Tumutumu mission insisted that missionaries teach them to "pray properly."[60] Missionaries taught them several prayers, especially the Lord's Prayer, the first text translated into Gikuyu. Converts prayed the prayer continually, sometimes praying and singing through the night. Missionaries worried lest the prayers become incantations, losing their meaning to the nighttime liturgists.[61]

Gikuyu wordplay tended to make writing and praying ends in themselves. Wanjiko's indecipherable letters, Wamagara's reading of the mission box, writing as tattooing, and reciting prayers from rote all detached the techniques of missionary pedagogy from their moorings, from the meaning to which they were supposed to refer. A similar debate over technique developed around the practice of biomedicine. From the earliest days of the mission Tumutumu doctors cured the sick in spectacular, public displays of surgery. Surgery was a discipline of modern subjectivity. As Paul Landau has shown, in cutting the body and extracting teeth, missionaries alienated Africans from the social matrix that had previously made them sick or well.[62] Cutting the body and preaching about conversion were alike: both were founded on and called into existence the individualized self. But Gikuyu watchers seemed more inclined to dwell on the techniques of missionary medicine than on the lessons about self and sickness which missionaries hoped to convey. The performance of Western medicine drew appreciative crowds. The first practitioner, a Gikuyu dispenser named Kitoto, daily dispensed iodine and purgatives before a crowd exceeding sixty people.[63] The missionary doctor Philp was ambivalent about the congregations that attended his surgeries, as he wrote in 1910: "A large number come to gaze at the white man and his doings. If a tooth is extracted quickly there is a murmur of approval, and for the next ten minutes each of the onlookers has to explain to his neighbor exactly how the [doctor] did it. . . . But if a tooth does not come out at the first pull, they like it even better, but there is no such thing as sympathy for suffering here. If a patient complains of pain they all seem to think it a very great joke, and shouts of derisive laughter greet the patient's protestations."[64] Gikuyu watchers were more interested in the technique than in the lessons about disease and wellness which missionaries sought to convey. It was as a contest over techniques of medical treatment—over needles, salves, and vaccines—that early struggles over healing at Tumutumu took shape. In 1916–1917 Philp, backed by the district commissioner's policemen, began a program of vaccination for smallpox throughout Nyeri district. He hoped that vaccinations would convince Africans of the superiority of modern medicine. But even chiefs were unable to prevent their people from hiding en masse at the appearance of the doctor.[65] When they were successfully vaccinated, Philp reported that, as soon as the doctor's back was turned, they smeared the vaccination with dung and leaves and washed the area with water.[66] Characteristically, Philp attributed their resistance to "native prejudices." But their evasion of the doctor's needles was not merely a conservative response to missionary medicine. What was at stake here were contending techniques of healing and contending evaluations of danger. Leaves and cow dung were emblematically cool in Gikuyu thought: they balanced the heat of disease and restored health to the body. And missionaries' vaccines, at least in 1917, were "hot": more often than not they led to an onset of the disease, as Philp himself admitted.[67] Even more immediately, vaccination was a disaster for smallpox sufferers: those who Philp identified as diseased had their huts burned to the ground by the chief as insurance against an epidemic. Philp's smallpox vaccinations literally ruined his victims by identifying them as individual sufferers, subjecting them to government law.

Gikuyu distrust of missionary needles was a medically astute, politically critical evaluation of a medical practice that ruined its patients. Rubbing vaccination wounds with leaves and dung was more than a traditional reply to missionary medicine. It was an act of criticism, an effort to compass missionary medicine within a wider healing framework, an effort also to deflect the individuating dangers of the needle.

In reply to the missionary demand that they speak as subjects about their religious beliefs, early Gikuyu hearers replied with random talk, rubbed-out vaccines, and strikingly material readings of schoolbooks and needles. Gikuyu confronted missionaries not as subjects, speaking for authentic African traditions or beliefs, but as gamblers, creatively thinking with the techniques of missionary culture. Their intricate, political criticisms disrupted the religious conversation that missionaries worked to evoke.

Even as they deconstructed the religious world taught at the mission, Gikuyu hearers used European ideas and practices to forge new identities for changed social times. For at least some inquirers, converts to a material religion, adopting some of the markers of missionary culture opened up new avenues by which to achieve the old Gikuyu goal of a respectable adulthood. A history of how they used new Christian ideas to embody old virtues is the starting point for a popular history of colonialism in Kenya, a history framed not by the binary choices of tradition and modernity but, instead, attentive to the changing strategies with which Gikuyu gambled.

Tea and Marriage in Converts' Rhetoric of Adulthood

I want to discuss briefly disputes over marriage and tea at Tumutumu, as a way of illuminating how young converts used missionary resources to claim Gikuyu adulthood. Gikuyu marriage was enacted through a series of exchanges of livestock and beer from the family of the young man to the bride's family. Beer condensed women's reproductive labor: it was made of millet, a crop that women grew, and kept by the bed of the mother of the young man the night before the marriage. The exchange of beer and cattle, both reproductive resources, for the bride at marriage bound families together. Husbands lubricated in-laws by continuing to offer small gifts of beer and livestock after marriage. Bridewealth, the proverb went, was never finished. Gikuyu marriage was a vital process of incorporation, working girls securely into families and families into accord.

Scots missionaries, hoped their cooking would civilize their converts and wean them from beer, began serving *cai,* tea with milk, to the first inhabitants of the mission boarding school. By 1913 young men from locations far distant from Tumutumu were asking missionaries for the tea leaves.[68] Early converts argued that the cai they drank at marriage ceremonies made them as virtuous as beer drinkers. The first recorded occasion, in 1915, at which the Church of Scotland's Gikuyu converts, all young men, met to debate church doctrine went as follows:

> It was entirely a native *shauri* [dispute] and a straight fight between the young men who were all out, not only not to drink, but to forbid it in the buying of their girls etc., and two or three of the older Christians who made the opposition. . . . In the end there were two plain issues: 1) That drinking or taking beer by Christians should be prohibited. Only two or three of the older ones admitted to still taking it. The motion was carried with only one dissident, 55 church members voting for it. 2) That beer in payment of buying a girl, or for work done, or as a friendly gift, should be prohibited. There was more discussion on this point, but in the end it, too, was carried, with perhaps three or four dissidents.[69]

The young men's stand against beer was a Christian commitment probably learned from teetotaling missionaries. But their principled objections to beer
were equally a rhetorical point directed at their fathers. Early converts used cai
to lay claims on marriageable women. The first Christian marriage conducted
at Tumutumu wed two inmates of the boarding school. They served tea at the
conclusion of the festivities.[70] The young man paid sacks of sugar to the father
of the woman he married, purchasing the sugar from Indian-run shops.[71] Sugar
was relatively inexpensive: it was given out in small quantities as *bakshish,* a
"thank you," in Indian stores and after World War I cost only twenty-five cents
a kilo.[72] But tea leaves were costly, and so was milk. Men drank cai at Christian
weddings, while wives drank millet porridge. As one woman put it, "Tea was
for when the men came."[73] Tea embodied a new kind of civility, no less gendered
than the old.

Angry elders protested that sugar and cai carried little worth in marriage
transactions. Beer had compensated the reproductive value of women with a
proximate reproductive value. Tea carried none of these meanings. Young converts' failure to brew beer was one of the most frequently voiced objections to
their marriage practices.[74] We can hear the echoes of elders' objections in one
woman's memory of her father's complaints about her going to school: "The
reason why girls were being told not to go to school was because if they went
to school, the elders would be refused to drink beer. . . . So when a man would
hear that the girl was going to school, he would be very angry. At the same time,
the elders were saying—the girls who are going to school, they will become
prostitutes. If they go, and if we don't drink beer, where will they get sexual
relations?"[75]

In elders' thinking converts' failure to produce beer at marriage negotiations alienated women from their families. Beer in bridewealth negotiations
brought common accord between families, binding in-laws together in consumption. Sugar and tea leaves in marriage exchanges brought only prostitution; it
made marriage into alienation, not incorporation. Elders had good reason to think
so. Girls who went to school lived far away from home, isolated from their families in mission-run boarding schools. Their physical alienation from home made
some elders wonder about their morality. Mission boarders in the 1910s and
1920s were rumored to eat wild animals, gazelles, and pigs.[76] They drank their
tea from human skulls and ate human flesh.[77] In an economy in which eating
together made for civil sociability and gendered order, in which food valorized
productive work, the rumors commented on the immoral alienation of schoolchildren from home.

Stung by elders' criticisms, youthful converts hoped to parlay their drink
into the substance of Gikuyu virtue. Cai became for them a means to prove themselves worthy of respect both to missionaries and to elders. The Tumutumu marriage crisis of 1914–1915 gave shape to converts' claims that cai could make

them respectable. Missionaries in the earliest years refused to allow catechumens to marry anyone outside the church. But until 1916 the catechumenate at Tumutumu was exclusively male.[78] Missionaries' intransigence threatened to keep young male converts in perpetual childhood. Elders called the Christian God the "God of children," mocking the young converts for their immaturity.[79] The young men, desperate for brides, made payments of sugar and tea for girls outside the mission.[80] By 1914 many of the young men of the mission had long-standing engagements with unbaptized girls whom they hoped, eventually, to marry.[81] But missionaries insisted on the ideal of Christian marriage, complacently counseling anxious young men to "wait patiently for the time when there will be Christian girls who would make worthy partners and helpmeets in their lives."[82]

The lengthy suspension of young men's marriages created a crisis of missionary law in 1914. Hoping for protection from government war recruitment, some young catechumens attempted to force their marriages. They demanded an increase in the wages they earned for teaching, using the extra cash to complete bridewealth payments.[83] A few, both ambitious and desperate, attempted to force missionaries to alter their rigid stance by beginning the series of feasts and dances that marked the fulfillment of Gikuyu marriage. One young convert, Macaria, completed paying his bridewealth and convened a feast near the mission. His family brewed beer for their in-laws. The missionary Marion Stevenson, together with twelve mission adherents, marched to the scene and announced that "this was not a Christian marriage, that those two were acting as heathens."[84] Stevenson hoped that her actions would help "make a break in the eyes of the people" between things Christian and things Gikuyu. But her young converts refused to make such harsh divisions between Christianity and paganism. They worked to keep religious categories negotiable.

One young man, Samsoni, waited for four years to complete his marriage to a girl from the nearby village of Njebere. She, tiring of the wait, married another man.[85] Samsoni hoped to use his wages to make payments for another woman, an unbaptized girl named Cai. He looked for the missionaries' approval by asking two questions of Stevenson: "1) Would we not allow them be married (as if it lay in our hands and was a caprice of ours!) because he had had to wait for Njebere? 2) Would it be wrong if he married a heathen (!) girl and had her come to school afterwards!!!"[86] Stevenson replied to Samsoni's sly interrogation by making a forceful distinction between marriage and her personal caprice. She insisted that marriage was not an arbitrary figment of missionary will; rather, it was "for Christians all over the world. This marriage law is not for *athungu* [whites] only!" Marriage in missionary thought was a socially autonomous institution, a ritual practice independent of political or social context. In contrast, Samsoni's questions insisted that marriage was a human process, not a matter of inanimate laws. He questioned the objectivity of the marriage law itself, refusing to recognize the distinctions that missionaries made between their personal will and the law. His careful, deconstructive critique blurred the lines between Christianity and paganism, opening up a rhetorical space with which to challenge missionary efforts to regulate young converts' lives.

It is important to recognize that the 1914–1915 struggles over readers' marriages were struggles over law itself and, by extension, over the textualized world that missionaries sought to create. To missionaries, Gikuyu marriage stubbornly refused to present itself as a ritual that could be legislated on. The very indeterminacy of marriage allowed young readers to challenge missionaries' right to control their lives, and wives, as Stevenson discovered later in 1914:

> I have just come from explaining marriage to the boys. They are in great puzzlement as to when it can be said that the sheep are finished being paid for a girl, seeing they say the *shauri* is never finished here. I said I did not believe that: that there must be a point when these sheep were really gifts from the son in law to the father in law and not really payment. Further I said that if there was no *muhaka* [boundary] where a man could say "the girl is now mine and not her father's" that we must make one! I certainly think that if the father allows the banns of marriage to be proclaimed he should be precluded after that from demanding further payment for the girl. Let them protest if he is not satisfied.[87]

Stevenson's quandary over marriage highlights the limits of missionaries' efforts to turn Gikuyu practices into laws. Gikuyu marriage offered no points of definition, no contractual end point that would allow missionaries to name it as complete. Marriage was always in a process of becoming because Gikuyu homesteads, bodily health, and social order itself were themselves vital processes, carefully won bargains with a threatening wilderness. Marriage, part of the larger process by which Gikuyu made social order of the unproductive forest, was a substantial transaction that defied attempts to resolve it into law.

The Tumutumu marriage crisis highlights, again, just how much is at stake in understanding the radical nature of missionary evangelism as a form of power. By making predictable rituals of complex processes, missionary evangelism worked to create a mechanical world, a society structured by law. Laws allowed missionaries to pass judgment on converts, determining, for example, whether Macaria's festival amounted to a real marriage. Over time these rules would be codified and made into the stuff of customary law, the textbook for colonial government.

But converts like Samsoni were not easily caught up in the world of laws established by missionaries. They diagnosed missionary religion not through abstract laws or religious dogmas but through its techniques. Young converts experimentally incorporated cai into marriage exchanges, made writing a bodily discipline, and rubbed vaccines with dung and leaves. Their physical diagnoses of Christianity refused missionary attempts to elicit disembodied conversations comparing religious propositions. And as they deconstructed the hierarchies of reality along which missionary evangelism worked, converts challenged missionary efforts to create abstract rules with which to govern their lives. Some actively played with laws by asking slyly deconstructive questions. By speculating on missionary techniques, by turning impersonal laws into intensely personal arguments, converts challenged missionary structuralism. As they embodied foreign substances and techniques, they knit together new identities for a changed world.

Notes

As part of a larger project on writing and religion in central Kenya, my research was funded in 1993–1994 by a Fulbright (IIE) grant, in 1996 by the University of Minnesota's MacArthur Program, and in 1998 by the Research Enablement Program, a grant program funded by the Pew Charitable Trusts. For their comments on earlier drafts of this essay, I thank John Lonsdale, Allen Isaacman, and Jean Allman.

Archival sources are referenced as follows: *KNA:* Kenya National Archives, Nairobi; *PCEA:* Presbyterian Church of East Africa archives, Nairobi; *TT:* Tumutumu church archives, Karatina, Nyeri district; *AIM:* Africa Inland Mission archives, Nairobi; *EUL:* Edinburgh University Library, Scotland. Transcripts of oral interviews are held at Tumutumu and will shortly be deposited at the Kenya National Archives.

1. H. E. Scott, letters no. 15 and 16, *Kikuyu News* 14 (October 1909).
2. Arthur Barlow, "Evangelistic Work at Kenia," *Kikuyu News* 35 (May 1912).
3. Marion Stevenson, letter no. 4, *Kikuyu News* 7 (October 1908).
4. H. Philp, "The Evening Service," *Kikuyu News* 47 (February 1914).
5. Barlow, "Tumutumu Notes," *Kikuyu News* 17 (March 1910).
6. John Mbiti, *African Religions and Philosophy* (New York: Praeger, 1969). See also Mbiti, *Introduction to African Religion* (Portsmouth, N.H.: Heinemann, 1975).
7. This paragraph draws from Rosalind Shaw, "The Invention of 'African Traditional Religion,'" *Religion* 20 (1990): 339–353; and Paul Landau, "'Religion' and Christian Conversion in African History: A New Model," *Journal of Religious History* 23 (1999): 8–30.
8. Talal Asad, *Genealogies of Religion: Discipline and Reasons of Power in Christianity and Islam* (Baltimore: Johns Hopkins University Press, 1993).
9. David Chidester, *Savage Systems: Colonialism and Comparative Religion in Southern Africa* (Charlottesville: University Press of Virginia, 1996).
10. Louis Leakey, *The Southern Kikuyu before 1903* (London: Academic Press, 1977), 1107–1109.
11. *EUL,* Gen. 1785/1: A. R. Barlow, entry on *gita.*
12. H. E. Lambert, *Kikuyu Social and Political Institutions* (London: International African Institute, 1956), 83.
13. For these examples of *thahu,* see C. W. Hobley, *Bantu Beliefs and Magic* (London: H. F. and G. Witherby, 1922), 105–125.
14. For descriptions of *tahikio,* see Hobley, *Bantu Beliefs,* 134–145; Leakey, *Southern Kikuyu,* chap. 26.
15. Leakey, *Southern Kikuyu,* 1180.
16. Stanley Gathigira, *Miikarire ya Agikuyu* (1933; rpt., Nairobi: Scholars Press, n.d.).

17. Leakey, *Southern Kikuyu,* 1107–1109; Jomo Kenyatta, *Facing Mount Kenya: The Tribal Life of the Gikuyu* (London: Secker and Warburg, 1953), chap. 10.

18. Barlow, "A Sacrifice for Rain," *Kikuyu News* 3 (May 1908).

19. *TT,* Notes for Catechists file: Barlow, *Guthura Uhoro wa Gikuyu na wa Ukristiano,* n.d. (but 1930s).

20. G. Barra, *1000 Kikuyu Proverbs* (1939; rpt., Nairobi: Kenya Literature Bureau, 1994), nos. 573, 618, 640, and 963.

21. *PCEA,* I/Z/13: Marion Stevenson, "Specimens of Kikuyu Proverbs," lists *Ngai ni nene* and *Ngai ni nguru* as expressions of misfortune or resignation. Barlow, in marginal notes appended to Stevenson's manuscript, doubted whether such proverbs existed before Christian evangelism.

22. *TT,* Notes for Catechists file: Barlow, *Uhoro wa Ukristiano na Ugikuyu.*

23. *EUL,* Gen. 1785/3: Barlow, notes on *guthathaiya.*

24. *PCEA,* I/A/4: Barlow to Scott, 28 June 1909.

25. Barlow, "Beginnings at Tumutumu," *Kikuyu News* 14 (October 1909).

26. *PCEA,* I/A/5: Barlow to Scott, 15 July 1909.

27. John William Arthur, "A Visit to Tumutumu," *Kikuyu News* 19 (May 1910).

28. *PCEA,* I/A/13: Arthur to DC Fort Hall, 3 January 1912.

29. Cf. Timothy Mitchell, *Colonising Egypt* (Berkeley: University of California Press, 1991).

30. Interview: Kariuki Muturi and Joseph Muthee Muriuki (Tumutumu, 14 September 1998).

31. *PCEA,* I/A/11: Barlow to Arthur, 8 February 1912.

32. Charles Muhoro Kareri, *Muoyo wa Charles Muhoro Kareri* (MS in possession of Muthoni Mwihaki, Tumutumu).

33. *TT,* Notes for Catechists file: Barlow, "The Choice between Christianity and Gikuyu Things," n.d.

34. Leakey, *Southern Kikuyu,* 202; Hobley, *Bantu Beliefs,* 19, for natural religion.

35. Barlow, "Good and Evil in the Kikuyu Mind," *Kikuyu News* 37 (August 1912).

36. *EUL,* Gen. 1786/5: Leakey, "Notes on the Meeting of Native Christians in Nairobi," 8 January 1910.

37. *EUL,* Gen. 1786/5: UKLC meeting, 25 September 1914.

38. *EUL,* Gen. 1786/5: UKLC meeting, 13–14 August 1913.

39. Stevenson, "How Do You Begin?" *Kikuyu News* 44 (September 1913).

40. *TT,* Ministers file: Alliance, "Syllabus for Instruction of Those Being Prepared for Baptism," 14 January 1918.

41. *AIM,* box 9: UKLC meeting, 13–14 August 1913.

42. Mahmood Mamdani, *Citizen and Subject: Contemporary Africa and the Legacy of Late Colonialism* (Princeton, N.J.: Princeton University Press, 1996).

43. Barlow, "The Tree of Fat," *Kikuyu News* 31 (October 1911).

44. *PCEA,* I/Z/6: Tumutumu logbook, entry for 24 March 1930.

45. *TT,* Hospital Board file: Ronald Keymer, "What in the World?" 2 December 1967.

46. Stevenson, "Village Work," *Kikuyu News* 16 (January 1910).

47. *PCEA,* I/Z/12–13: *Kabuku ga kuurania* (Church of Scotland Mission, British East Africa Mission, 1919).

48. H. E. Scott, "The Heathen Belief in Spirits," *Kikuyu News* 33 (February 1912).

49. Stevenson, "A Corner of the Vineyard," *Kikuyu News* 50 (August 1914).

50. "Three Kenia Lads," "Lions in the Path," *Kikuyu News* 51 (September–October 1915).
51. Philp, "Smallpox at Tumutumu," *Kikuyu News* 42 (May 1913).
52. Stevenson, "A Corner of the Vineyard," *Kikuyu News* 50 (August 1914).
53. Stevenson, "The Kikuyu Language Committee," *Kikuyu News* 37 (August 1912).
54. Stevenson, "After a Year in Kenya," *Kikuyu News* 46 (January 1914).
55. Stevenson, "Sidelights on School Work," *Kikuyu News* 9 (January 1909).
56. A. Hemery, *Handbook of the Kikuyu Language* (Nairobi: RCM Press, 1903), 75; A. W. McGregor, *English-Kikuyu Dictionary* (London: SPCK, 1904), 191.
57. For *retemuo,* see McGregor, *English-Kikuyu Dictionary,* 100; for *ruoora* and *ndemwa,* see L. Beecher, *A Kikuyu-English Dictionary* (Nairobi: CMS Bookshop, 1938), 185, 196.
58. Stevenson, letter no. 7, in *Kikuyu News* 7 (October 1908).
59. *PCEA,* I/A/10: Scott, "In Far Fields," 24 June 1910. See also Bernard Cohn, "The Command of Language and the Language of Command," in *Subaltern Studies IV: Writings in South Asian History and Society,* ed. Ranajit Guha (Delhi: Oxford University Press, 1985), 276–329.
60. Stevenson, "After a Year in Kenya," *Kikuyu News* 46 (January 1914).
61. *EUL,* Gen. 762: Arthur, 25 January 1907.
62. Paul Landau, "Explaining Surgical Evangelism in Colonial Southern Africa: Teeth, Pain and Faith," *Journal of African History* 37 (1996): 261–281. Gyan Prakash similarly writes about the materialization of the body under colonial therapy in *Another Reason: Science and the Imagination of Modern India* (Princeton, N.J.: Princeton University Press, 1999), chap. 5.
63. *PCEA,* I/A/5: Barlow to Scott, 15 October 1909.
64. Philp, "Medical Work at Strategic Sites in Kenia," *Kikuyu News* 24 (December 1910).
65. *PCEA,* I/J/2: Philp, Nyeri District Surgeon Report, 1918.
66. *PCEA,* I/J/1 and 3: Philp, "Report on the Health of the Native Reserves in Nyeri District," April–August 1918.
67. *PCEA,* I/J/1 and 3: Philp to Paterson, 23 March 1925.
68. Mrs. Philp, "Notes on Itinerating," *Kikuyu News* 40 (January 1913).
69. *PCEA,* I/D/3: Arthur to Peel, 21 September 1915.
70. M. Jack, "The First Christian Marriage in Kenia," *Kikuyu News* 59 (April–May 1916).
71. Interviews: Gerard Gachau Kingori (Gitugi, 19 June and 8 July 1998); Grace Mukunya (Kagere, 7 July 1998).
72. Interviews: Grace Gathoni (Ngorano, 10 August and 16 September 1998); Monica Muumbi (Magutu, 12 August 1998).
73. Interview: Jerida Kirigu (Magutu, 12 August 1998).
74. See interviews: Maritha Gakeria (Tumutumu, 2 March 1998); Idis Kahiga (Tumutumu, 7 August 1998); Alice Wanjeri (Magutu, 13 May 1998); Esther Mbau Mwihaki (Mahiga, 13 June 1998).
75. Interview: Grace Gathoni Gachigua (Iruri, 10 August 1996).
76. Interview: Jerida Kirigu.
77. For skulls, see interviews: Gerard Gachau Kingori; Paul Thuku Njembwe (Gitugi, 18 June and 10 July 1998); for human flesh, see interview: Elijah Kiruthi (Mahiga, 15 June and 16 September 1998).
78. *PCEA,* I/B/7: annual report, Tumutumu, 1916.
79. "Three Kenia Lads," "Lions in the Path," *Kikuyu News* 51 (September–October 1915).

80. Philp, "Tumutumu Notes," *Kikuyu News* 48 (July–August 1913).

81. *PCEA,* I/A/19: Stevenson to Barlow, 9 January 1915.

82. Barlow, "Kikuyu Marriage Customs," *Kikuyu News* 40 (January 1913).

83. *PCEA,* I/A/19: Barlow to MacLachlan, 7 April 1915.

84. *PCEA,* I/A/19: Stevenson to Barlow, 16 January 1914.

85. *PCEA,* I/A/17: Filipu Mathenge to Barlow, 3 January 1915.

86. *PCEA,* I/A/19: Stevenson to Barlow, 16 January 1914.

87. *PCEA,* I/A/19: Stevenson to Barlow, n.d. (but 1914).

CHAPTER 4

Here (We) Are the Haredim

INTERTEXTUALITY AND THE VOICE OF AUTHORITY
IN THE REPRESENTATION OF A RELIGIOUS
FUNDAMENTALIST MOVEMENT

JEREMY STOLOW

*I*t seems increasingly difficult to ignore the rise of a new religio-politics on the world stage so readily, but perhaps also misleadingly, associated with the name *religious fundamentalism.* The contents of almost any daily newspaper offer ample evidence of how religious fundamentalism has made its mark on the popular imagination, by gathering under a single rubric such diverse phenomena as Protestant evangelical revival meetings, Islamist insurgencies, Hindutva protest marches, or published rulings from Orthodox rabbinic authorities. Intense debates of academics and scientists about the place of religion in the modern world have also reinforced the prominence of fundamentalism. Over the past two decades numerous demographic studies, ethnographies, taxonomies, psychoanalyses, philosophical debates, and political prognostications have appeared in the form of monographs, conference proceedings, and even encyclopedic compendia, including most prominently the internationally coordinated, multiauthored, five-volume *Fundamentalism Project.*[1] But what is at stake in this compulsion to document the new forms of religio-politics as varieties of religious fundamentalism? Is the specter of religious fundamentalism simply a product of moral panic, an invented enemy, a convenient foil for other, yet-to-be identified social ills in the body politic? Or is there something else underlying the visibility of religious fundamentalism, demanding our critical attention and collective deliberation?

Before broaching these questions, we should first acknowledge the immense profits that have been reaped from recent scholarly work on the current global conjuncture of religion and politics. This scholarship has done much to refine the sweeping generalizations one often encounters in the popular media. In the media fundamentalism is often represented as a regressive, atavistic social tendency that has failed to embrace modernity, as connoted by the apparent devotion of its adherents to hidebound sexual conservatism or absurd notions such as scriptural inerrancy or by their blind submission to punctilious scholars and rabid prophets. Recent scholarship, in contrast, has enhanced our appreciation of fundamentalist movements as markedly untraditional. Adherents appear in this work as people deeply implicated within, and circumscribed by, social and cultural formations more readily associated with a secular modernity they claim to oppose: from chartered tourism to real estate investment, welfare provision, consumer awareness campaigns, Internet sites, rock music and comic books, election campaigning, and political punditry on television and radio talk shows.

Despite its admirable advances, much of the work that purports to account for the origin and influence of fundamentalist movements, ideas, and beliefs suffers from a sort of blindness about the religio-politics it represents. This blindness can be inferred from the way many studies narrow their focus on the statements and textual products of elites. A typical account of religious fundamentalism proceeds by tracing fundamentalist worldviews and modes of discourse directly back to the aboriginal source of individual (elite) creators, only thereafter considering how these ideas might have trickled down from "a surface of clearly stated propositions to a subsoil of incoherent but common opinion."[2] From this perspective a rich variety of intermediary institutions and networks of intellectual producers—such as those of publishers, translators, editors, proselytes, recruiters, and other popularizers—are presumed to function simply as passive conduits for the unidirectional spread of the ideas and doctrines of religious elites and are therefore viewed as unworthy of sustained independent study.[3]

In avoiding explicit consideration of the institutional constraints and media forms that enable religious fundamentalist messages to circulate and have effect in the modern world, many scholars also repress the terms by which fundamentalist social tendencies are made intelligible to them in the first place. In this essay I explicate some of the key conditions and consequences of this act of repression. My specific point of departure is the work of a cadre of writers constellated around an Anglo-Judaica press, ArtScroll-Mesorah Publications (hereafter, ArtScroll). Based in Brooklyn, New York, ArtScroll is an innovative publisher of Jewish books that span liturgical, scholarly, and popular genres, distributed throughout the English-speaking world (Canada, the United States, the United Kingdom, Australia, South Africa, and the anglophone community in Israel). This press is also linked to one of the preeminent Orthodox Jewish movements of the twentieth century, Agudat Israel: a society founded in 1912 to represent the interests of *Haredism* (Jewish "ultra-Orthodoxy") on the world stage. Situated within the transnational space of the contemporary Jewish imaginary, the texts of the ArtScroll cadre are thus illustrative of the broader social discourse about religious fundamentalism in our global present.

Let me begin by reconstructing a moment in my research when I began to reflect upon a number of polemical texts penned by haredi authors associated with ArtScroll and Agudat Israel. In book reviews, editorials, prefaces, and letters of protest, I kept coming across detailed rejoinders to scientific scholarship about the development of Haredism, the current state of the haredi world, or the different political positions of haredi authorities with respect to Israel or to Jewish life in the diaspora (and often with specific reference to the situation of North American Jewry). In retrospect it should not have surprised me to discover these texts, which so deftly challenged a scientific monopoly over the representation of Haredism. Nor should I have been surprised at the existence of haredi authors who exercised command over the textual traditions out of which the European and North American human sciences have developed. After all, there have always been haredim living in urban centers where scientific forms of anthropology, sociology, and history have been produced. Many of the cultural canons that inform haredi society are inculcated and transmitted within advanced academies in the heart of the metropole, contiguous with "secular" institutions such as the university. This surely placed numerous haredi readers and authors alike in a position to comment extensively upon the scientific representations that have been produced about them.

But there seemed to be little precedent in the scientific disciplines in which I had been trained to give serious weight to this kind of work. How was I to incorporate the fact that haredi authors are busily involved in producing journal articles, book reviews, and other sorts of texts that aim to redress "errors of representation"? Was this simply another body of materials to be plumbed for evidence of a haredi worldview? Would my attempt to interpret these texts require me to ignore the fact that their authors offer competing or entirely incommensurable accounts of Haredism and, even more troubling, that one of their principal goals is to challenge the representational authority upon which my own scientific practice is based?

In the following pages I shall try to address these questions by considering a variety of representations of Haredism produced by authors who possess very different assumptions and goals. My aim is not to account for Haredism itself but, rather, to attend to some of the dynamics of competition, polemical distinction, and (often unacknowledged) collaboration between academic scientists and haredi authors, as they form two distinct groups of intellectual producers working within a single discursive field. This presupposes that a study of the points of intertextual contact between the two groups will be fruitful in throwing light on some of the political stakes underlying knowledge claims about Haredism as a kind of religious fundamentalism. How, I would like to know, ought one to represent a historical trajectory that has situated both fundamentalists and nonfundamentalists in an ongoing struggle for the authority to define the historical truth of fundamentalism itself?

Scientific Authority

In enunciating their truths, scientific discourses are always articulated as relations of authority with other discourses that they either exclude or subordinate through the very act of representing them.[4] Not all scientists, however, are explicit about the authority they claim for themselves, having sublimated it into the descriptions they offer of their work as reportage or analysis. Such dissimulation is certainly at work in the scientific discourse about religious fundamentalisms, in which the effort to gain insight into such movements and to account for their social logic is simultaneously a practice aimed at demonstrating the illegitimacy of fundamentalist discourses and the marginality of fundamentalist social agents. This is evident in the many ways that the language of adherents, believers, and practitioners comes to be distinguished from the professional protocols, the competencies, and the standards of verisimilitude which define scientific discourse. Ongoing and widespread commitments of professional academics to disinterestedness or methodological agnosticism thus serve as sources of distinction for the legitimacy of scientific practice itself, in opposition to the discursive practices of competing authorities. Among these "competitors" we might include intellectual producers situated within communities such as the haredim, who have very different interests at stake in the representation of Haredism.

The assertion of representational prerogatives is no doubt endemic to all scientific accounts of religion, at least insofar as they attempt to comprehend religious phenomena by "asking something else of them than what they meant to say."[5] One can envisage a study that gauges the subordination of nonscientific or "religious" knowledge to the authorizing discourse of science according to the various acts of displacement which the latter performs: in which religious truths are converted into social functions; a religiously inscribed history becomes a history of religious society; or beliefs are translated into social effects among populations. Through such procedures sacred discourses and sacred sources of legitimation—and by extension the social actors who participate in their circulation—would appear to be systematically excluded from the formation of legitimate representations of the meaning of the sacred and of religious action.

But this is not the place to review in detail the variety of analytical mechanisms and hermeneutical procedures available for the scientific study of religion. Nor is there room here to consider the merits of the contrasting interpretive schemata or protocols for defining standards of evidence, as they have been elaborated within positivist, Marxist, structuralist, Durkheimian, or Weberian accounts of religious belief and practice—although, I should hasten to add, it

would be impossible to ignore the favor shown by scholars of religious fundamentalism for Weber's *verstehende* approach to religious social action and religious meaning.[6] I only want to signal here the presence of some more elementary
axioms underpinning the scientific study of religious fundamentalism: first, that
the very attempt to constitute authoritative scientific inquiry depends upon the
displacement of religious discourse from the orbit of its participants; and, second, that this displacement is effected through a reification of the social-discur-
sive context in which scientists encounter those others destined to become their
objects of representation.

This displacement should not be confused with the so-called insider-out-
sider (or emic-etic) debates in the social sciences.[7] However self-reflexive, methodological arguments about how to constitute authoritative representations of
social phenomena—and especially the ideas, beliefs, and signifying practices
of others—are waged within the scientific community itself. As such, they depend upon the exclusion of nonscientific interlocutors through the enforcement
of professional protocols and related mechanisms for consecrating legitimate authorship. Therefore, even the attempt to present scientific accounts of the meaning of beliefs and practices "from the point of view of the believers and
practitioners themselves" does not abnegate the exercise of representational authority among scholars concerned with religious fundamentalism. On the contrary, empathic identification merely reproduces authority in more insidious ways,
by continuing to rely upon a social and textual divide separating legitimate scientific authorship from the discordant and unruly voices of fundamentalist competitors. By supposing that the words and actions of religious fundamentalists
are constituted as expressive or meaningful texts, the truth of which only trained
scientists are equipped to recognize and assess, voices proposing competing interpretations cease to be heard as voices that challenge the authority of scientific truth. They are instead transformed into new texts: into new objects of
circumspection and new forms of expression, the meaning of which can be established authoritatively through scientific methods.[8]

These are admittedly sweeping generalizations about the scientific study
of religious fundamentalism. But perhaps they serve the purpose of throwing
into relief the peculiar situation of academic historians, sociologists, anthropologists, and others who are concerned with the production of representations of
Haredism. This situation is one of competition and struggle for the monopoly
of legitimate authority over the representation, and thus the social significance,
of Haredism itself. In order to gain insight into this struggle, it will be necessary to cast one's eye beyond the borders of the scientific text in search of certain repressed moments of encounter. I shall proceed by first offering a thumbnail
sketch of the current scientific literature on Haredism and then considering some
of the ways this work has been dealt with by haredi authors of the ArtScroll
cadre.

Haredism Made Visible

With disparate points of focus, and varying accents, the scientific literature has sought to represent the social pressures that have combined to make
Haredism an effective force in the modern world, particularly within the context of the contemporary Jewish imaginary. We can infer a general picture from
the plethora of local studies that conceive Haredism as the product of: (1) the
dramatic convulsions that have reshaped "traditional" Jewish communal structures over the course of the past century (especially in Eastern Europe), such as
political emancipation, the confessionalization cum privatization of Jewish social identity, intercontinental migration, the Nazi Holocaust, and the founding
of the state of Israel; (2) the new opportunities presented to elite Orthodox scholars, increasingly detached from traditional obligations and local customs and
implicated in a reinvigorated and inwardly directed academic culture; (3) new
principles of theoretical organization insinuated into those apparatuses of public order which secure the hegemony of this emergent scholarly elite, as reflected
in the imposition of "Torah-true" standards of verification upon secular knowledge, the redaction and re-translation of canonical texts, and the dismissal of
lenient interpretations of Jewish law; and (4) the irruption of new forms of charismatic authority along the lines of communication between the scholarly elite
and the masses who "voluntarily" constellate around it, subjecting themselves
(and others) to the word of these Torah sages.

These tendencies have been the subject of various normative assessments,
the details of which cannot be given the attention they deserve in this discussion.[9] Nevertheless, there does appear to be a consensus that Haredism is best
understood in terms of a progressive (or, in certain cases, a sudden) detachment
from "traditional" Jewish practices and forms of social identity. Within this
scheme the rise of Haredism is commensurate with the loss of a prior, more integral, or more "balanced," manifestation of everyday practice, religious obser-
vance, and structures of authority. This loss is registered in the haredi drift toward
excessive punctiliousness and stringency in the interpretation of religious law;[10]
in a foreboding emphasis on scripturalism and a narrowly defined Jewish canon
as the basis for legitimate discourse, at the expense of other, "un-Jewish" sources
of knowledge;[11] in the growing demagoguery of haredi scholars, who displace
their own, post-traditional "status anxiety" onto their authoritarian assertions of
exclusive legitimate interpretation of Jewish law and tradition;[12] and, more glo-
bally, in a progressive disconnection from the numinous experience of the divine itself in everyday Jewish practice. We might take as emblematic of this
scientific viewpoint the following conclusion, extracted from Haym Soloveitchik's widely circulated commentary on the haredi scene: "It is this rupture
in the traditional religious sensibilities that underlies much of the transformation of contemporary Orthodoxy. Zealous to continue traditional Judaism un-
impaired, religious Jews seek to ground their new emerging spirituality less on
a now unattainable intimacy with Him, than on an intimacy with His Will, av-

idly eliciting Its intricate demands and saturating their daily lives with Its exactions. Having lost the touch of His presence, they seek solace in the pressure of His yoke."[13]

The Dispute over Da'at Torah

Even while certain assessments of Haredism have been enveloped in the authoritative gown of science, their rejection by haredi writers has been vociferous. Haredi intellectuals do not regard Haredism as evidence of a post-traditional effusion. For them it is the manifestation of an unbroken tradition of religious thought and practice that must be defended at all costs. Their rejection of scientific typologies and categories thus serves as a means for calling into question the terms by which Haredism, and more generally the very category of religion, has been defined in so-called modern, secular society.

There are numerous specific points of confrontation which deserve our attention, including arguments over the interpretation, translation, and redaction of canonical Jewish texts, the identification of "corrupt" texts, the assessment of specific historical documents, and other matters relating to the definition of legitimacy and "authentic" Jewish practice in modern society. Among these instances of intertextual contact between scientific and haredi authors, I shall consider one conflagration that I take to be particularly symptomatic, since it touches on the combined problems of legitimate authority, historical representation, and normative assessment regarding the position of the haredim in the modern world. This debate concerns the significance of the term *da'at Torah* (knowledge of the Torah) for contemporary haredi textual politics and the constitution of haredi social formations.

As various academic scholars have described it, da'at Torah comprises a specifically charismatic source of authority for the interpretation of canonical Jewish texts and the promulgation of Jewish law. Haredi scholars who are recognized as possessors of this esoteric knowledge are authorized, by virtue of this charismatic possession alone, to produce interpretations of the canon which constitute the *halakhic* (religious-legal) norms for the communities in which they reside. Da'at Torah thus forms the basis for any "pronouncement of the halakhists *ex cathedra,* made binding upon religious Jewry and with its authority based simply upon the general prestige conferred upon the halakhists."[14] Authoritative opinions, prohibitions, legal rulings, and other decrees are thus issued by rabbinic figures who themselves are not required to explain or defend their interpretation of halakhic sources, "their sole authority being their position as rabbis immersed in the study of Torah."[15]

Perhaps because of its charismatic quality, da'at Torah has also been characterized in the scientific literature as a historically unprecedented mechanism for legitimating rabbinic authority. There is in fact wide agreement that the promotion of da'at Torah, or what Lawrence Kaplan has called the "oracular nature" inherent in appeals to the authorities who embody this principle, lacks a firm precedent in canonical sources and, more specifically, that it is of relatively recent provenance in Jewish religious social practice.[16] More precisely, da'at Torah is said to have gained prominence only at the moment of dissolution of traditional structures of authority in Jewish communities. As Kaplan puts it:

> A key factor, if not the key factor, in the rise of the ideology of Daas Torah was . . . the breakdown of traditional communal structures, the concomitant weakening of the power of communal rabbis and lay religious leaders, and the emergence of the *rashei yeshiva* [headmasters of religious academies], with their Torah scholarship and personal charisma, to center stage. This process has, of course, been going on since the nineteenth century, but it reached its climax only with the Second World War and the destruction of the great traditional Jewish communities of Eastern Europe. Thus, the climax of this process, of this change in leadership, coincides with and would seem to be partially, if not largely, responsible for the emergence of a full-blown concept of Daas Torah.[17]

Having located da'at Torah outside the confines of traditional Jewish communal structures and modes of legitimate authority, scientific authors have also positioned themselves to comment upon its "social function." This social function, say scientists, is to legitimate haredi approaches "to the wide range of issues and challenges posed by the modern world and the breakdown of tradition" and at the same time to delegitimate other approaches, grounded in "reasoned debate."[18] In Kaplan's assessment:

> Daas Torah . . . requires the *suppression* of one's own critical faculties and submission to the superior, if at times incomprehensible, wisdom of the *gadol* [great scholar]. And one must submit to the views of the gadol not simply because the halakhic system, in terms of its complex rules for resolving disputes, ascribes greater authority to his decisions. Rather, the views of the gadol are true and authentic, while my differing views are false and inauthentic. What is required of me, then, is, again, intellectual submission and faith in the gadol and his superior wisdom. . . . That being the case, it follows that the ideology of Daas Torah is a central, perhaps the central, element in the ethic of submission to authority, the authority of halakhah, of the gadol, of God, is the highest religious value and *one that is absolutely opposed to the modern values of intellectual autonomy and self-expression.*[19]

From the scientific vantage point da'at Torah is converted into a source of social demagoguery. Set against the Enlightenment standards of "intellectual autonomy and self-expression," the possessors of da'at Torah are not viewed simply as patriarchal sages, steeped in recondite texts and devoted to *Talmud Torah lishma* (the study of Torah for its own sake). They are now figured as danger-ous rabble-rousers, who sway the masses, who brook no dissent, and whose very retreat into an abstract textualism has compelled them to displace their newfound "status anxiety" onto their followers through exacting and uncompromising demands.

And what of the haredi response to this imagery of a narrow-minded, au-thoritarian anti-modernism? One commentator, Rabbi Berel Wein (author of a popular series of Jewish history published by ArtScroll), has replied directly to those scientists who have deigned to account for the social sources and mean-ing of haredi authority. He writes: "Kaplan does not like the 'ethic of submis-sion' because it 'is absolutely opposed to the modern values of intellectual autonomy and self-expression.' So what? These 'modern values' have yet to bring much benefit to a suffering twentieth century. If 'modern values' conflict with basic Torah beliefs and precepts, then a Jew must sacrifice some 'modern val-ues.'"[20] Another haredi critic, Rabbi Yaakov Feitman, has suggested:

> While the concept of Daas Torah as a source of authority is a *funda-mental* Jewish teaching, some find it troubling. For, although many of us live by this principle and make the most important decisions of our lives based upon it, we are hard-pressed to identify its mechanism or even define its criteria. . . . [On the other hand, the claim that] "no one is going to tell me what to do," can be rationalized as *an expression of free will,* but it is actually *the natural retrogression into childlike defi-ance of parents and teachers,* even when their inherent claim to authority should be obvious. One of the most subtle yet pernicious manifestations of this phenomenon is the often *emotional,* occasionally outright *illogical hostility* to the concept of Daas Torah.[21]

It is noteworthy that Rabbi Feitman's reply to the academic critics is concerned with the definition of *free will,* since, as we saw in Kaplan's analysis of da'at Torah, this is also one of the chief criteria against which the legitimacy of this charismatic form of authority is measured within scientific discourse. Rabbi Feitman, however, draws free will into juxtaposition with a new series of terms—*retrogression, childlike defiance, emotionalism, illogical hostility*—thereby di-rectly inverting Kaplan's account of what constitutes a legitimate source of halakhic interpretation. Moreover, this inversion of the meaning of *free will* is only made intelligible in connection with Rabbi Feitman's proposition that da'at Torah is not of recent provenance within Jewish thought and social practice. As he insists, against the scientists, da'at Torah can only be understood as a doc-trine that has maintained a continuous presence in the thought and practices of legitimate Jewish authorities, perhaps dating back to the moment of reception of the Torah itself at Sinai:

> As the critics of Daas Torah themselves perceive in moments of candor and honesty, it is ludicrous to impute major corruptions of ancient

tradition to *those whose lives are defined by being repositories of that tradition* [namely, the *Hafetz Hayyim* and Rabbi Elchonon Wasserman: two haredi authorities who have been "wrongfully impugned" in Kaplan's text]. So *while they are correct in not finding the phrase in the writings of earlier generations, they missed the fact that, in truth, the concept is not new;* through the use of the term, *a time-honored tenet had simply been reaffirmed.*

For what many of us, living in a century polluted by the sputterings of politicians, academics, and "experts" of every type, have forgotten, is that *for all our history until very recently, it was the Torah leadership, and it alone, that was the spokesman for the people of Israel.* It has always been unthinkable for any major decision affecting the nation to be made by someone other than a Torah sage. And so, the term *Daas Torah* was *superfluous* because everyone knew that *Daas Torah* with any other suffix was an oxymoron.[22]

In sum, the debate over the provenance of the term *da'at Torah* is simultaneously a debate over the historical meaning and normative constitution of modernity itself. Insofar as academic critics of da'at Torah have succeeded in establishing this concept as a post-traditional mode of rabbinic authority, they have marked it as a merely charismatic effluence, and to that extent as an arbitrary (and presumably unwelcome) intrusion of haredi halakhists into public social arenas: exercising their anti-modernist ethic of submission to the harsh, ascetic norms which they have established in their isolated academies; and disrupting the constitutive norms of participatory, democratic social processes, which themselves depend on the existence of autonomous, free-willed moral and political subjects.

But, on the other hand, for haredi critics such as Rabbi Feitman and Rabbi Wein, the idea of da'at Torah is rooted in the very structure of the revelation at Sinai and is linked by a continuous chain extending from the formation of rabbinic Judaism through the long history of Jewish scholarship down to the present. Situated within this tradition are "those who have the ability to be 'unquestioning,' so great is their trust in their mentor (who possesses da'at Torah)"—and then there are others who fail to recognize that "submission to G–d and His Torah [is] the *entire* basis of Jewish faith . . . the theology of *mitzvos* [commandments], of tradition and family."[23] From this perspective the unwillingness of scientific authors to submit to contemporary haredi halakhic authorities becomes evidence of their arrogant hostility to legitimate Jewish practice. By the same token the valorization of Enlightenment notions of free will and autonomy serves as an index for measuring what is wrong with modernity itself. The greater the value accorded to these un-Jewish norms, the more pronounced the challenge to the authority of the *gedolim* to deliver their da'at Torah and, therefore, the more indisputable the evidence that secular definitions of scholarly practice and political subjectivity threaten to subvert a divine message, of which current haredi elites are merely a repository. As Rabbi Nosson Scherman, the general editor of the ArtScroll press, puts it:

> The Torah specifically enjoins each generation to accept the authority of his own contemporary elders and priests. In this injunction there is a deeper motive than the plea of a President that the nation support him because "I'm the only President you have." To the nation of Torah, leadership has far greater significance. As the first *Mishna* in *Avos* makes clear, succeeding generations are Hashem's [God's] means for perpetuating Torah. The concept of *Mesora* [tradition] contains far more than adherence to tradition through ancestor worship. "The Torah that is in our hands today is the one that was given to our teacher, Moshe"—this is one of the basic elements of our belief. And it is in our hands today because of the chain of the Mesora—the Torah authorities of each generation who received the Torah from their predecessors and hand it on to their successors. . . . Without this belief, we could not claim legitimacy as a Torah nation.[24]

According to this line of interpretation, the gedolim are not demagogues; they are heroic defenders of tradition. If scientific academics fail to appreciate the legitimacy of this heroism, this only demonstrates the extent of their unwillingness to participate in those structures of belief which underpin the transmission of tradition and, therefore, their distance from the truth over which they claim authority. In Rabbi Wein's shrewdly worded conclusion, "The reason this admittedly sophisticated concept is so difficult for 'modern' circles to accept is because many scholars (and others) [are] looking at Daas Torah from the outside, and not experiencing it from within."[25] The circle of belief in which Rabbi Wein situates himself and his fellow haredim is thus presented as an impenetrable wall: an invisibility structured by the very representational mechanisms that make up the scientific gaze.

A Field of Encounter

The dispute over the meaning of *da'at Torah* exemplifies how definitions of Haredism are subject to competing normative assessments and competing conceptions of what counts as truthful discourse. It is also noteworthy that the debate is focused on the very historical transformations that are presumed to have facilitated the existence of haredi cultural formations and haredi tendencies in the present. Are haredi halakhic innovations signs of a drift toward extravagant forms of punctiliousness and zealous intolerance? Or are they a return to "correct" halakhic practice, the stringency of which is constituted as a necessary measure in the face of "degenerating moral standards" and the cancerous spread of social anomie of modern society? Is the articulation of Torah-true knowledge a defensive retreat into a narrow dogmatism, a deafening of the ear to the promises heralded by science and liberal moderation? Or is this a regaining of lost ground in the search for truth itself, which has been buried under the weight of confusing misdirections and vacuous generalizations? Is the promotion of da'at Torah a sign of the demagoguery of haredi elites, indexically referring to the haredi assault on free will, rationalism, and autonomy in halakhic interpretation and other forms of Jewish practice? Or does it illuminate the legitimacy of a "traditional" form of authority, which has been reasserted in the attempt to reverse a dangerous slide toward solipsism and anarchy marked by secularist, "un-Jewish" notions of individualism or moral relativism?

And how might one adjudicate between these contradictory positions? More particularly, what is at stake for a scientific discourse that is cognizant of its potential displacement by a competing source of intellectual authority? No doubt, some scientists would choose to ignore direct challenges to their authority, perhaps by folding haredi rebuttals into their ongoing commentary about the structure of haredi ideology itself. Others might invoke familiar claims of theoretical relativism or methodological agnosticism in the attempt to shield themselves from the moral consequences of speaking on behalf of others. But the foregoing discussion makes room for a third line of response. This would involve asking how science itself is implicated in an enunciative context, in which scientists and religious actors encounter one another and propose diverging accounts of the truthful meaning of religious claims and religious actions. In this regard my investigation into the ways that authoritative claims about Haredism and authoritative representations of the haredim have been produced (and contested) at the level of written texts has not purported to offer an authoritative account of the meaning of haredi beliefs and ideas per se. Rather, I have only sought to trace the movement of beliefs and ideas within a textually mediated social field, occupied by different intellectual producers who, from their specific positions within this field, have been locked into competitive struggles over the flow of authoritative discourse itself.[26]

This method might now invite theoretical generalization. Rather than attempting to escape from itself and to fuse with another "truth" it claims simply to represent (but in which it invariably discovers the reflection of its own mirror image), I would like to suggest that a scientific discourse about religious fundamentalism might be better served by abandoning the effort to represent the meaning of beliefs and practices from the believers' and practitioners' point of view. If we were to make the drama of encounter itself a primary object of analysis—that is, by treating representations of the beliefs and practices of others as nothing but *effects of discourse,* produced by the apparatus of those texts which mediates the encounter between representor and representee—we might relieve scientific inquiry of the demand to predicate understanding on the discovery of an isomorphism between social groups, their interests, and the intentionality of their discourses: an isomorphism that, I have intimated, is only sustained by silencing the dissenting interpretations of the "truthful meaning" of these discourses propagated by others.[27] In other words, by refusing to identify the work of understanding with the degree of success in empathically fusing with the objects of one's representations, one might at the same time call into question the very desire to establish authoritative claims about the interior experience of religious beliefs or practices.

While this shift in focus might leave scientists with much less to say about what beliefs and practices mean from the point of view of the believers and practitioners themselves, I suspect that it may open up new, and ultimately more fruitful, opportunities for exploring the discursive apparatus by virtue of which statements about belief are enunciated and made effective in the world: assertions of belief; efforts to defend them or to explain them ("scientifically" or otherwise); attempts to induce others to believe, to declare one's conviction, or to define oneself as someone who has come under conviction. Conceived in this way, it would be the proper business of a science of religious fundamentalism to represent ideas and beliefs only as they have been inscribed in texts (broadly defined) and only as they have been constituted by the social spaces in which texts are materially produced and institutionally enacted and in which they occasion various responses among listeners and readers.

Let me also stress that I do not imagine that this reorganization of the mode of inquiry will somehow offer scientists an opportunity to escape the problems associated with representational authority. I do think, however, that a shift toward questions of encounter and competition, attending to the production process of authoritative representations, can advance scientific inquiry beyond its rather specious tendencies to naturalize (and thereby disguise) its own authority, to deny the presence of others who challenge this authority, or to proclaim the impossible task of speaking the truth "unauthoritatively." For when discursive confrontation itself becomes the object of focus, as in the instances of textual exchange between haredi and scientific authors, the possibility is opened up for scientists to recognize ourselves. By placing ourselves in relations of competition with others, we are forced to acknowledge that the very persons about whom we speak do not give any credence to the truth we articulate. It also makes explicit the inescapable moral dilemma facing all scientists who choose to speak about social movements including so-called fundamentalisms: that the production of knowledge is inextricably linked with the production of effects upon others, who must bear the consequences of "being represented."

It should also be said that acknowledging the structures of representational authority is not at all tantamount to foreclosing the possibility of critical rejoinders. Recognizing one's responsibility as a participant in an authoritative discourse does not necessarily mean that one accepts the terms under which challenges to that authority have been constituted by others. With respect to disputes with, between, or for or against so-called religious fundamentalisms, in which much of the position taking has been organized either by the advancement of moral panics and demonizations or by apologetics, polemical rejoinders, and seductive entreaties, it would seem especially urgent to revisit the question of how to define responsibility.[28] Indeed, we might want to ask, must one submit to imperatives issued by others in the field, who demand allegiance to one or another of the positions that they have constituted in their struggle to monopolize legitimate authority? In the case of Haredism, for instance, is there no room for alternatives to the binary opposition between, on the one hand, a willful submission to the authority of haredi gedolim—constituted within haredi discourse as the sole authorized interpreters of canonical truths and the sole legitimate arbiters of moral and legal decision making—and, on the other, the shrill denunciation of this discourse as an antimodern effusion of demagoguery or fanaticism?

Perhaps it is in a refusal to align him- or herself unequivocally with already constituted positions that the student of intertextual encounters has the most to offer. Perhaps, in other words, the most fruitful course is to explore the conditions under which moral agency itself is possible within this field, by identifying the ways this agency has been institutionally enacted, enforced, challenged, dissipated, or even rendered innocuous. For, if one takes as given the idea that, when it comes to political action, the suppression of effects depends upon the identification, isolation, and suppression of their causes, then it may follow that a study of the ways in which the causes of fundamentalism have been constituted and disputed will constitute a crucial intervention into the field of dispute that has made the effects of religio-politics so visible on the contemporary world stage.

One way to conceive of this intervention is in terms of a discussion about the disavowed relations of mutual debt existing between differently positioned players in the field or about other forms of discursive hybridity or complementarity of cultural practices, which the polemics of position taking have kept hidden from purview. In this respect I would suggest that scientists are uniquely positioned to recognize certain unacknowledged points of conjuncture. For when haredi authorities, such as those of the ArtScroll cadre, speak and write—and particularly when they reject scientific claims—they are often obligated to use distinctively un-haredi words. It is not merely incidental, for instance, that in their defense of da'at Torah as a legitimate mode of authoritative discourse, Rabbis Feitman, Scherman, and Wein make use of terms such as *free will, autonomy,* and perhaps also *modernity,* even if they appear to do so quite disdainfully. Disdain, after all, is a mark of their participation in a discourse they share with others, the rules for the successful enactment of which are not of their own choosing. From this we might infer that the effort to promote da'at Torah is not so far removed from other modes of participation in so-called modern, liberal-secular society or from the discursive practices of social science.

If for some these points of discursive overlap appear as contaminants—threatening, as the case may be, the original purity of traditional beliefs or the autonomy of social scientific inquiry—for others they should emphasize how the words of so-called fundamentalists, just as much as the words of the social scientists who study fundamentalism, are never the exclusive property of their speakers. They are always, of necessity, being displaced, recontextualized, and reinterpreted by others. Accounts of belief and faithful practice (as authorized by science) and defenses of belief and faithful practice (and especially the claims of their inscrutability to science) are beholden to the imperative of making these truths intelligible to others. Scientific and haredi interlocutors are inevitably locked into mutual relations of addressivity and answerability. Of course, both parties have had recourse to a considerable rhetoric in order to obfuscate this "mutual contamination," and both have hotly denied the existence of such relations of interdependence. But the complicities between haredi and scientific discourses, and the institutional positionalities of their producers, are complex and mutually sustaining, even, and perhaps especially, at the point at which these producers attempt to distinguish the validity and legitimacy of their own practices as unique and inexchangeable.

Notes

I would like to thank Lisa Disch, Barbara Godard, Derek Peterson, Ato Sekyi-Otu, and the attendees of the "After Secularism/Religion" conference for insightful commentary and discussions. Financial support for this work was provided in part by the Social Sciences and Humanities Research Council of Canada.

1. Martin Marty and R. Scott Appleby, *The Fundamentalism Project,* 5 vols. (Chicago: University of Chicago Press, 1991–1995).
2. Fritz Ringer, *Fields of Knowledge: French Academic Culture in Comparative Perspective, 1890–1920* (Cambridge, U.K.: Cambridge University Press, 1992), 11.
3. There are, however, several encouraging exceptions to this trend. These include: Linda Kintz, *Between Jesus and the Market: The Emotions That Matter in Right-Wing America* (Durham, N.C.: Duke University Press, 1997); and Susan F. Harding, *The Book of Jerry Falwell: Fundamentalist Language and Politics* (Princeton, N.J.: Princeton University Press, 2000), which both devote sustained attention to the outpouring of books, videotapes, and other popular materials disseminated by contemporary Protestant evangelical organizations in the United States. Cf. Yves Gonzalez-Quijano, *Les gens du livre: Éditions et champ intellectuel dans l'Égypte républicaine* (Paris: CNRS Éditions, 1998), for an illuminating discussion of the Islamization of the book industry in Egypt since the 1950s; and Arvind Rajagopal, *Politics after Television: Hindu Nationalism and the Reshaping of the Public in India* (Cambridge, U.K.: Cambridge University Press, 2001), for a sensitive reading of the relationship between televised national broadcasts of the Ramayana serial and the Birthplace of Ram movement, at the heart of recent Hindu nationalist politics.
4. I define *authority* here as the product of a struggle to win or maintain support from others through the imposition of claims to legitimacy. This definition is loosely based on Weber's notion of "legitimate domination," encompassing a category of commands that are obeyed because there exists an "interest in obedience" (Max Weber, *Economy and Society* [New York: Bedminster Press, 1968], 212; cf. 31–38). I do not depend strictly on Weber's typology of legitimate order, however, or on the sources of legitimate expression as he identified them. For one thing, these categories are based

on a conception of "belief in legitimacy," the discursive conditions of which Weber did not find necessary to explicate in any detail.

5. Michel de Certeau, *The Writing of History* (New York: Columbia University Press, 1988), 138.
6. See, e.g., Alan L. Mittelman, *The Politics of Torah: The Jewish Political Tradition and the Founding of Agudat Israel* (Albany: State University of New York Press, 1996). It is well known that Weber considered it insufficient to rest claims about the social significance of religious ideas and beliefs upon positivist standards alone. As he insisted, "An *understanding* of [religious] behavior can be achieved *only from the viewpoint of the subjective experiences, ideas and purposes of the individuals concerned*—in short, from the viewpoint of *the religious behavior's meaning*" (Weber, *Economy and Society,* 399; emph. added).

   This tradition of hermeneutical practice—which could be traced back via Weber to Dilthey and thence to the early-nineteenth-century Romantic hermeneuticists such as Schleiermacher (although the methodology in question is more widespread than this lineage might suggest)—has consistently equated understanding with the *exposure* of a unique articulation of "truth" inhering in texts, cultural formations, or historical traditions. Such exposure is said to be accomplished through acts of "empathic identification" (what Schleiermacher called *Einfühlung*), "re-living" (Dilthey's category of *Nacherleben*), or "thick description" (Geertz). Thus we find, underlying the work of empathic understanding, a presumption of the accessibility of the inner life of authors or cultural practitioners, embedded in the texts they produce, which the interpreter is positioned to "uncover" or "recuperate" through a succession of approximations.
7. See, e.g., Russell T. McCutcheon, *The Insider/Outsider Problem in the Study of Religion: A Reader* (London: Cassell Press, 1999).
8. Writing about the "ethics" of representation, Marty and Appleby establish as a goal for the scientific study of religious fundamentalists that "the people described therein would recognize themselves in the portrait" (Marty and Appleby, *Fundamentalism Project,* 2:17). But it is striking that nowhere do they suggest how one would be able to confirm whether these acts of "self-recognition" have taken place. Nor do they explicitly broach the more difficult question of whether the objects of these studies want to be represented at all and what ought to be done in such cases. In other words, however commendable the fact that these scientists seek to elicit the "approval" of their informants, the hermeneutical model of empathy upon which their discourse depends must not escape critical scrutiny.
9. In addition to Mittelman, key studies of Agudat Israel, Haredism, and the haredim include: Gershon Bacon, *The Politics of Tradition: Agudat Yisrael in Poland, 1916–1939* (Jerusalem: Magnes Press, 1996); Menachem Friedman, "Life Tradition and Book Tradition in the Development of Ultraorthodox Judaism," in *Judaism Viewed from Within and from Without: Anthropological Studies,* ed. Harvey Goldberg (Albany: State University of New York Press, 1987), 235–255; Samuel Heilman, "The Holy and the Orthodox," in *Events and Movements in Modern Judaism,* ed. Raphael Patai and Emanuel S. Goldsmith (New York: Paragon House Press, 1995), 91–101; Samuel Heilman and Menachem Friedman, "Religious Fundamentalism and Religious Jews: The Case of the Haredim" in Marty and Appleby, *Fundamentalism Project,* 1:197–264; William B. Helmreich, *The World of the Yeshiva: An Intimate*

Portrait of Orthodox Jewry (New Haven, Conn.: Yale University Press,1982); Lawrence Kaplan, "Rabbi Isaac Hutner's 'Daat Torah Perspective' on the Holocaust: A Critical Analysis," *Tradition* 18 (1980): 235–248; Lawrence Kaplan, "*Daas Torah:* A Modern Conception of Rabbinic Authority," in *Rabbinic Authority and Personal Autonomy,* ed. Moshe Sokol (Northvale, N.J.: Jason Aronson Press, 1992), 1–60; Jacob Katz, "Orthodoxy in Historical Perspective," *Studies in Contemporary Jewry* 2 (1986): 3–17; Jacob Katz, "*Da'at Torah*—The Unqualified Authority Claimed for Halakhists," *Jewish History* 11 (1997): 41–50; Barry B. Levy, "Our Torah, Your Torah, and Their Torah: An Evaluation of the Artscroll Phenomenon," in *Truth and Compassion: Essays#/n Judaism and Religion in Memory of Rabbi Dr. Solomon Frank,* ed. Howard Joseph, Jack N. Lightstone, and Michael D. Oppenheim (Waterloo, Ont.: Canadian Corporation for Studies in Religion / Wilfred Laurier University Press), 137–189; Lawrence J. Silberstein, ed., *Jewish Fundamentalism in Comparative Perspective: Religion, Ideology, and the Crisis of Modernity* (New York: New York University Press, 1993); and Haym Soloveitchik, "Rupture and Reconstruction: The Transformation of Contemporary Orthodoxy," *Tradition* 28 (1994): 64–130.

10. See Soloveitchik, "Rupture and Reconstruction"; Heilman, "The Holy and the Orthodox."
11. See Friedman "Life Tradition"; Levy, "Our Torah."
12. Kaplan, "Rabbi Isaac Hunter," 284.
13. Soloveitchik, "Rupture and Reconstruction," 103. Cf. Heilman, "Holy and the Orthodox," 98.
14. Katz, "Da'at Torah," 41.
15. Katz, "Da'at Torah," 43. Cf. Bacon, *Politics of Tradition,* 55.
16. Kaplan, "Rabbi Isaac Hunter," 246. Kaplan argues that the modern usage of the term *da'at Torah* has no clear basis, either in the Talmud or in the *Responsa* literature. At best, he argues, it is based on a selective and motivated reading of classical sources. See Kaplan, "Daas Torah," 28–50. There is nevertheless a lack of agreement among scholars concerning the precise origins of *da'at Torah.* While Gershon Bacon and Jacob Katz both locate it rather strictly within the context of the emergence of Agudat Israel in the early part of the twentieth century, Kaplan emphasizes instead its roots in hasidic notions of charismatic leadership which were prevalent throughout Eastern Europe in the nineteenth century and eventually penetrated *mitnagdic* (i.e., nonhasidic) circles, including those out of which Agudat Israel emerged. See Kaplan, "Daas Torah," 54 n. 84. Cf. Bacon, *Politics of Tradition,* 50–57, and Katz, "Da'at Torah."
17. Kaplan, "Daas Torah," 12–13.
18. Kaplan, "Daas Torah," 22–23.
19. Kaplan, "Daas Torah," 23–24; emphasis added.
20. Rabbi Berel Wein, "*Daas Torah:* An Ancient Definition of Authority and Responsibility," *Jewish Observer* 27 (1994): 5–6.
21. Rabbi Yaakov Feitman, "Daas Torah: Tapping the Source of Eternal Wisdom," in *Torah Lives: A Treasury of Biographical Sketches,* ed. Nisson Wolpin (Brooklyn, N.Y.: Mesorah Publications, 1995), xii; emphasis added.
22. Feitman, "Daas Torah," xiv; emphasis added. Cf. Wein, *Daas Torah,* 5.
23. Wein, *Daas Torah,* 5.
24. Rabbi Nosson Scherman, "The Crisis of Leadership," *Jewish Observer* 10 (1975):

6; emphasis added.

25. Wein, *Daas Torah,* 8.

26. My use of the term *field* is based loosely on Pierre Bourdieu's notion of a "field of cultural production." See, for example, "Intellectual Field and Creative Project," in *Knowledge and Control: New Directions for the Sociology of Education,* ed. Michael F. D. Young (London: Collier-MacMillan Publishers, 1971), 161–188; and Bourdieu, *The Field of Cultural Production: Essays on Art and Literature* (New York: Columbia University Press, 1993).

   Following Bourdieu, my methodological orientation to specific intellectual agents, texts, and ideas emphasizes their positional properties, including networks of shared meanings, relations of collaboration, functional complementarity or competition, and distributions of power. This orientation supposes that, whenever individual players engage in the practices that define a given field, wittingly or unwittingly they enact strategies that reproduce and sustain the dynamically competitive structure of the social order in which they are situated. In other words, the practitioners in every field have an "interest" in securing legitimacy, even though they might deny, repress, or misrecognize their role in this struggle by proclaiming the "disinterestedness" of their activities (see, e.g., Bourdieu, *Field of Cultural Production,* 76–82).

27. I should hasten to add that the debate I have reconstructed in this discussion is at best partial. Certain cadres of intellectuals have not been given any explicit consideration here. These include haredi women writers or movement activists representing other modes of Jewish identity and practice (e.g., "modern" Orthodox, Conservative, Reform, Reconstructionist, secular Zionist)—to say nothing of the various adherents to competing world religions and to other powerful ideological movements, such as consumerism or nationalism—with which the voices of specific haredi authorities have become intertextually related in a shared system of global communication. Trying to accommodate these other voices would radically complicate the present account of discursive exchange, competition, and complementarity.

28. Mikhail Bakhtin invented the term *otvetstvennost,* translated into English either as *responsibility* or *answerability,* that is, as simultaneously discursive and normative. See *The Dialogic Imagination* (Austin: University of Texas Press, 1981); *Speech Genres and Other Late Essays,* ed. Caryl Emerson and Michael Holquist, trans. Vern McGee (Austin: University of Texas Press, 1986); and *Art and Answerability: Early Philosophical Essays* (Austin: University of Texas Press, 1990). Following Bakhtin, I would suggest that all scientists are necessarily located in a flux of dialogue, within which their representations are constituted both as responses to the previous utterances of others and as solicitations for responses from others.

PART II

CHAPTER 5

Republicizing Religiosity

MODERNITY, RELIGION, AND THE MIDDLE CLASS

❦

SANJAY JOSHI

$\mathcal{T}$he writings of Talal Asad, among others, have recently demonstrated how modernity restricted the meaning of religion to matters of private belief, its domain to the otherworldly and the esoteric, and its legitimate place to the world of rituals rather than the public and the political realm.[1] Broadly defined, *modernity* in this sense refers to new models of organizing social, political, and economic relations, which, we are told, draw their inspiration from the ideas of the Enlightenment and material circumstances following from the triumph of industrial capitalism. While there is no doubt that modernity does in many ways define the world we live in, one wonders if we must assume such a one-way traffic between religion and modernity. Must we, in our representations of the world, empower modernity with such a totalizing force? Can we not, and given the evidence to the contrary that we see around us, should we not perhaps, consider the possibility of a more dialogic process—in which religiosity is undoubtedly transformed by modernity but also in some way helps to shape and define the contours of the modern world? It is to explore such a possibility that this essay examines the emergence of what I term "republicized" Hindu religiosity in colonial north India. Focusing on the city of Lucknow, I demonstrate how a modernity shaped by Indian middle-class activists sought to transform multiple strands of beliefs and practices into a more or less monolithic Hinduism and purge it of its divisive and hierarchical aspects so as to suit their own public sphere projects.

A close examination of these efforts also reveals, however, that this recasting of religion created powerful discursive templates that were then deployed in many different ways, for a variety of different political agendas. Not only did a transformed Hindu religiosity allow for the imagination of "Hindu pride," often better known in its modern incarnation of *Hindutva*, or Hindu nationalism, but such templates also served the project of a more liberal "secular" nationalism. Exploring in some detail the nature of the modern political world fashioned by middle-class activists in India, therefore, raises some interesting possibilities of reinterpreting the relationship of religion and modernity. Not only does the modernity fashioned by this middle class bring religion back into the political realm, but this republicized religiosity becomes a central and constitutive feature of a political modernity. Such a modernity, this scenario suggests, allows for and perhaps makes necessary the simultaneous avowal of secular and the religious, thereby smudging the boundaries between two terms so often read as binary opposites.

Why did religion become so important for middle-class nationalists in colonial India? Partha Chatterjee has offered us one of the best-known recent explanations. Chatterjee argues that the middle-class intelligentsia of colonial India from the late nineteenth century onwards constructed an "inner domain of cultural identity," from which to ready the nation for contesting colonialism. He locates the concern with religion in the failure of middle-class projects in the "outer" domain of politics. Middle-class intellectuals sought to claim complete sovereignty over their "inner domain," which they defined primarily in spiritual terms. [2] In other words, the concern with religion is born out of a failure, a lack. Failures in the realm of "true" public sphere politics, which in colonial India was governed by the "rule of colonial difference," animated middle-class concerns with religion.[3] Although Chatterjee is very aware of how middle-class activists then deploy religion to attempt their own counterhegemonic project, religion in this work, as in many others, necessarily functions as an alternative to modernity, rather than a part of it. In the larger picture Chatterjee's focus on middle-class religiosity helps explain why "our modernity," the modernity of the colonized, had to be different from Western modernity.[4]

Yet there is a serious danger here of reifying religion as possessing a timeless and unchanging essence. In accepting Chatterjee's thesis in toto, we open up the possibility of simply reinforcing the notion that the domain of the religious, by definition it seems, excludes negotiations over political power conducted in the public sphere. This is also one of the dangers posed by some recent postcolonial readings of Indian history, in which religion figures as a resource for academic critiques of modernity. Scholars, such as Chatterjee himself, have found in the presence of religion in politics a position from which to critique the universalist claims of western modernity.[5] This is a valuable critique, both to show the limits of modern history and to push all historians toward understandings of the past which do not simply universalize a particular ideal-typical modernity, so often attributed to the history of Europe.[6] One wonders, however, if the best way to demonstrate the limits or indeed the partiality of a Eurocentric modernity's self-image is to reaffirm religion as something outside of, and an alternative to, the modern. At a time when religious chauvinism is on the rise, there is, for one, a danger of unwittingly valorizing this very different (and extremely modern) vision of religiosity.[7] Moreover, deploying religion in this fashion also appears to reaffirm the notion of religion as the essence of the nonmodern, bringing us surprisingly close to colonial readings of the non-West. Religion, after all, was the basis on which Orientalist scholarship "othered" India, to establish both the incapacity of Indians to rule themselves and to reaffirm the rationality and the capacity of the West to rule over others.[8] This essay seeks to offer an alternative, by first examining the ways in which the concern with religion of the middle class brought religion firmly into the realms of public sphere politics and then analyzing the larger implications of this republicized religiosity.

Republicizing Religiosity

A study of Lucknow's middle class bears out Chatterjee's thesis to some extent. The tropes of what Sudhir Chandra termed an "oppressive present" appear as important components of the middle-class imagination of the late nineteenth century.[9] Images of desolation and powerlessness abound in many of the writings of Westernized middle-class men of nineteenth-century Lucknow. P. C. Mookherji, himself evidently well educated in English and probably in government service as well, chose his own kind as the target of a scathing attack. In his book on the city he describes the "educated native" of his times: "A little big fellow with hollowness within . . . a heterogenous phenomena for self glorification [whose] walk is oblique . . . deportment foreign, his conduct conceited; his religion is no binding back to his soul; his conception is almost denational, his production is abortive." Mookherji was concerned with the lack of achievement, the inability of the educated Indians, actually to do anything to assert their presence in the city. As Mookherji said: "With all that vast bookish knowledge, the so called educated native is helpless to the last degree. . . . They talk and speechify well—but cannot show any matter."[10] The realization of the limits of their own participation in liberal politics initiated by colonial rule was, as Chatterjee suggests, evidently one factor prompting the despairing vision of the colonial middle class.

Although full of despair, and evidently dissatisfied with the amount of influence they were able to exercise over society, the autocritique of the late-nineteenth-century middle-class activists was hardly nihilistic. Contemporaries from differing ideological persuasions agreed that religion in some way constituted an answer to their problems. The England-educated barrister, social reformer, and future president of the Indian National Congress, Bishan Narain Dar, attributed the absence of "genius" in modern India to the lack of moral fiber in young men of his time, which in turn he attributed to their lack of religion. "Morality," he said, "has been so closely connected with religion, since history began, that whenever religious sanction has grown weak, serious moral injuries have occurred to mankind."[11] A present thought of as oppressive, corrupt, and alienating was blamed on the fact that society had gone astray from its religious ideals. Not only that, but the lack of religion was seen as one of the causes for their lack of freedom and strength. Partha Chatterjee's thesis, it seems, stands vindicated with this evidence. The religiosity of the nineteenth-century middle class in Lucknow, as in the Bengali case Chatterjee studies, appears to reflect closely a concern with overcoming their perceptions of inadequacy and disempowerment, which, in turn, were seen by them as a direct product of the colonial experience.

Yet there are significantly different possibilities of reading this history. The concern of middle-class activists with religion was very evident in the controversy surrounding cow protection in the 1890s. The cow protection movement did not have direct impact on the city of Lucknow. It was at its strongest in the Bhojpuri-speaking region, particularly the district of Azamgarh, where in 1893 a group of Hindu peasants attacked Muslim property and killed many Muslims to liberate cows in the name of Gaurakshini Sabhas. In his study of this movement Gyanendra Pandey has pointed to the multiple meanings that participants brought to their actions. He especially points to the cohesion as well as the contradictions present in the invocation of a Hindu identity in the mobilization efforts of leaders and participants in the movement.[12]

Bishan Narain Dar, in his capacity as a lawyer, was called upon to defend some Hindus convicted of rioting in Azamgarh. He visited the area and independently published a report blaming the "meddlesomeness" of colonial authorities for the trouble between Hindus and Muslims.[13] His agenda was fairly explicit: "I have no particular liking for the [*Gaurakshini*] *Sabha* myself as I think that such institutions whether they be Hindu or Mohammedan, do more harm than good in the long run, yet I do not see the wisdom and even the justice in interfering with other people's religious persuasion."[14] While turning a blind eye to the "interference" that Hindu Sabhas had practiced, Dar highlighted the actions of British officials in Azamgarh as evidence of governmental interference in the religious practices of Hindus. He represented the prosecution of Hindu rioters as "religious persecution, pure and simple."[15] Expressing grief at the partisan attitude of the colonial government toward Hindus, Dar depicted the whole affair as one in a series of happenings in which "Hindu religion is insulted and Hindu practices are treated with unconcealed scorn."[16]

One could, with Chatterjee, argue that the roots of this imagination lay in the middle-class perception of their oppression at the hands of the colonial state, especially if we add to Chatterjee's thesis the gendered dimension of a perceived emasculation though the workings of a "colonial masculinity."[17] It was to overcome this perception of oppression, to seek new sources of self-respect, that middle-class activists such as Dar sought to selectively celebrate aspects of what they perceived as evidence of "Hindu manliness" in Azamgarh. In his report, for instance, Dar complained that Hindus "have for years and years been treated like the proverbial dog whom any stick is good enough to beat with."[18] What he celebrated through this report was the possibility that Hindu peasants' actions had opened up for the imagining of a strong and virile community in contrast to a disempowered and oppressed one. It was the desire to celebrate a strong, virile, "native" self that led Dar to adopt a position valorizing the collective violence against Muslims enacted in Azamgarh. Despite distancing himself from the actions of the rioters, Dar demonstrated pride in the actions of the Hindu Sabha activists of Azamgarh, simply because their actions proved to him "that the Hindus are not quite such a meek, unmanly, and contemptible race as they have been imagined."[19]

Dar's report, no doubt, contains an element of the desire to contest the colonial domination of public sphere politics through the valorization of religion, which could be construed here, too, as an inner domain, a place of one's own. Yet this was hardly a retreat into any domain, uncolonized or otherwise. On the contrary, Dar used the report to criticize colonial official actions and bring the question of religion very much into the domain of public contestation with the state and its administration.[20] Of equal significance is how he did so. In titling his report *An Appeal to the English Public on Behalf of the Hindus of North-western Provinces and Oudh,* Dar explicitly made his criticism as a self-appointed representative of the Hindu community. His report, however, completely appropriated the complex web of events and ideas which had contributed to the disturbances in Azamgarh to the agenda of middle-class politics. The multiple meanings of "Hindu-ness" present in Azamgarh were submerged in Dar's report. The report also made it evident that Dar's concerns were not really with Azamgarh or even the cow protection movement. Despite acting as their lawyer, Dar described the cow protection movement as "humane, though somewhat impractical."[21] Moreover, in his report he was quite willing to acknowledge what he termed the "good deal of latent barbarism" among the participants. The interventions of men such as Dar produced a new, and specifically middle-class, discourse of Hindu religiosity. No doubt serving to overcome perceptions of middle-class inadequacy, the striking point about this modern Hindu religiosity was that, on the one hand, it distanced itself from the latent barbarism of the religious practices of illiterate peasants of Azamgarh, yet, on the other hand, it used the opportunity to celebrate "Hindu valor" and defend "Hindu rights" in the domain of public sphere politics.

There is little doubt that middle-class men did indeed find in religion a resource for overcoming their perceptions of disempowerment vis-à-vis the colonial state. But seeing religion—at least the religiosity of those of the middle class in their political projects—as only constituting an inner, or "uncolonized," domain seriously limits our understanding both of the nature of the middle-class agenda and of the category of religion. For one, treating "religion" as a synchronic entity ignores the ways in which religiosity itself was recast in very new terms through middle-class interventions in colonial India. Second, exclusively looking at religion as a way of contesting colonial hegemony glosses over the ways in which religion, like other middle-class interventions, was actively concerned with the empowerment of this social group over others. Together, these two lacunae obscure important historical connections between religion and power as they were being created anew through the politics of nationalism in India.

A number of studies of precolonial South Asia testify to the fact that religious institutions were very much a part of processes through which power and authority were constituted. The centrality of religion in political processes also made it a powerful locus for the creation of collective identities well before the advent of colonialism.[22] This was certainly the case in Lucknow, where Shia Islam played a significant role in the way politics and power were configured in the Nawabi courts.[23] Colonial rule entailed the severing of many of these connections and contributed in important ways to the transformation of religious identities in India. Whether through Orientalist reinterpretations of texts,[24] or new administrative and legal categories and practices,[25] colonialism created the circumstances for very different perceptions and possibilities of imagining religious communities. Central to this process, however, is also the often-overlooked role of middle-class activists who resisted the attempts of the state to push religion into the realms of the personal, by successfully republicizing religion through harnessing it to their interventions in the colonial public sphere. Such interventions not only created new understandings of religion but also decisively shaped the nature of modern politics in India.

The Possibilities and Limits of a Publicized Religiosity

References to Hindu religious practices or beliefs in Dar's report were either condescending or derogatory, even though he was representing the Hindus of his province and offered a spirited defense of their rights. Dar lived at a time when debates between Hindu reformers and revivalists were particularly keen. In fact, Dar was himself at the center of a controversy about religious practices, when his decision to go to England to study law led to a split in the Kashmiri Brahmin community of north India, and his own temporary ostracism from the community.[26] Despite that, however, and the fact that he left behind copious amounts of writing, much of it stressing the importance of religion, we are left with no clue as to Dar's own position on matters of devotional practice—whether, for instance, he advocated a "return" to *varnashram dharma* (in which the fourfold caste hierarchy would be central), or some reformed variant of Hinduism. In fact, Dar, like many of his middle-class contemporaries, was articulating a new sort of religiosity, forged out of concerns of middle-class activists as they sought to create a larger place for their own endeavors in the public sphere.

Traditional conceptions of religion, prevailing religious practices and beliefs, could not easily serve projects that were part of the agenda of the emerging middle class. Existing Hindu religiosity—with multiple traditions, metaphysical speculations, and, most obviously, social practices governed by hierarchical principles—was particularly unsuitable as the basis of an ideology to mobilize a public and create a community which could be represented by the middle class. Middle-class constructions of Hindu religiosity therefore stressed its active, this-worldly orientation as well as its nondivisive aspects. Through such reinterpretations activists sought to create a religiosity that could most effectively be deployed in the public sphere. This republicized Hindu religiosity emphasized community rather than hierarchy, unity rather than divisions and difference, activism rather than "mere" contemplation, and the exercise of reason over "blind faith." Much like other aspects of their public sphere politics in colonial India, however, this vision of a singular Hindu community was also riven with contradictions. Attempts to mobilize this community often made these contradictions visible, especially as the vision of an undivided Hindu community came into conflict with hierarchical beliefs and practices equally important for the middle class to maintain their social hegemony.

In addition to lay public sphere activists, religious specialists or those who had taken ascetic vows were involved in efforts at redefining religion. Swami Vivekanand was probably the most famous of such "patriotic *sanyasis*."[27] In Lucknow it was Swami Rama Tirtha, and later his disciple Narain Swami, who caught the imagination of the middle class. After earning a master's degree in mathematics, Rama Tirtha became a professor of mathematics at the Mission College in Lahore by 1896.[28] His decision to adopt the path of *Advaita Vedanta* (a monist philosophy based upon the Upanishads) and to lead the life of an ascetic monk has been linked to his meeting with Vivekanand in Lahore in 1897. It is certainly to Vivekanand that Rama Tirtha owed his philosophy of "Practical Vedanta," blending philosophical monism of the Upanishads with "patriotism and humanity."[29]

Swami Rama Tirtha's religiosity was quite the opposite of any sort of otherworldly speculation. "Vedanta locked in cupboards will just not do," he wrote, thus breaking from the path of Upanishadic philosophical abstraction and firmly establishing his Hindu religiosity in the public sphere.[30] Rama Tirtha's Vedanta had no place for rituals either. Rather than traditional animal sacrifices (*yagna*), he urged disciples to use the ingredients normally used in such sacrifices to feed the poor.[31] In the contemporary world, Rama Tirtha argued, "sacrifice (*yagna*) requires, not innocent animals, but rather to consign to the flames of love, all our feelings of groupism, that is, caste and religious differences (*jati-bhed*) and envy, which alone can bring us heaven on earth."[32] Real religion—politicians and poets, activists and ascetics, alike seemed to agree—did not lie in philosophical abstractions or blind devotion or ritual practices. Rather, real religion was intimately tied up with the world, with the concerns and problems of people. For the Kashmiri Pandit Brij Narain Chakbast, lawyer, poet, and nationalist, real religion lay in practices connected to the world. "One cannot be called a Brahmin by merely wearing the sacred thread," wrote Chakbast. His own conception of religion, according to his biographer, was intimately connected to "service of man and upholding of human freedom."[33] Such an anthropocentric view of religion, tied to ideas of humanity and national uplift, was a defining quality of the middle-class religiosity of the late nineteenth and early twentieth century.

These newly created standards of a "real" Hinduism were also deployed by middle-class activists to try to control or change existing traditions and practices. The *sadhu*s (wandering ascetics) of India were a favorite target, particularly for what was termed their "indolence." Undoubtedly, the fractious and fiercely independent nature of many ascetic sects added to the desire to "reform" the sadhus.[34] Rama Tirtha, despite his own ascetic vows, was highly critical of Indian sadhus, comparing them to "unhealthy scum" on a lake and as "suckers and parasites to the tree of nationality."[35] His disciple, Narain Swami, attempted to discipline these wandering ascetics and set up a "Sadhu Mahavidyalaya" (University for Sadhus) at Hardwar so that "illiterate sadhus" could be given what was considered an appropriate Sanskrit education.[36] Narain Swami was also active in the *Dharma Rakshana Sabha*, which sought to make Hindu charitable endowments more accountable to the public and in 1927 persuaded the government to set up the Hindu Religious and Charitable Endowments Committee to suggest measures for their better management.[37]

Equally important was the disciplining and reformulation of everyday religious practices. Here women were a particular target of reforming zeal, not only because they were perceived as inherently more religious but also for their ability to produce and shape future, appropriately religious subjects.[38] Sannulal Gupta's didactic manual aimed at middle-class women, *Strisubodhini,* sought to educate and improve women in this crucial aspect of their behavior, in addition to offering other advice. Gupta warns women against "superstition" and against "charlatans" who adopt a religious guise. Most religious specialists, but particularly wandering ascetics claiming powers of divine possession or sorcery (though also venal Brahmin priests), are shown to be frauds in Gupta's manual. The miracles of these soothsayers he shows to be based on simple scientific chemical reactions that an educated woman can be taught to see through.[39] Rather than depend on these unreliable and ultimately greedy religious intermediaries, the middle-class Hindu woman was, through this book, taught that *her* religion consisted of simply worshiping God in her own home and not entangling herself in "the webs of deceit of spirits, demons, and possession."[40] Ultimately, a woman's true religion, Gupta suggests, consists in following *stridharma* (literally a woman's religion/duties, effectively a religion of domesticity), and for that she has no need of either religious specialists or indeed to participate in fairs, festivals, or other public rituals.

Like contemporaneous movements among the Sikhs and those led by middle-class Muslims, many of the innovations coming from middle-class Hindus at this time consisted of drawing boundaries between religions. At the level of religious practice, for instance, it was common for Hindus, and particularly women, to seek boons and blessings at the shrines of Muslim *pirs,* or renowned holy men. This form of popular worship, which often cut across caste, class, sectarian, and religious boundaries, was unacceptable to middle-class reformers, who, undoubtedly influenced by a modern colonial epistemology, found such practices "irreligious." Reformers such as Gupta took it upon themselves to wipe out syncretic religious practices among Hindus. *Strisubodhini,* accordingly, contains a major diatribe against worshiping at the tombs of Muslim pirs, invoking fear (such worship may make women barren) and castigating such worship for demonstrating a disrespect for one's "own religion" because the shrines glorified individuals who were responsible for killing many Hindu men.[41]

Although many of the changes initiated by reformers in the late nineteenth and early twentieth centuries were couched in terms of rediscoveries of eternal truths about Hindu Dharma, there is little doubt that such innovations were recasting, if not reinventing, religious traditions.[42] This new Hindu religiosity not only allowed greater facility in constructing bounded religious communities to represent but also the opportunity for greater social control through the power or authority to define what did or did not constitute appropriate religious practice. This period also saw the emergence of a new middle-class notion of religiosity, in which religion was separated from superstition, became more rational and more amenable to the sensibilities of middle-class educated men and to their public sphere projects as well. Of course, middle-class religiosity of the late nineteenth century was not the first time that people speaking broadly within the Hindu ambit had dissented from or criticized existing social and cultural traditions, including the ideas and institutions of caste society. At the same time, however, the critical reformulation of religious ideas taking place in colonial India represented significant departures from existing traditions. The attempt to fashion, address, and mobilize a singularly imagined Hindu community in the nineteenth century was a unique attempt and one that reflected the concerns of members of the middle class and the new possibilities that were open to them in the colonial public sphere.[43]

Yet, as much as the writings of middle-class men reveal the tremendous confidence they had in their ability to transform social practices and beliefs at will, their projects remained necessarily partial and incomplete. At one level, conservatives in their own ranks resisted them. A man such as Shivanath Sharma, a prominent Hindi journalist and humorist of Lucknow, used his journal *Anand* to lampoon savagely the dress, eating habits, and even newer ways of relieving oneself that the Anglicized "Babu" unthinkingly copied from his masters.[44] At another, more quotidian level, middle-class efforts at transforming religious practices were resisted simply by being ignored. Arya Samaj sources inform us that the Lucknow branch of the Samaj was particularly strict in its enforcement of rules of conduct, even prohibiting members from participating in rituals with origins in superstitious Hinduism or syncretic popular practices blending Islamic and Hindu rituals.[45] Yet, at the level of actual practice, these rules were evidently ignored. A report from the Lucknow newspaper the *Advocate,* in 1904, reveals that "for some years" the president of the Lucknow Arya Samaj had been a gentleman by the name of Umrao Bahadur, who was born of a Hindu father and Muslim mother and who had himself married a Muslim woman.[46] When even the president of a branch of the Arya Samaj, which prided itself on orthodoxy, so evidently transgressed boundaries the organization was seeking to reinforce, then we can only conclude that there was a considerable gap between ideas and practice. Efforts by men seeking to create a monolithic, singular Hindu community were bound to remain unconsummated.

But a more serious limitation of the project of creating a public Hinduism, perhaps even more so than resistance at the level of praxis, was the fact that contradictions constitutive of the new modernity sought to be forged by middle-class activists worked to undermine their own efforts to construct this new entity. Nothing shows up these contradictions better than the vexed issue of caste. Caste was foremost among the variety of social, cultural, and devotional practices that needed to be tamed and disciplined to produce the new Hindu religiosity. With the principle of hierarchy at its center,[47] caste ideology as well as practices such as untouchability, interdictions on commensality, and restrictions on interaction between different castes were the biggest obstacles to realizing the sort of unity desired by public sphere activists in colonial Lucknow. Rama Tirtha made the criticism of caste one of the central motifs of his writing.[48] In fact, he attributed the decline of Indian civilization, the weakness of India itself, to the growing narrowness and divisions of Indian society: "Caught in distinctions of caste and religion, we have become separated from each other and hence, weak."[49]

A true Hindu, he said, "must not observe any discrimination against anybody. For him there is no differentiation between the rich and the poor, high and low, and a Brahmin and Shudra."[50] He insisted that the caste system, *as it existed,* did not conform to "*shastric* [scriptural] ideals." An originally harmonious system of division of labor, Rama Tirtha said, over a period of time became "stultified, ossified, mummified, or petrified."[51] The modernity of Rama Tirtha's interpretation is most evident in his critique of the *Manu Smriti,* a fourth-century canonical text that most explicitly and unabashedly sets out caste and gender hierarchies and prescribes draconian punishments for transgressions. "Instead of serving the people," Rama Tirtha argues, the *Manu Smriti* acted as "a despotic tyrant."[52]

Despite the theoretical rejection of caste by reformers, for many middle-class men upper-caste status was an important marker of their social respectability and their distance from lower classes and castes. Sannulal Gupta's book shows him to be a great supporter of the Arya Samaj, whose formal ideology also rejected notions of hereditary caste privilege or disability.[53] Yet Gupta's book demonstrates how the attempts at constructing a singular, rational, and modern religious tradition were often undermined by very traditional ideas of separation and hierarchy which were equally part of the way "Aryadharma" was imagined by him. It is when criticizing the superstitious practice of worshiping at the shrines of local pirs that Gupta most evidently reveals the limits of his imagination of the category of Hindu. The most convincing reason he can offer to dissuade women from worshiping "un-Hindu" pirs is to point to the low-caste origins of these saints. "Isn't it a matter of shame," Gupta asks, "that even though we are high-born (*uchha kul*), we worship a base-born person?"[54] Worshiping these saints, he points out, is to worship *Chamars* (an "untouchable" caste) and, even worse, *Bhangis* (scavengers, even lower on the caste scale). "Ram! Ram!" writes this Arya Samaj supporter, "have we Aryas become so *irreligious and backward* that we should fold our hands to and worship Bhangis, Chamars, Koilis, Chandalas, etc."[55] Clearly, neither the religion nor the progress that Gupta or his kind were seeking to construct in colonial India included any association with the lower castes. Rama Tirtha's fond hopes were evidently at odds with the sentiments and practices of many of the people he addressed. The new religiosity of the middle-class imagination revealed contradictions almost at the moment of its creation.

By the 1920s caste issues were very much at the forefront of political debate in nationalist circles. This was also the time when an assertive Hindu nationalism, building on the templates of a new religiosity, was seeking to play a larger role in political affairs by championing the "rights" of a Hindu political community.[56] To represent the rights of Hindus successfully and to create a stronger, more assertive, Hindu self in colonial north India, it was crucial to the project of Hindu publicists in the 1920s to reiterate, at least rhetorically, the notion of a single Hindu community. There were, for instance, many highly charged, emotional articles in support of allowing "Untouchables" entry to Hindu temples in *Madhuri*, the prominent Hindi journal of Lucknow. One of them compared the Untouchables' situation with children prevented from embracing their father.[57] Yet, much like the earlier efforts of people such as Dar to represent a single Hindu community, the Hindu nationalism of the 1920s also betrayed its limitations as a project of male, upper-caste, middle-class empowerment.

Caste was not only an integral part of brahmanical Hindu religious discourse but also an important part of the privileges enjoyed by the upper-caste men. There should be little surprise, then, that caste practices always sat uneasily with representations of a homogeneous Hindu community. This became one arena in which the limits of the modern Hindu religiosity stood revealed most clearly. Immediately after an impassioned plea on behalf of allowing Untouchables temple entry, *Madhuri,* for instance, warned against taking such reformism too far. While it was important to recognize certain "Hindu birthrights," *Madhuri* argued, showing Untouchables "more compassion than was necessary" would only divide Hindu society and therefore harm the Hindu movement. Even allowing lower castes access to traditional markers of upper-caste status, such as wearing the sacred thread, would only alienate orthodox Hindus and hence harm Hindu society as a whole, the editors argued.[58] On an earlier occasion, *Madhuri*'s upper-caste editors had also criticized the attempts to force Hindu Sabha members to eat a meal cooked by Untouchables. Their objections were expressed through a rhetorical question, asking if "the natural and bodily impurity which made such *jatis* [castes] untouchable in the first place [had] disappeared all of a sudden?" "The Hindu Sabha," the journal said, "should be an organization which a Hindu of any caste or sect should feel is his own."[59] However much the editors may have liked to believe otherwise, fault lines based on caste and class limited not only the Hindu Sabha members but the very imagination of a modern publicized Hindu religiosity.

It is important not to dismiss such contradictions in middle-class Hindu nationalism as evidence of a simple political duplicity or to suggest that this avowal of a single Hindu community was merely using religion as a guise for more real material or political interests. That would be tantamount to arguing that Bishan Narain Dar went to Azamgarh with the real agenda of undermining the religious sensibilities of the peasants there, even while claiming to represent the Hindu community; or that the editors of *Madhuri* were simply upper-caste bigots who put on a facade of liberality while writing some articles in the journal but allowed their true feelings to surface in some pieces. There is really no historical justification for such conspiracy theories. In fact, such dismissals have lurking at their root the notion that "real" religion needs to be concerned with the otherworldly, with individual worship, rather than political power. What middle-class interventions actually did was to repoliticize religion in the contexts of the colonial public sphere. Of course, like all religiosities perhaps, the product of their efforts also reflected their own interests and the power configurations emerging in the late nineteenth and early twentieth centuries in colonial north India. This context included tensions and contradictions that were constitutive of the middle class. The coexistence of the old and the new, the hierarchical and the emancipatory, and the religious and the secular are therefore better seen as examples of inevitably fractured modernities characteristic of middle-class politics. A closer look at other deployments of this republicized Hindu religiosity will make this more evident.

Deploying Religiosity

Despite its many limitations, the reconstitution and disciplining of Hindu ideas and practices was an important development, enabling as well as limiting a variety of political and cultural initiatives in the public sphere. As an ideological construct, this republicized religiosity allowed the public sphere activists to represent a unified Hindu community and thus enabled a larger, more influential role for them in north India society and politics. Probably the most significant contribution of this new religiosity, however, was that it created a set of discursive templates for the deployment of religion in the public sphere. Emphasizing the novel idea of a Hindu community, the new Hindu religiosity sought to deny most of what divided this putative community as "false" religion or as later degenerations that needed correction. Once the lived religious practices and the multiplicity of traditions were either so characterized or subsumed as inferior versions of a more authentic religious tradition, then a publicized religiosity could be deployed in the public sphere for a variety of endeavors.

Tamed Hindu religiosity, liberated from specific contexts and practices, could and was deployed in different ways, as part of many political projects and in many sorts of discourses. A variety of explicitly nationalist projects were the most obvious among them. Having consigned caste and other inconvenient features of lived Hinduism to the realms of false religion and emphasized the pristine purity of Advaita Vedanticism, Rama Tirtha and the more famous Vivekanand deployed the new religiosity to impress upon foreign and native audiences the glories of Hinduism. It was equally necessary for caste and other parochial aspects to be defined as historical accretions upon a true Hindu essence, before India's first president and philosopher, S. Radhakrishnan, could claim that "Vedanta is not a religion, but religion itself in its most universal and deepest significance."[60] A range of hierarchical precepts reinforcing caste and gender distinctions and a significant history of sectarian conflicts within and between groups of rival Hindu religious specialists and ascetics needed to be marginalized, suppressed, or subsumed by this new notion of Hindu religiosity before Gandhi could define "nonviolence" as one of the essential virtues of Hinduism.[61] On the other hand, political activists such as Bishan Narain Dar were not so concerned with the history and philosophy of Hinduism. But, even for him to be able to appropriate subaltern religiosity in the name of representing the rights of a Hindu community against the "meddling" of the colonial state, it was necessary to have the idea of a Hindu community free of divisions, whose rights were to be defended by middle-class activists like himself.

Abiding faith in liberal values and commitment to the politics of nation building may have led Dar to emphasize, even in his celebration of Hindu might, shared aspects of the history and culture of Hindus and Muslims.[62] In other contexts, however, the cultural politics of Hindu assertiveness could, and was, used to construct a much less plural vision of the nation, underscoring Hindu superiority while compelling Muslims to recognize their status as the vanquished.[63] This aggressive Hindu nationalism also drew upon the templates of middle-class modernized Hinduism, celebrating a real Hinduism—one not divided by caste, class, language, or region—as the ideological basis for a Hindu community it sought to represent. A rhetoric of community and solidarity, rather than hierarchy, as the characteristic of a modern Hinduism is equally necessary for the middle-class proponents of Hindutva today when they tear down mosques or carry out systematic pogroms of Muslims or Christians in the name of "restoring Hindu pride."

But this is, by now, well known. What is more surprising, however, is that the discursive templates that allowed for the discourse of Hindu nationalism to emerge also underpin large parts of the most liberal and so-called secular discourse of Indian nationalism. Jawaharlal Nehru is almost universally regarded as a quintessential modernist. His rationalism, a belief in the progressive impact of Western science and technology and heavy industry, has often led to unfavorable comparisons with Mahatma Gandhi, the "indigenous" critic of modern industrial society.[64] In the India of the 1990s, moreover, Nehru's name has also been inextricably linked with the notion of secularism. Radical and right-wing Hindu critics alike allege that "Nehruvian secularism," which ignored the religious sensibilities of the majority of India's population, lies at the root of many of the problems besetting the Indian polity. Nehru's own disdain for "superstitious practices and dogmatic beliefs" and his outward rejection of religion, because its "method of approach to life's problems . . . was . . . not that of science," do, on the surface, appear to reinforce the image of Nehru the modern secularist.[65] What is quite surprising, therefore, is to note the extent to which Nehru's narrative, as recounted in his *Discovery of India,* also draws heavily upon a republicized Hindu religiosity.

One reason that Nehru could not unequivocally celebrate the Indian past was because that past contained much that was evidently unsuitable for a progressive, modern nation-state. Yet that past needed to be appropriated, made available, for the history of the modern nation. How, then, were hierarchical and nonmodern institutions and ideas, so much a part of that history, to be accounted for? How was Nehru to square his dislike for nonscientific superstition and dogma of religion with the need to celebrate and take pride in a past that so evidently consisted of much that was religious? Nehru's resolution was very much in the discursive pattern established by men such as Rama Tirtha or Vivekanand. Expressing his admiration for the vitality of the Vedas and the spirit of inquiry and philosophical insights of the Upanishads,[66] Nehru celebrated the "rational spirit of enquiry, so evident in ancient times, which might well have led to the further growth of science," but then notes a historical and intellectual decline when such a spirit of inquiry is replaced by orthodox, orthoprax religion and "irrationalism and a blind idolatry of the past." It is then that Indian life, in Nehru's view, becomes "a sluggish stream, living in the past."[67] It is this degeneration of an authentic tradition that leads to the sort of superstition and dogma Nehru associates with religion, which "petrifies" a system of reasonable division of labor and a mechanism of group solidarity into the oppressive caste system.[68]

In common with much of nationalist writing, Nehru exhibited what has variously been described as the "aporia" and the "Janus-faced" character of nationalism, asserting simultaneously the "objective modernity" and the "subjective antiquity" of the Indian nation.[69] The tension between the two is never quite resolved, as this quotation bears out.

> India must break with much of her past and not allow it to dominate the present. Our lives are encumbered with the dead wood of this past; all that is dead and has served its purpose has to go. But that does not mean a break with, or forgetting of, the vital and life-giving in that past. We can never forget the ideals that have moved our race, the dreams of the Indian people through the ages, the wisdom of the ancients . . . nor can we forget the myriad experiences which have built up our ancient race and lie embedded in our subconscious minds. We will never forget them or cease to take pride in that noble heritage of ours. If India forgets them, she will no longer remain India and much that has made her our joy and pride will cease to be.

The only way Nehru could appropriate history for the Indian nation was to fall back on notions almost identical to those of a real Hinduism deployed by the middle-class activists in the nineteenth century. What India needed, therefore, was not to reject the "vital and life-giving" past but to break with "all the dust and dirt of the ages that have covered her up and hidden her inner beauty and significance, the excrescences and abortions that have petrified her spirit, set it in rigid frames, and stunted her growth. We have to cut away these excrescences and remember afresh the core of that ancient wisdom."[70]

A tamed, disciplined, religious heritage, unencumbered by the "dust and dirt of the ages," was the essence of Nehru's "wisdom of the ancients." Such a heritage, liberated from lived practices as well as a host of hierarchical and nonmodern notions, could be polished, selectively appropriated, to serve as a glorious and untarnished resource available to the emerging Indian nation. Ironically, therefore, it is the discursive template of republicized religiosity that allows Nehru, the arch-secularist, to detach religious ideas from their contexts, from religion itself as he understands the term. It is only a new way of thinking about religiosity that allows Nehru to celebrate the wisdom of the ancients and their spirit of inquiry while condemning the rest as the "dust and dirt," as "excrescences and abortions." It is this religiosity that allows the secularist to first construct and then condemn only one part of a tradition as religion.

Conclusion

Nationalist modernity in India evidently did not relegate religion to the realms of the private or personal belief. On the contrary, actions of middle-class men in colonial India brought the discourse of religiosity firmly into the domain of public politics: far from a being a "consciousness other than a consciousness of reality," a republicized religion became constitutive of the realities of nationalist politics in India. Liberated from specific devotional beliefs and so-cial and cultural practices and detached from the worldviews from which they emerged, republicized religiosity was easily deployed for a variety of modern projects in which the middle class played a central role. Such interventions, of course, also transformed religion. The republicized Hindu religiosity of the middle class was considerably different from the myriad customs, beliefs, and practices that had previously characterized Hinduism. Undoubtedly a modern phenomenon, this middle-class vision of Hindu religiosity cannot be dismissed either as nonreligion, however, or reduced to a duplicitous drive to acquire po-litical power. Looking at this phenomenon in the context of a longer history, in fact, we could well see this as yet another instance in which transformations in religious ideas both reflected and contributed to struggles over political power. Moreover, the very visible presence of religion in the modern arena of nation-alist politics also allows us to question the ideal-typical model of modernity itself.

A close examination of middle-class interventions bringing religion into the domain of modern politics certainly reveals a number of contradictions. While their interventions modernized religion, it appears that religion in turn under-pinned their constructions of the modern as well. Even as their recasting of re-ligion sought to transform it to the ends of modern public sphere politics, their modern political idiom contained elements drawn from much older and hierar-chical ideas about political and social organization. Modern notions of secular-ism drew on the same discourse of religiosity which fostered what has been termed "communalism."[71] In short, the cultural reinscriptions of the middle class were not recorded on a tabula rasa. Their efforts very obviously deployed newer ideas and used new possibilities that opened up with colonial rule yet also re-tained many older resources of respectability, not quite consistent with the rheto-ric of Enlightenment freedoms.

But how are we to understand the contradictions of middle-class politics, and particularly the presence of religion in the very modern realm of national-ist politics? Are these contradictions simply pointers to the impossibility of a true modernity in a world peopled by *Homo hierarchicus,* as Louis Dumont's work suggested, echoing the sentiments of many generations of Orientalist schol-ars and colonial administrators before him?[72] Or should we follow the lead of-fered by Partha Chatterjee, among some other scholars of the Subaltern Studies collective, and trace the contradictions of the middle class to the colonial mi-lieu that compelled the Indian middle class to define its modernity in ways very different from that of the West?[73] Underlying all these questions, ostensibly about the peculiarities of the Indian case are comparisons between the failures, lacks, or deviations of the Indian case, and certain "originary" models.

This essay suggests an alternative. As empirical evidence from other parts of the colonial as well as metropolitan world mounts, scholars are coming to the conclusion that the model of an ideal-typical modernity, which has nothing to do with religion, is increasingly difficult to square with historical experience.[74] Although the narrative of modernization emphasizes the decline of religion and the growing secularization of society as an essential part in the emergence of the "modern West," recent scholarship questions these assumptions. Jose Casanova's work on the place of religion in modern society points out that "deprivatized" religion can, under certain circumstances, have a formative role to play in modern politics.[75] Peter van der Veer warns against accepting the secularization thesis too easily by pointing to the important role played by Evangelical Christianity and the revival of Roman Catholicism in producing the modern subject and shaping political culture in Victorian Britain. Van der Veer, in fact, makes a case for arguing that modernity was "sacralized" at the moment of its production, not just in India but also in Europe.[76]

If modernity in the West, despite its ideal-type representations, did not automatically usher in a new secular order but indeed was constituted by existing religious discourses, then the case for Indian exceptionalism—whether based on primordialism or guided by the intent of demonstrating the radical heterogeniety of a colonial modernity—becomes weaker. Rather than understand the Lucknow middle-class religiosity as a lack or failure, in which they strive for and ultimately fail to achieve the secular-modern ideal, we can look at them as active producers and the products of a sacralized modernity, which in turn produced a modernized religiosity in colonial India. This was a modernity shaped by their own concerns and contexts, and their rhetoric and politics were in turn shaped by it. Religion, or rather self-definitions based on religious categories, became a critical part of the modern self, created by the colonial middle class. The modernity that middle classes constructed in colonial India, therefore, used the new and the old and looked ahead as well as back. The modern in this case was built on the traditional and coexisted with it, belying neat dichotomies between the modern and the traditional, the religious and the secular. It is this fractured modernity,[77] built upon but never erasing existing traditions, which allows for the simultaneous articulation of the traditional and the modern, the religious and the secular, which are so characteristic of modern politics not only in India but also across much of the colonial and postcolonial world.

Notes

I am grateful to the organizers for providing me the opportunity to present an earlier version of this essay at the "After Secularism/Religion" conference organized at the University of Minnesota in May 2000. The essay benefited considerably from comments offered by Shampa Biswas as well as other participants. Perceptive and helpful suggestions by the conference organizers, particularly Derek Peterson, helped bring it to its present form. The final essay has been shaped by the close reading and comments offered (as always) by Sanjam Ahluwalia.

1. Talal Asad, *Genealogies of Religion: Discipline and Reasons of Power in Christianity and Islam* (Baltimore: Johns Hopkins University Press, 1993).

2. Partha Chatterjee, *The Nation and Its Fragments: Colonial and Postcolonial Histories* (Princeton, N.J.: Princeton University Press,1993), 6–7.
3. Chatterjee, *Nation and Its Fragments,* 16–18.
4. Partha Chatterjee, *Our Modernity* (Rotterdam, Neth., and Dakar, Senegal: SEPHIS and CODESRIA, 1997).
5. Dipesh Chakrabarty, "Postcoloniality and the Artifice of History: Who Speaks for 'Indian' Pasts?" *Representations* 37 (winter 1992); Chatterjee, *Our Modernity;* Ashis Nandy, "The Politics of Secularism and the Recovery of Religious Tolerance," in *Mirrors of Violence: Communities, Riots, and Survivors in South Asia,* ed. Veena Das (Delhi, India: Oxford University Press, 1990).
6. Chakrabarty, "Postcoloniality."
7. Sumit Sarkar, *Writing Social History* (Delhi, India: Oxford University Press, 1997).
8. Ronald Inden, *Imagining India* (Cambridge, Mass.: Basil Blackwell, 1990); Gyanendra Pandey, *The Construction of Communalism in Colonial North India* (Delhi, India: Oxford University Press, 1990).
9. Sudhir Chandra, *The Oppressive Present: Literature and Social Consciousness in Colonial India* (Delhi, India: Oxford University Press, 1992).
10. P. C. Mookherji, "The Pictorial Lucknow" (unpublished galley proofs dated 1883, Oriental and India Office Collection, London), 145–46.
11. Bishan Narain Dar, *Collected Speeches and Writings of Pt. Bishan Narain Dar,* ed. H. L. Chatterjee (Lucknow, India: Anglo-Oriental Press, 1921), 1:89.
12. Pandey, *Construction of Communalism.*
13. Bishan Narain Dar, *An Appeal to the English Public on behalf of the Hindus of Northwestern Province and Oudh* (Lucknow, India: G. P. Varma and Brothers Press, 1893).
14. Dar, *Appeal to the English Public,* app. 6.
15. Dar, *Appeal to the English Public,* app. 9.
16. Dar, *Appeal to the English Public,* app. 10.
17. Mrinalini Sinha, *Colonial Masculinity: The "Effeminate" Bengali and the "Manly" Englishman in Nineteenth Century Bengal* (Manchester, U.K.: Manchester University Press, 1995); John Rosselli, "The Self-Image of Effeteness: Physical Education and Nationalism in Nineteenth-Century Bengal," *Past and Present* 86 (February 1980).
18. Dar, *An Appeal to the English Public,* 30.
19. Dar, *An Appeal to the English Public,* 28.
20. This is also how it was primarily read by the administration. Dar's report was widely cited and criticized within the administration for its antigovernment tone. For one such interpretation, see the official report on Dar written at the time he was elected president of the 1911 session of the Indian National Congress (Government of India, Home Political, January 1912, B121–123, National Archives of India).
21. Dar, *Appeal to the English Public,* 8.
22. Peter van der Veer, *Religious Nationalism: Hindus and Muslims in India* (Berkeley: University of California Press, 1994); Susan Bayly, *Saints, Goddesses, and Kings: Muslims and Christians in South Indian Society, 1700–1900* (Cambridge, U.K.: Cambridge University Press, 1989); Arjun Appadurai, *Worship and Conflict under Colonial Rule* (Cambridge, U.K.: Cambridge University Press, 1981).
23. J. R. I. Cole, *Roots of North Indian Shi'ism in Iran and Iraq: Religion and State in Awadh, 1722–1859* (Delhi, India: Oxford University Press, 1989).

24. Peter van der Veer, "The Foreign Hand: Orientalist Discourse in Sociology and Communalism," in *Orientalism and the Postcolonial Predicament,* ed. Carol Breckenridge and Peter van der Veer (Philadelphia: University of Pennsylvania Press, 1993); Inden, *Imagining India;* Romila Thapar, "Imagined Religious Communities? Ancient History and the Search for a Hindu Identity," *Modern Asian Studies* 23 (1989).

25. Bernard Cohn, *An Anthropologist among the Historians and Other Essays* (Delhi, India: Oxford University Press, 1987); Appadurai, *Worship and Conflict under Colonial Rule;* Robert E. Frykenberg, "The Emergence of Hinduism as a Concept and as an Institution: A Reappraisal with Special Reference to South India," in *Hinduism Reconsidered,* ed. Gunther-Dietz Sontheimer and Hermann Kulke (Delhi, India: Manohar, 1997); J. D. M. Derrett, "The Administration of Hindu Law by the British," *Comparative Studies in Society and History* 4 (1961); Gregory C. Koslowski, *Muslim Endowments and Society in British India* (Cambridge, U.K.: Cambridge University Press, 1985); Lata Mani, *Contentious Traditions: The Debate on Sati in Colonial India* (Berkeley: University of California Press, 1998).

26. Henny Sender, *The Kashmiri Pandits: A Study of Cultural Choice in North India* (Delhi, India: Oxford University Press,1985).

27. Tapan Raychaudhri, *Europe Reconsidered: Perceptions of the West in Nineteenth Century Bengal* (Delhi, India: Oxford University Press, 1988); Sumit Sarkar, "'Kaliyuga', 'Chakri' and 'Bhakti': Ramakrishna and His Times," *Economic and Political Weekly,* 18 July 1992.

28. Pt. Brijnath Sharga, *Life of Swami Ram Tirtha,* 2d ed. (Lucknow, India: Rama Tirtha Pratishthan, 1968); Puran Singh, *The Story of Swami Rama: The Poet Monk of India,* rev. ed. (Lucknow, India: Rama Tirtha Pratishthan, 1974); S. R. Sharma, *Swami Rama Tirtha* (Bombay: Bhartiya Vidya Bhavan, 1961).

29. Singh, *Story of Swami Rama,* 87.

30. Swami Rama Tirtha, *Bharat Mata: Bharatiya Ekta aur Unnati ke Mool Mantra,* Rama Tirtha Granthavali, vol. 7 (Lucknow, India: Shri Rama Tirtha Pratisthan, 1982), aphorism no. 83, 15.

31. Rama Tirtha, *Bharat Mata,* aphorism no. 16, 3.

32. Rama Tirtha, *Bharat Mata,* aphorism no. 60, 11.

33. Saraswati Saran Kaif, *Chakbast* (Delhi, India: Sahitya Akademi, 1986), 35.

34. See William R. Pinch, "Soldier Monks and Militant Sadhus," in *Contesting the Nation: Religion, Community, and the Politics of Democracy in India,* ed. David Ludden (Philadelphia: University of Pennsylvania Press, 1996).

35. Sharga, *Life of Swami Ram Tirtha,* 155.

36. Sharga, *Life of Swami Ram Tirtha,* 25.

37. Sharga, *Life of Swami Ram Tirtha,* 408–409.

38. Sanjay Joshi, *Fractured Modernity: The Making of a Middle Class in Colonial North India* (Delhi, India: Oxford University Press, 2001), 59–95; Anshu Malhotra, "Pativratas and Kupattis: Gender, Caste, and Identity in Punjab, 1870s–1920s" (Ph.D. diss., School of Oriental and African Studies, University of London, 1998); Gail Minault, *Secluded Scholars: Women's Education and Muslim Social Reform in Colonial India* (Delhi, India: Oxford University Press, 1998).

39. Sannulal Gupta, *Strisubodhini,* ed. Pandit Rupnarayan Pandey (Lucknow, India: Tejkumar Press Bookdepot, 1954), 635–676.

40. Gupta, *Strisubodhini,* 678.

41. Gupta, *Strisubodhini,* 643–645.
42. See Harjot Oberoi, *Construction of Religious Boundaries: Culture, Identity and Diversity in the Sikh Tradition* (Delhi, India: Oxford University Press, 1994); Kenneth W. Jones, *Arya Dharma* (Delhi, India: Manohar,1989); van der Ver, *Religious Nationalism.*
43. After the death of Rama Tirtha, for instance, his disciple Narain Swami decided that the most fitting memorial for his spiritual mentor was the establishing of the "Rama Tirtha Publication League," which later became the "Swami Rama Tirtha Pratishthan," and undertook the task of publishing and disseminating the message of his Guru to the largest possible audience (Swami Rama Tirtha Pratishthan,"*Swami Narayana: Some Reminiscences with a Brief Life Sketch* [Lucknow, India: Rama Tirtha Pratishthan, 1975], 26).
44. Shivanath Sharma, *Mister Vyas Ki Katha* (Lucknow, India: Ganga Pustakmala, Vikram Samvat 1984, c. 1927).
45. Satyaketu Vidyalankar and Haridutt Vedalankar, *Arya Samaj ka Itihas,* vols. 1–2 (Delhi, India: Arya Swadhyaya Kendra, 1984), 1:589–590 and 2:288.
46. *Advocate,* 27 October 1904, cited in the report of "City Arya Samaj, Lucknow" *Report of the Nineteenth Indian National Social Conference* (Benaras, 1905), xlv–xlvi.
47. Louis Dumont, *Homo Hierarchicus: An Essay on the Caste System,* trans. Mark Sainsbury (Chicago: University of Chicago Press, 1970).
48. Singh, *Story of Swami Rama,* 221; Rama Tirtha, *Bharat Mata,* 42.
49. Rama Tirtha, *Bharat Mata,* 102.
50. Rama Tirtha, *Sanatan Dharma* (Lucknow, India: Rama Tirtha Pratisthan, n.d.).
51. Sharga, *Life of Swami Ram Tirtha,* 146.
52. Sharga, *Life of Swami Ram Tirtha,* 146.
53. Jones, *Arya Dharma,* 33.
54. Gupta, *Strisubodhini,* 645.
55. Gupta, *Strisubodhini,* 647; emphasis added.
56. Van der Veer, *Religious Nationalism;* Pandey, *Construction of Communalism;* Joshi, *Fractured Modernity.*
57. *Madhuri,* 30 April 1925, 564–566.
58. *Madhuri,* 30 April 1925, 564–566.
59. *Madhuri,* September 1924, 275.
60. Van der Veer, *Religious Nationalism,* 68.
61. M. K. Gandhi, *Hindu Dharma* (Delhi, India: Orient Paperbacks, 1995), 8.
62. Dar, *An Appeal to the English Public,* 23.
63. Van der Veer, *Religious Nationalism;* Pandey, *Construction of Communalism.*
64. Chandra, *Oppressive Present,* 6–10; see also Gyan Prakash, *Another Reason: Science and the Imagination of Modern India* (Princeton, N.J.: Princeton University Press,1999), for a different reading of the issue.
65. Jawaharlal Nehru, *The Discovery of India* (1946; rpt., Delhi, India: Jawaharlal Nehru Memorial Fund and Oxford University Press, 1982), 13–14.
66. Nehru, *Discovery of India,* 78–95.
67. Nehru, *Discovery of India,* 47.
68. Nehru, *Discovery of India,* 284–295.
69. Tom Nairn, "The Modern Janus," *New Left Review* 94 (November–December 1975); Benedict Anderson, *Imagined Communities: Reflections on the Origin and Spread*

of Nationalism (London: Verso, 1983); Prasenjit Duara, *Rescuing History from the Nation: Questioning Narratives of Modern China* (Chicago: University of Chicago Press, 1995).

70. Nehru, *Discovery of India,* 620.
71. Pandey, *Construction of Communalism.*
72. Dumont, *Homo Hierarchicus.*
73. Partha Chatterjee, *Our Modernity.*
74. Lila Abu-Lughod, *Remaking Women: Feminism and Modernity in the Middle East* (Princeton, N.J.: Princeton University Press, 1998).
75. Jose Casanova, *Public Religion in the Modern World* (Chicago: University of Chicago Press, 1994).
76. Peter van der Veer, "The Moral State: Religion, Nation and Empire in Victorian Britain and British India," in *Nation and Religion: Perspectives on Europe and Asia,* ed. Peter van der Veer (Princeton, N.J.: Princeton University Press, 1999).
77. For an elaboration of this argument, see Joshi, *Fractured Modernity.*

CHAPTER 6

A Religion That Was Not a Religion

THE CREATION OF MODERN SHINTO
IN NINETEENTH-CENTURY JAPAN

⚜

SARAH THAL

Explanations of what it means to be
Japanese have frequently invoked the influence of Shinto, widely understood as
the unchanging, ancient, indigenous religion of Japan. Yet Shinto—an amorphous
conglomeration of shrines and priests, charismatic movements and political pressure groups, self-consciously distinct from Buddhism, dedicated to the worship
of reputedly native *kami* (gods) according to rituals ostensibly unchanged for
over a thousand years—is a relatively recent creation. Developed in conjunc-
tion with the Japanese nation-state itself in the political, social, and intellectual
ferment of the nineteenth and early twentieth centuries, Shinto (literally, "the
Way of the Kami") is neither ancient, unchanging, nor peculiarly indigenous.
Nor is Shinto self-evidently a religion, as that term is used to define movements
such as Christianity or Buddhism which lay claim to historical founders and doctrinal creeds. Indeed, throughout the history of modern Shinto, advocates and
critics have alternately defined it as both a religion and not a religion, thereby demonstrating the difficulty of confining the reputed embodiment of Japaneseness within the conceptual categories of church and state, religion and
secularism.

It was not accidental that the politics of nativeness and the nation-state
became intimately tied to the problem of religion in nineteenth-century Japan.
Well-known historical episodes had long linked opposition to foreign influence

with opposition to foreign worship. In the sixth century, defenders of kami worship fought against the introduction of Buddhism by immigrants from the Korean peninsula. A thousand years later, the Tokugawa shogun evicted Portuguese missionaries on charges of fomenting rebellion and promoting allegiance to the Catholic pope and required all Japanese to prove their repudiation of Christianity by registering with Buddhist temples. During the nineteenth century, as European and American ships repeatedly sought and finally gained entry to Japanese ports, a nativist movement gained vigor in part by reviving attacks on Buddhism and Christianity as foreign forms of worship.[1] Thus, when the term *religion* (translated as *shūkyō,* "sectarian teachings") was introduced into Japanese in the 1860s as part of treaties guaranteeing the rights of resident foreigners, the concept quickly became associated with "evil, foreign teachings" antagonistic to native tradition and subversive of native authority. As advocates of kami worship attacked, adopted, then once again vilified religion, they succeeded first in establishing the Way of the Kami as a state-supported creed, then in distinguishing it from religion and setting it up as a Way superior to mere preachings of doctrine. By invoking a series of powerful, rhetorical contrasts between true Shinto and evil religion, priests, politicians, and public speakers created a realm of discourse and practice in which Shinto, the Way of the Kami, became the embodiment of the reputedly natural, civic-minded, and civilized essence of the Japanese nation. The processes through which advocates sought to unify the population of Japan, creating modern Shinto as both religion and above religion, have in turn left an indelible mark on attitudes toward religion, identity, and the Japanese nation throughout the twentieth century.

The term *Shinto,* referring to the worship of kami—powerful gods of the sun, creation, and other natural forces or objects—has existed since at least the eighth century of the common era.[2] Often adopted by ancient clans as tutelary or ancestral deities, kami were thought to guarantee good weather and prosperity to those who worshiped them correctly and to punish those who offended them with pain, illness, death, or natural calamities. Although at first considered antithetical to the buddhas and Buddhist rites that were imported from the Asian continent in the sixth century, the kami were soon absorbed into a combinatory religious universe of esoteric Buddhism and mountain worship. For approximately one thousand years, from the ninth century until the mid-nineteenth century, worship of the kami was interwoven with Buddhist rituals, teachings, and institutions. The Way of the Kami existed within a combinatory system dominated by Buddhism. It was neither a fully independent set of institutions nor a distinct philosophical tradition during most of the millennium before 1868.[3]

It was in the second half of the nineteenth century, during the decline of the Tokugawa shogunate and the establishment of a centralizing, imperial government in its place, that worship of the kami emerged from the activities of scattered scholars and priests to coalesce into a widely recognized entity called Shinto central to the political and intellectual life of the emerging nation-state.

This new Way of the Kami arose primarily from a nativist intellectual movement that spread among the educated gentry in the eighteenth and nineteenth centuries.[4] Seeking a native aesthetic to contrast with the dominance of Chinese writing, Confucian political thought, and Buddhist institutional controls in the late seventeenth and eighteenth centuries, scholars reconstructed a style of worship of the native kami, based on ancient texts, which they equated with naturalness, sincerity, emotionality, and the sacred power of the Japanese language. In the early nineteenth century, as Russian and American ships repeatedly encroached on Japanese waters, one prominent nativist, Hirata Atsutane (1776–1843), called for immediate action based on his own version of the kami Way. The source of all problems in society and government, Hirata argued, was the anger of powerful kami who were offended at being worshiped according to foreign rituals and under foreign names. Peace and prosperity could only be possible when worship of the kami had been purged of all foreign elements, especially Buddhism.

By the mid-nineteenth century many educated leaders were familiar with, if not actively committed to, Hirata's argument for the worship of pure Japanese kami. For many, this commitment included reverence and obedience to the only living kami, the emperor, who despite embodying the will of his ancestor, the Sun Goddess, was confined to the imperial court in Kyoto by the recognized ruler of the land, the Tokugawa shogun. By 1868 such nativist-inspired loyalty to the kami and the emperor helped shift attention to the imperial court, topple the Tokugawa shogunate, and establish in its place a new government focused on the young emperor Meiji.

In the early months and years of the new government, nativists exercised great power. It was their study of the ancient texts, for instance, that provided the blueprint for the earliest forms of the Meiji state, in which the emperor presided over a system that, for a short while, placed rituals in honor of the imperial kami above organs of general administration. Nativists in the new government seized the moment to proclaim, in the name of the emperor, a nationwide "separation of kami and buddhas (*shinbutsu bunri*)." This decree provided the authority for nativists throughout the countryside to "purify" local sites of worship, defining enshrined objects as kami, chasing out Buddhist priests, burning or selling off Buddhist ritual implements, and, in their place, setting themselves up as priests of the newly purified shrines (*jinja,* literally "shrines of the kami"). Within weeks of the edict and during the years that followed, thousands of priests who had presided over rituals to both buddhas and kami in the combined shrine-temple complexes of Tokugawa-period worship sites either confirmed their commitment to their Buddhist vows, thereby losing their homes and their livelihoods, or—in an effort to maintain control of their institutions—renounced Buddhism altogether, adopting new lay names and promising to embrace worship of the kami exclusively. While at times incurring the sometimes violent opposition of local worshipers, this officially condoned eradication of combinatory worship established throughout Japan tens of thousands of Shinto shrines, now entirely distinct from Buddhist temples.[5]

In 1871, while combinatory sites were still being transformed into Shinto shrines, the Meiji government moved to bring the newly established shrines under closer state control. Building on the precedent of the Tokugawa shogunate's oversight of temple administration and responding to petitions from shrine priests for official recognition, status, and privileges akin to those they had enjoyed or envied under the previous regime, the highest government body established a hierarchical system of shrines governed, and in part funded, by the state.[6] Declaring that "shrines of the kami (*jinja*) are for the worship of the state (*kokka no sōshi*)," not for the benefit of a single person or family, the Meiji leaders banned hereditary priesthood, asserted the right of the government to appoint priests, and established the principle that shrines were government, not private, property.[7] The institutional framework of nationwide, nativist worship was set in place.

State sponsorship of kami worship took shape amid widespread concerns over the growing presence of Christianity. The treaties concluded with foreign powers during and after 1854 stripped the Japanese government of the ability to control imports, whether economic or religious. Foreign signatories set tariffs, opened ports, and claimed the right of extraterrioriality for their subjects living in those ports. While the treaties did not permit overt Christian proselytizing within Japan, they did allow the free exercise of religion by resident foreigners, who frequently used the opportunity to spread their beliefs. Most alarming to nativists, Buddhists, and political leaders of first the shogunate and then the Meiji regime, however, were the numbers of hidden Christians who suddenly appeared with the arrival of the foreigners.

Early in the seventeenth century, after the forces of the third Tokugawa shogun succeeded in subduing a four-month-long uprising of peasants and (Catholic) Christians on the island of Kyushu only after calling on the assistance of Dutch ships, the shogun evicted all Europeans (except the nonproselytizing, Protestant Dutch) and enforced a ban on Christianity as an "evil" religion. The desire to eradicate Christianity—as a foreign, politically subversive belief—shaped shogunal policies toward Buddhism, foreigners, and the domestic population for over two hundred years. When the descendants of those early Japanese Christians began making contact with newly arrived French Catholic missionaries in 1865, the specter of insurrection was raised again. Amid the unraveling of the shogunate in the mid–1860s, the demonstrated strength of Christianity seemed to embody all of the ways in which the social and political establishment was under attack. Not just content to challenge the powers and propriety of the buddhas and kami, Christians—whether foreign missionaries or domestic insurgents—seemed to pose a serious threat to the shaky authority of the tottering shogunate and, later, the fledgling imperial regime, by encouraging people to follow the teachings of a foreign church instead of the laws of the Japanese state. As a result, both shogunate officials and the Meiji leaders who replaced them reiterated the ban on Christianity and followed a policy of Christian suppression, imprisonment, and execution.[8]

The problem of Christianity seemed especially dire to the leaders of the new Meiji regime as they sought to assert their right to rule. Both nativist and Buddhist proselytizers were dispatched to preach to Christians about the importance of emperor and kami. This mission to the hidden Christians formed the core around which a wider campaign was built to preach the ideology of the new regime to all people throughout the country. In 1870 the Meiji government announced the Great Teaching Campaign (Taikyō Sempu Undō), in which Shinto and Buddhist priests, as well as village headmen and public entertainers, were appointed to preach on the virtues of reverence for the kami, acceptance of (Confucian) morality, and obedience to the will of the imperial court to all residents of the Japanese islands.[9] Although Buddhists were instrumental in initiating the effort, the campaign quickly became dominated by the rhetoric and rituals of kami worship. The Way of the Kami was thus effectively established as the official orthodoxy of the state: a "national religion" (*kokkyō*), literally "national teaching," analogous to "sectarian teaching" (*shūkyō*), that is, religion.

As Japanese leaders became aware of intellectual trends in Europe and the United States regarding separation of church and state, however, overt state support of kami worship and doctrine came under attack. During the early years of the Meiji period, many leaders toured and studied abroad, absorbing foreign concepts and practices and advocating their selective incorporation into the government and society of the new era. Among those ideas was the principle of separation of church and state. In 1872 Mori Arinori, a close associate of many of the new Meiji leaders and later minister of education, published an influential treatise in English while he was in the United States, pointing out the invented nature of the state's new Shinto and calling for "religious freedom in Japan." "[The government's] attempt to impose upon our people a religion of its creation cannot receive too severe condemnation," he asserted, "because such an attempt not only disregards our sacred liberty of conscience, but its effect is to crush the very soul of man."[10]

Domestic politics and foreign pressure soon forced a reversal of religious policy as administrative pragmatists in the Home Ministry forced the most radical nativists out of the government. In 1875 the Ministry of Doctrine officially recognized the right to "freedom of religious belief" (*shinkyō no jiyū*) of both the proselytizers of the Great Teaching and the people to whom they preached, as long as such freedom did not prove "an impediment to acceptance of imperial proclamations and the government of the emperor."[11] Although these restrictions on religious freedom rendered the acknowledgment virtually meaningless (as did similar language in the Meiji Constitution of 1890, which stated that "Japanese subjects shall, within limits not prejudicial to peace and order, and not antagonistic to their duties as subjects, enjoy freedom of religious belief"), the government set a precedent recognizing the principle of freedom of religious belief.

The declaration of religious freedom heralded the demise of the Great Teaching as a "national religion."[12] It also prompted the dispersal of the variety of movements, institutions, and doctrines that had begun to coalesce by 1875 as a general entity called "Shinto."[13] Through the activities of the Great Teaching Campaign, organizations of all types had been able to gain government recognition and protection if they accepted and propagated the state teachings. The 1875 statement on freedom of religious belief enabled these groups, which had gathered under the auspices of the Great Teaching for the sake of institutional security, to seek recognized status apart from the semi-governmental Shinto movement. Over the next few years, the Great Teaching movement fell apart, and the several groups that had come to be known collectively as Shinto diverged, taking their new Shinto identities with them. Thus, new religions founded by visionaries as well as shrine priests eager to promote their institutions remained Shinto in the eyes of beholders, as did government-appointed priests at officially recognized Shinto shrines.

With Shinto leaders no longer tied to the role of government ritualists and teachers, it became increasingly difficult for officials to justify the special treatment given to the worship of the kami. By 1879 the Home Ministry (which had taken over administration of shrines and temples in 1877) publicly announced a solution to the problem. Distinguishing between "worship of the state" and "popular celebrations" (*minsai*), the ministry declared that priests of all shrines below the sixty-nine nationally ranked and funded shrines, and by extension all ritualists outside this state system, would be considered specialists in "popular celebrations" and would thus be treated similarly to Buddhist priests.[14] Shinto at nationally ranked shrines, then, constituted official ritual, commissioned by the state; Shinto outside that system was akin to the religion of Buddhism.

This distinction corresponded to another dichotomy drawn on the basis of understandings of *religion* itself. Religion was conceived of as a doctrine (*shūkyō,* "sectarian teachings")—an understanding that was further promoted by the Protestant missionaries and diplomats who argued for the protection of the Christian "faith." The charismatic movements that stood outside the shrine system and each had their own teachings (even if they were influenced by the Great Teaching Campaign) could therefore be designated as religion. Pursuant to this logic, the government in 1882 distinguished Shinto preachers and sites of preaching (i.e., *kyōkai,* or "churches," literally "teaching meetings") from the shrines themselves, forbidding priests to hold office simultaneously as preachers. In turn, churches could not be located within the formal precincts of shrines.[15] Shrines were thus designated as sites of worship or ritual; doctrinally based activities, in contrast, constituted religion. In the years that followed, then, Shinto came to be divided into two institutional categories: the religions of "Sect Shinto" (*shūha shintō*) and the rites of "Shrine Shinto" (*jinja shintō*).

    This institutional distinction plagued the government until 1945, and its legacy continues to trouble Shinto and Japanese politics today. How was it that identical rituals and prayers to identical deities could be considered religion when performed by "the people" but constitute ritual when performed by the state? How could seemingly religious practices, such as bowing, praying, and buying amulets, not constitute religion when performed at state-supported shrines? From the 1880s through the early twentieth century, prominent Shinto priests and apologists attempted to address this contradiction by calling for all shrines to be classified as sites for state worship. Their overlapping statements, repeated in newspapers, policy statements, and public speeches throughout Japan, informed and drew from broader trends toward national self-definition during economic recessions, failed attempts at treaty reform, and—after the revision of the unequal treaties in 1894—the pursuit of two international wars. Elaborating upon the opposition that had already been established between Shinto and "evil, foreign teachings" (i.e., religion), priests, politicians, and public intellectuals drew analagous oppositions between the public and the private, between the natural and the artificial, and between civilization and superstition. The Way of the Kami, always associated with the best of each pair, thus became the embodiment of the civic-minded, natural, and civilized essence of the Japanese nation.

    The fundamental rationale for state sponsorship of Shinto—first of the teaching and then only of the shrines—was that its public nature placed it within the proper realm of governmental affairs. Confucians, Buddhists, and nativists (now Shinto advocates) had over the centuries each insisted that alignment with Heaven, protection of the Buddhist Law, and appeasement of potentially troublesome gods were inextricable from the process of good government. There was a predisposition to view rituals and worship as the responsibility of the ruler.

    The government, in recognizing freedom of religious belief (literally, "belief in a teaching," *shinkyō*), had in some respects separated rituals from doctrine, assigning belief in teachings to personal choice but implying that the performance of rituals was a public duty. Ensuing rhetoric continued to draw distinctions between worship as a public act and belief as private. One Shinto advocate in the early 1880s explicitly drew upon this distinction between worship that supported the nation as a whole and beliefs as particular to each individual. "Shrines . . . are sites at which the kami of Heaven and Earth, the spirits of imperial loyalists, and the righteous heroes of patriotism are enshrined and worshiped by officials," he wrote. "Churches [i.e., sites of religious preaching] . . . are the places where people celebrate the spirits of each individual faith. . . . All shrines should be established by national law, and all churches by the private contracts of believers." Indeed, he went on to say, "There is fundamentally no distinction between the spirits of shrines . . . and the deities of churches . . . : only the distinction between their histories and their official or private [nature]."[16] In this view, as in many others, the purview of shrines included public worship of the heroes of the nation and the kami of all of creation, while that of churches consisted of private belief.

This preoccupation with public worship over private religion bespoke a broader concern of the times: a desire for unity. During the 1870s and early 1880s, the Meiji leaders instituted rapid changes, not only establishing new governmental structures but also pushing through such controversial measures as community-funded education, tax reform, and a national military draft. Opposition to these dramatic changes of policy erupted in protests, riots, arson, and assassinations around the country. In this context emphasis by priests and politicans (i.e., the educated elite, whose welfare was most threatened by the violence and destruction) on public worship and private religion resonated as code words for social unity and disunity, respectively. "Public" worship, which united people into a peaceful society, was desirable; religion, or the pursuit of "private," "selfish" beliefs, was not.

The focus on unity also arose from a perceived sense of threat from outside. Politicians and intellectuals increasingly called for national unity in the face of intransigent world powers. The public, and therefore areligious, nature of Shinto thus became a point of national pride and uniqueness. Beginning with a warning of the Russian "eagle" and the Chinese "dragon" poised to attack and reminding his readers of the inroads of Britain and France in Asia, "whether through religious invasion or military invasion," an official of the Shinto head office dryly noted in 1887 that, "when it comes to religion (*shūkyō*), everyone praises their own and degrades others." Because Shinto was a universal, public Way, however, it could not be considered a self-promoting religion: "There can be no question of committing the evil deed of viewing our Way of the Gods (*Shintō*)—the public way of Heaven and Earth, the spirit of the world—as identical with religion in general. Indeed, it is our most pressing need to promote this Way and cultivate in our people the original spirit of reverence for the kami, reverence for the Emperor, and love of the country: we feel the need to explain that this Way cannot be included in 'religion' any more than can ice in ashes, that the distance between the two is as far as between Heaven and Earth."[17] Shinto, in this reading, was not a religion but a Way—a public way shared by the subjects of the Japanese emperor, if not by all peoples of the world.

Praise of the public and vilification of the private was a common ideological strategy in the mid-Meiji period. In a process that historian Carol Gluck has called the "denaturing" of politics, elites throughout Japanese society sought in the 1880s to align themselves with the public good, attacking their opponents for "selfish interest" and, ultimately, destroying popular confidence in parliamentary democracy, based as it was on competing claims and partisan representation.[18] In this context accusations against religion which pointed out the personal or private nature of belief contributed to the poisoning of the very idea of religion itself as a symptom of selfishness and a source of disunity.

Almost inevitably tied to avowals of the public nature of Shinto were assertions of its naturalness. Borrowing from the strategy of Chinese Taoists, who
espoused a "Way" (Chinese: *Tao;* Japanese: *Dō* or *Tō*) in contrast to the "teachings" of Confucius, Shinto advocates in Japan insisted that the Way of the Kami,
the "public way of Heaven and Earth, the spirit of the world," arose spontane-
ously from nature. Religion, in contrast, had been artificially created: it both
reflected and encouraged the problematic, selfish, conflictual behavior of humankind. One nativist-turned-Shinto priest clarified this distinction for readers
of a shrine-published souvenir magazine in 1892, as he sought to distinguish
Shinto shrines from the Buddhist temples of which they had been a part before
1868. "Buddhist temples," he wrote, "are nothing but sites for the preaching of
a man-made religion (*jinzō shūkyō*). Shinto shrines are different from this: they
arise from the moral feelings that are the origins of social cohesion."[19]

Accordingly, it was the Shinto kami who made possible the peaceful unity
of people, not the teachings of a religious leader such as Buddha, Moses, Christ,
or Mohammed. Proof of this moral uniqueness of Shinto shrines was their intimate relationship to the land itself. Shrines, wrote the priest, could be established through either divine or human action, "but, whether [enshrined] by kami
or by man, they have an affinity with their site [of enshrinement]" which causes
local inhabitants to offer up their gratitude.[20] Because of the organic connection between kami and place, he asserted, the "belief or disbelief of individuals" was irrelevant. Shrines, wrote the priest, "have the characteristic that if one
lives in that place, one cannot help but revere them."[21] Shinto thus constituted
the Way of acknowledging reality, of recognizing the power of deities that existed naturally in the world; religion was a set of teachings that created false
deities.

Because of this intimate tie with nature, then, Shinto was coeval with all
of existence. Rather than having been invented by man, the Way of the Gods
had always existed since the kami created the world. Like the Imperial line, which
the Heavenly Imperial ancestor, the Sun Goddess Amaterasu, had decreed in her
last testament would reign forever, Shinto—which arose from nature itself—
would always exist: "Shinto has its origins in the final instructions of the sacred Heavenly ancestor and in the foundation of those instructions, the Heavenly
principles of Nature. It is the original spirit of the world: eternally unchanging,
one with the universe, unlimited by Heaven or Earth. It is the essence [literally,
the "national body," *kokutai*] of our nation."[22] The Way of the Gods, then, was
identical with the laws of nature. Shinto was to be accepted not because of personal faith but as an acknowledgment of the world itself. The existence of the
kami was a matter of concrete, physical reality.

By associating kami, shrines, and Shinto with the physical landscape in
particular and all of nature in general, advocates successfully hid the created
nature of Shinto itself. Shinto kami, associated as they often were with mountains, rocks, caves, or other natural phenomena, reinforced this idea of perma-

nent, unchanging existence. The use of the term *Shinto* (Way of the Gods), instead of *shinkyō* (Teaching of the Gods), a term that had been used during the
short-lived Great Teaching Campaign, likewise removed any appearance of human agency. By defining Shinto as a natural Way instead of a man-made teaching and eschewing mention of the nativist intellectual movement that had
"unearthed" and formulated that Way through study of the ancient texts, advocates of Shinto erased any sense of human founders or agents in the creation of
the tradition. By the early twentieth century the eradication of origins, so necessary to a successful ideological campaign, was complete.[23]

Despite its formulation in the context of national law and imperial myth,
Shinto as natural and public was not only—or, for many people, even primarily—a political phenomenon. It was instead a marker of civilization, defining
the place of the kami and, indeed, the Japanese people themselves in the intellectual and social hierarchy of the modern world. Bureaucratic and priestly
shapers of Shinto consistently kept an eye on the opinions of the foreign powers, as is evident in the state's recognition of freedom of religious belief and
Shinto apologists' recognition of the need to work within that framework. But
the push to "civilize" the Japanese people was not aimed solely at demonstrating equality with Europe and the United States in order to revise the unequal
treaties. "Civilization" (*bun, bunka, bunmei*) was a long-cherished goal within
Japan as well. Both for the purposes of treaty revision and to justify their own
positions as leaders in society, advocates of Shinto expended a great deal of en-
ergy on equating the Way of the Kami with civilization itself.

Drawing upon Confucian ideas of a decorous, moral civilization, state-
sponsored, ritual Shinto was set up not as an embodiment of magic and prayer
for personal advantage (as were many of the "religious" Shinto sects under the
leadership of charismatic founders) but as a model of reverential thanks to the
creator gods and ancestral deities. Shrine priests preached on "respect for the
gods and love of country," exhorting listeners to pay back the benevolence of
the gods, not to seek more from them. They taught the correct order of clap-
ping and bowing now prescribed for Shinto prayer, demonstrating obeisance to
the deities. And they conferred upon worshipers sanctified sake and special amulets to symbolize their membership in a community consisting of both humans
and kami.[24]

This decorous civilization of the educated elite conveniently coincided with
the efforts of Shinto advocates to affiliate their Way with modern, Western science and technology. By aligning the Way of the Kami with nature and natural
law, instead of human teachings, apologists argued that Shinto was more compatible with modern science than were "superstitious" religions based on
miracles. Priests therefore sought to show how the kami worked in the modern
world, redefining worship to accommodate the scientific viewpoint of the late
nineteenth century.

Such modernization of the kami posed a problem. The presence of kami in a place could only be known through a miraculous occurrence; moreover, most people worshiped the kami in hopes of receiving a similar miracle for themselves. As a consequence, the priests could not deny the existence of miracles altogether, for then they would undermine the very reason for their existence. How, then, could they reconcile the miracles of the kami with a modern world in which human agency, not reliance on the gods, was the key to success? In an article addressed to worshipers of the guardian kami of sailors in 1892, a pseudonymous author set forth a solution to this problem. He divided the intercession of the gods in the lives of humans into two kinds. Before the scientific advances of the Meiji period, he explained, the deity had displayed a bright light or a golden wand to guide shipwrecked sailors to safety: this, he wrote, was the "divine virtue of an uncivilized age" (*mikai no yo no shintoku nari*). Now in the 1890s, however, the kami had inspired educated men to study navigation and meteorology and had encouraged them to build lighthouses and place lights on boats. This, he said, was the "divine virtue of the age of civilization" (*kaimei no yo no shintoku nari*).[25] The role of the gods and their miracles was therefore, in this interpretation, to inspire the human efforts that made scientific and human progress possible.

For priests and rural gentry, Shinto constituted civilization in two ways: it embodied the cultured decorum of the educated elite while simultaneously accounting for the scientific advances of modern society. The Way of the Kami now pointed out the proper Way of the modern imperial subject: the good citizen as well as the good worshiper of the kami would seek to educate himself, act decorously in obedience to the imperial government and its representatives, work hard, and worship the kami with thankful reverence. The Way of the Kami—natural, public, and equivalent with civilization itself—had become the Way of the Subject, unsullied by the selfishness, artificiality, and superstition associated with religion.[26]

The rhetoric of Shinto as "not a religion" was never entirely convincing. Because even state-supported shrines relied for most of their income on the donations of worshipers and the purchase of amulets, questions repeatedly arose concerning the religiosity of even the most public, nationally ranked shrines. During the first decade of the twentieth century the journal of shrine priests was filled with attempts to address these concerns through appeals to a higher, national good. As a graduate of the Institute for Study of the Shinto Classics wrote in 1902, "Has not [the focus on Shinto as a set of rituals and moral teachings] raised among people suspicions that prayers and petitions to shrines are meaningless and . . . that these are actions that do not escape uncivilized thought, that they are deeds inspired by religious superstitions (*shūkyōteki meishin*)?" Yes, he remarked, but because proper shrines affirm the actual presence of a true kami, prayers do have an effect and are therefore not only acceptable, but are an important influence on the "national feeling."[27]

During the Russo-Japanese War this national justification became even

stronger. "Some writers criticize [the distribution of protective amulets to soldiers, saying that they] inspire superstition," commented a lawyer during the war
in 1904. "But if [the amulets] advocate the naturally majestic spirits of the imperial kami, if they pray for a fruitful harvest or petition for the flourishing of
the national military, then this constitutes national faith (*kokkateki shinkō*), and
I believe that even those writers cannot call it superstition."[28] Such justifications of the areligious, nonsuperstitious nature of Shinto through alignment with
the explicitly national (as opposed to just public) good received a strong boost
near the end of the Russo-Japanese War, when Admiral Tōgō Heihachirō was
quoted as attributing the unexpected victory of the Japanese navy over the Russian fleet to "the grace of Heaven and the help of the kami"—a statement upon
which Shinto apologists elaborated for years thereafter.[29]

Even though the distinction between Shinto and religion or superstition
remained problematic, this very slippage prompted apologists to appeal ever more
directly to the status of Shinto as a national, not simply a public, tradition in the
decades that followed. The wartime need for military miracles, in particular, encouraged the elaboration of Shinto as a national cult. During the final years of
the Pacific War in the 1940s, the politics of wartime mobilization merged with
the rhetoric of Shinto in public praise of the emperor as a living kami, adding
an aura of supernatural protectiveness to the leader and symbol of the nation as
well as to the young suicide pilots popularly known as kamikaze (the wind of
the gods).

Shinto as an officially enforced national cult gained such power and no-
toriety by the end of the Pacific War that one of the first actions taken by Occupation officials was the disestablishment of "State Shinto" in December 1945.
At that time all government support of Shinto shrines, teachings, rituals, and
institutions was expressly forbidden in order "to separate religion from the state,
to prevent misuse of religion for political ends, and to put all religions, faiths,
and creeds upon exactly the same legal basis."[30] After years of denying the religiosity of Shinto, priests and apologists found themselves suddenly defined as
religious, limited by the very principle of freedom of religious belief which they
had once overcome by defining themselves against religion. While now institutionally religious, registered as religious organizations and members of purely
voluntary Shinto organizations, many Shinto shrines still retain a bureaucratic,
semigovernmental, and thus areligious image. Whether priests now consider
themselves protectors of Japan's environmental legacy, defenders of the prestige of the imperial house, or promoters of civic nationalism among an ever more
apathetic citizenry, they continue to draw on the definitions of Shinto as natural, public, civilized, and national which developed originally in the attempt to
avoid religion.

The strength of rhetoric deployed over the years to support the idea that
Shinto is not a religion has not only shaped Shinto but has informed broader
attitudes toward religion and religiosity as well. Distrust of religion in contemporary

Japan—where approximately 65 percent of the population has claimed to have no religious belief since at least the 1950s[31]—is not just a product of the sarin gas attack on the Tokyo subway by a violent religious group in 1995. Influenced by decades of Shinto rhetoric, many Japanese view doctrines with suspicion, mistrust movements based upon the insight of individual founders, and feel uncomfortable with the dedication and belief of active practitioners.[32]

Instead of worship as an expression of belief, worship as an expression of tradition is considered much more acceptable. By removing Shinto from the realm of religion, the accumulated rhetoric of decades succeeded in establishing Shinto, in its nineteenth-century form, not as a religious belief but as the fundamental expression of Japanese identity. As advocates insisted, in language that pervaded public discourse until at least 1945, the Way both of the kami and of the Japanese people as a whole was natural and timeless, public and civic minded, civilized and therefore compatible with the modern, indeed the postmodern, age. Through their skillful development of such values in opposition to foreign culture in general and religion in particular, writers and speakers in Meiji Japan succeeded in a project dear to the hearts of many peoples outside the industrialized nations of Western Europe and North America: they defined themselves as simultaneously modern and unique—indeed, as superior to Western countries whose modernity was still caught up in the artificiality, selfishness, and superstition of religion. Using the concept of religion as a political tool, advocates of Shinto confounded the boundaries of church and state, religion and secularism, to shape the very idea of Japaneseness itself.

Notes

I would like to thank Gauri Viswanathan, Allison Sneider, Carl Caldwell, Andrew Bernstein, Eva Haverkamp, and Joel Wolfe for their comments on earlier versions of this essay.

1. Nineteenth-century attacks on Buddhism frequently used antiforeign rhetoric to disguise a more fundamental opposition to the institutional ties of Buddhism to the Tokugawa government.
2. Kuroda Toshio provides a concise history of the term *Shinto* in his classic essay, "Shinto in the History of Japanese Religion," first published in translation in the *Journal of Japanese Studies* 7 (winter 1981): 1–21. My argument builds upon Kuroda's insistence that Shintō only achieved the status of an independent religion after 1868.
3. While this interrelationship of Buddhism and kami worship has been called both syncretic and assimilative, I follow the usage of Allan G. Grapard in emphasizing its "combinatory" or "combinative" nature, insofar as particular kami became associated with particular buddhas during this period according to what Grapard calls "rules of combination" (Grapard, *The Protocol of the Gods* [Berkeley: University of California Press, 1992], esp. 7–10). Ian Reader and George J. Tanabe Jr. have emphasized assimilation in an attempt to clarify the variety of levels of interrelatedness between kami and buddhas, ranging from combination to transformation (*Practically Religious: Worldly Benefits and the Common Religion of Japan* [Honolulu: Univer-

sity of Hawaii Press, 1998], esp. 147–155; see also Kuroda, "Shintō in the History of Japanese Religion").

4. Several of the most influential leaders of the nativist movement (*kokugaku,* or national studies) came from families of shrine priests, including Kada no Azumamaro (1669–1736), born into a priestly lineage at Fushimi Inari Shrine, and Kamo no Mabuchi (1697–1769), born into a family of priests in eastern Japan. The movement they fostered, however, grew far beyond the boundaries of ritual studies, attracting adherents from throughout the educated elites of the time.

5. For estimated figures in English on the number of Buddhist institutions destroyed—that is, converted into Shinto shrines—see Martin Collcutt, "Buddhism: The Threat of Eradication," in *Japan in Transition,* ed. Marius B. Jansen and Gilbert Rozman (Princeton, N.J.: Princeton University Press, 1986), 162; and Tamamuro Fumio, "On the Suppression of Buddhism," in *New Directions in the Study of Meiji Japan,* ed. Helen Hardacre and Adam L. Kern (Leiden, Neth.: E. J. Brill, 1997), 499–505.

6. In his study of the development of the state shrine system, Sakamoto Koremaru points out that it was shrine priests who first petitioned the government for special status; the initiative apparently came initially from the priests, not from the government itself (*Kokka shintō keisei katei no kenkyū* [Tokyo: Iwanami Shoten, 1994], 52 and 69 n. 21).

7. Dajōkan fukoku 234, reproduced in Umeda Yoshihiko, *Kaitei sōho Nihon shūkyō seidoshi* (Tokyo: Tōsen Shuppansha, 1971), 355–366.

8. Notto R. Thelle, *Buddhism and Christianity in Japan* (Honolulu: University of Hawaii Press, 1987), 35–36; Yasumaru Yoshio, *Kamigami no Meiji Ishin* (Tokyo: Iwanami Shoten, 1979), 69–70.

9. For analyses of the Great Teaching Campaign in English, see James Edward Ketelaar, *Of Heretics and Martyrs in Meiji Japan* (Princeton, N.J.: Princeton University Press, 1990), 96–135; and Helen Hardacre, *Shintō and the State, 1868–1988* (Princeton, N.J.: Princeton University Press, 1989), 42–59.

10. Cited in Ketelaar, *Of Heretics and Martyrs,* 127.

11. Kyōbushō kutatsu, 27 November 1875, reproduced in Umeda, *Kaitei sōho Nihon shūkyō seidoshi,* 394.

12. James Ketelaar analyzes this shift in terms of the subtle nuances of the morpheme *kyō:* "The redefinition of 'kyō' from a national doctrine (*kokkyō*) to a sectarian doctrine (*shukyō*), as forced by activists such as Shimaji, successfully altered the rules of the game" (Ketelaar, *Of Heretics and Martyrs,* 131).

13. On the coalescence of "Shinto" by 1875, see Hardacre, *Shintō,* 58.

14. Sakamoto, *Kokka shintō keisei katei no kenkyū,* 288.

15. For this reason, even today, the headquarters of lay associations or religions associated with particular shrines are frequently located just outside the main gates or along the borders of shrine precincts.

16. "Shinkan kyōdōshoku bunri ni tsuki ikensho" (c. 1883), in *Shūkyō to Kokka,* ed. Yasumaru Yoshio and Miyachi Masoto (Tokyo: Iwanami Shoten, 1988), 66.

17. Nishizawa Koresuke, "Shintō wa shūkyō ni arazaru no ron" (October 1887), in *Shūkyō to Kokka,* 76–80.

18. Carol Gluck, *Japan's Modern Myths: Ideology in the Late Meiji Period* (Princeton, N.J.: Princeton University Press, 1985), esp. 49–67.

19. Matsuoka Mitsugi, "Jinja butsuji no kubetsu," *Kotohira miyage* 1 (1892): 1r. The

magazine can be found in the Matsuura collection of the Seto Naikai Minzoku Rekishi Shiryōkan.

20. Matsuoka, "Jinja butsuji no kubetsu," 1v.
21. Matsuoka, "Jinja butsuji no kubetsu," 3v.
22. Nishizawa, "Shintō," 81.
23. Herman Ooms has drawn upon the theories of Habermas and Bourdieu to uncover similar development of "synchronic consciousness" and "genesis amnesia" in the construction of early Tokugawa ideology (*Tokugawa Ideology* [Princeton, N.J.: Princeton University Press, 1985], 63–108).
24. Sarah E. Thal, "Rearranging the Landscape of the Gods: A History of Kompira Pilgrimage in Modern Japan" (Ph.D. diss., Columbia University, 1999), examines these priestly efforts at a popular pilgrimage site.
25. "Yo no keishinsha ni hitogoto su," *Kotohira miyage* 1 (1892): 10v–11r.
26. In 1941 a booklet entitled *Shimmin no Michi* (The Way of the Subjects) was published to exhort Japanese to fight for the emperor. Like motivational writing through the years until 1945, it incorporated the themes of public, natural, civilized Shinto into a single-minded focus on the imperial house while avoiding explicit reference to Shinto as such. The Way of the Gods had been completely naturalized.
27. Nukaga Hironao, "Jinja to kigan," *Jinja Kyōkai Zasshi* 6, 15 August 1902, 26.
28. Nakagawa Yūjirō, "Gunjin ni taisuru mamorifuda juyo ni tsuite," *Jinja Kyōkai Zasshi,* 15 June 1904, 5–6.
29. Ogasawara Chōsei, ed., *Seishō Tōgō Zenden* (Tokyo: Seishō Tōgō Zenden Kankōkai, 1941), 3:27–28.
30. SCAP directive, 15 December 1945.
31. Ian Reader, *Religion in Contemporary Japan* (Honolulu: University of Hawaii Press, 1991), 5–6.
32. Ian Reader, *A Poisonous Cocktail? Aum Shinrikyō's Path to Violence* (Copenhagen: NIAS Publications, 1996), 109–110.

CHAPTER 7

Secularism and Religion in the Arab Middle East

REINVENTING ISLAM IN A WORLD OF NATION-STATES

JAMES L. GELVIN

Until a little over twenty years ago, chronicling the course of secularization in the Middle East was a simple matter. Following the axioms of nineteenth-century social theory, particularly Weberian sociology, and bolstered by the authoritative pronouncements of its less sophisticated but more directly prescriptive offshoot, modernization theory, historians and social scientists presumed that the waning of the doctrinal and institutional authority of Islam was well under way and that its imminent demise was a certainty. For those historians and social scientists the path to secularization in the Middle East would be as it purportedly had been in Europe and North America— linear and irreversible. Their reading of the apparent success of the secularizing activities of Mustafa Kemal in Turkey, Reza Shah and Muhammad Reza Shah in Iran, and Gamal ʿAbd al-Nasr and the Baʿth Party in the Arab world seemed to validate these assumptions.[1]

Then came the Iranian Revolution, followed by a number of events in the territories that had once comprised the Ottoman Empire: the assassination of Anwar al-Sadat in Egypt in 1981, Islamist uprisings in Syria from 1979–1982, the emergence of Islamist movements as the chief rivals to the secularist Palestine Liberation Organization (PLO) in the West Bank and Gaza Strip, the establishment of Islamist political parties, and renewed debates about the practicability of reinstituting Islamic legal practices in states throughout the region.[2] All of these events cast a pall on past sureties. Suddenly the path to secularization did not appear as linear and irreversible as it had once appeared, and the scramble to improvise an explanation, if not an entirely new theoretical framework, was on.

Some scholars have attempted to circumvent the disparity between theory and event simply by portraying the population of the region as perverse or by discounting its previous commitment to modernity. Often, this approach has been mixed with a civilizational critique steeped in the rhetoric of post–cold war Western triumphalism; as George Bush (père) once said of the Soviet Union, what can one expect from societies that never produced a Renaissance, Reformation, or Enlightenment?[3] Others who approach the Middle East and Islam with a less jaundiced eye have taken one step where two steps would have been more appropriate: while abandoning the social evolutionary schemas of their predecessors, they have continued to maintain a strict dichotomization between an unchanging religious sphere and its secular counterpart, often trotting out the two cultures thesis—incommensurable elite (secular) and popular (religious) cultures within a given polity—which had been all but abandoned in the more nuanced historiography of Europe. For this latter group the "return of Islam" still signified the abandonment of ideals associated with modernity and secularism.[4]

This is not meant to imply that historians and social scientists have failed to notice the modernness of the return of Islam phenomenon. Many have. But this modernness is, more often than not, situated within a paradox. The return of Islam is a phenomenon, it is affirmed, that was not only triggered by specific events that took place in the second half of the twentieth century (e.g., the retreat of the "post-populist" state from the increasingly intrusive role governments in the region had assumed over the course of the previous century); it could only have transpired under the social, economic, and demographic conditions unique to that century. Yet those Middle Eastern naïfs who propose for their polities a return to Islam seem not to have comprehended this—why else would they hang onto this "false consciousness"? Thus, the incommensurable and fixed categories are maintained: "radical Islam," according to one oft-cited author, represents a fusion of "medieval theology and modern politics;"[5] for another, the post-revolutionary compromises made by the Iranian government demonstrate "the triumph of politics over religion."[6]

Ironically, just as the scholars of the Middle East who wrote during the first three quarters of the twentieth century might be faulted for their blind emulation of nineteenth-century academic practices—practices that not only presented a mythologized and ideologized narrative of the rise of the secular state in Europe but lacked any empirical foundation for their assertions about the Middle East—their scholarly descendants might be faulted for precisely the opposite reason: few have paid attention to criticisms of the secularization thesis emanating from those unlikeliest of sources, the fields of sociology and comparative religion.

One of the most interesting and persuasive of those critics has been Karel Dobbelaere, whose most practical contribution to the debate about secularization has been to point out three problems about the "secularization thesis" which illuminate both the errors of its assumptions and the muddle-headedness of its reasoning.[7] All three problems are relevant to the arguments presented here.

First, Dobbelaere asserts that proponents of the secularization thesis have commonly conflated three levels of analysis: the societal, institutional, and individual. They have thus failed to distinguish among three measures of secularization: "laicization" of societal institutions (i.e., the transfer of institutions that govern public and private behavior from religious authority to nonreligious authority); "religious changes" (i.e., institutional changes, denominational changes, the emergence of new religious groups); and decline in personal belief and church involvement. It is my contention that, during the latter half of the nineteenth century, that which Dobbelaere identifies as laicization and religious changes took place in the Arab Middle East (although, as will be discussed shortly, the process of laicization is more complex than entailed in the notion of "transfer"). Laicization was encouraged in particular by the defensive developmentalist policies emanating from the ruling circles of the Ottoman state, which governed the region until 1918, while religious changes were encouraged both by the Ottoman state and from below. This essay will not address the issue of personal belief and church involvement simply because the former is unknowable and the latter unknown to historians.

Second, Dobbelaere argues that the notion of a process of secularization carries with it the presumption that there had previously existed a golden age of religious institutional dominance and that a slippage of that dominance took place in subsequent periods. In the case of Europe that golden age is commonly associated with the Middle Ages. This is a dubious proposition. As Carlo Ginzburg and others have demonstrated, the church's control over the minds and bodies of its adherents during the European Middle Ages, like that of the state, was anything but thorough—hence the Counter-Reformation and the Catholic Inquisition, campaigns engaged by church authorities in no small part to impose religious uniformity.[8] As a matter of fact, the argument could be made that it was not until the rise of the absolutist state and its nation-state successor that orthodoxy and institutional loyalty could achieve any semblance of dominance-cum-hegemony. I shall argue that a similar process of religious standardization took place in the territories of the former Ottoman Empire during the late nineteenth century. Supported by demographic, social, and economic change, the expansion of institutional capabilities led to what might be termed an "urbanification" of Islam—that is, the delimiting of creeds to those corresponding to a doctrinal synthesis emanating from centers of "high culture." The space for heterodox varieties of Sunni Islam, including certain forms of Sufism (i.e., those not manipulable and/or tolerated by the state and those that diverged from legalistic neo-Sufi movements),[9] narrowed, while the domain of a select set of fundamentally congruent Islamic forms—a revised orthodoxy, neoscripturalism, and modernism, for example—expanded.

This brings us to Dobbelaere's final point of criticism. In their rigid di-
*chotomy of institutions and doctrines that are relegated to a domain of religion and those that are relegated to the domain of the state, advocates of the secular-ization thesis understate or ignore the coherence and even symbiosis of what they purport to be two incommensurable domains. Religious institutions and state institutions share a history, evolve side by side, are subject to the same social and economic constraints, often mimic each other, and are, when not mutually supportive, at least locked in an uneasy embrace. Dobbelaere cites the example of the transformation of Catholic institutions and dogmas that took place in late-nineteenth-century Europe in response to the growth of state power, the emer-gence of mass politics, and the spread of market relations:

> In the nineteenth century, a specific form of Catholicism developed, to-
> tally different from ecclesiastical configurations in the *Ancien Régime.*
> The centralization of the Church, the sacralization of the organizational
> structure, and the sub-cultural boundary maintenance vis-à-vis the mod-
> ern world brought the Catholic religion more emphatically and more
> distinctly into the lives of the believers who remained. The differentia-
> tion of the Catholic religion from economic, political and other activi-
> ties, the specificity of the ecclesiastical organization—which stressed
> the clerical functions, the hierarchical structure, and the papacy, gave it
> theological legitimation—and the specificity of the Catholic identity
> contrasted sharply with a diffuse intertwining of the Church with the
> social world in the *Ancien Régime.*[10]

Obviously, a highly centralized structure abetted the Catholic Church's ability to respond to nineteenth-century events. Nevertheless, while it is undeniable that this centralization facilitated the institutional and ideological transformation of the Catholic Church, it was not indispensable for that transformation. It is the contention here that a similar process of religious institutional and ideological transformation, albeit with a very different outcome, took place in the Ottoman Empire, where religious structures had historically been far less centralized. This led to a privileging and, in many places, dominance of those Islamic institutions and doctrines that both the state and select religious elites found appropriate to the changed circumstances of the late-nineteenth- and early-twentieth-century world.

The choice to focus here on developments in the Ottoman Empire is de-liberate. While Islam was dominant in any number of polities in the nineteenth century, the Ottoman Empire was the predominant (and, to many Muslims both within and without, the preeminent) Muslim power of the time. At its height the Ottoman Empire ruled territories stretching from southeastern Europe through the Arab Middle East and across North Africa to Morocco. Although the geographic breadth of the empire had steadily shrunk over the centuries, the empire endured as an independent entity until it was dismantled by the victorious Entente powers in the aftermath of World War I. Before that final dismantle-ment, however, Ottoman governance left a lasting impression on the core terri-tories it ruled.

The ability of the empire to endure cannot be attributed merely to a fluke of history or to the strategic role it played in British imperial policy. In spite of its gradual territorial contraction, and in spite of Czar Nicholas II's description of the fin-de-siècle Ottoman Empire as the "sick man of Europe," the empire hardly lacked dynamism during the nineteenth century. Throughout that century two interconnected processes in particular both induced and set the parameters for far-reaching economic, political, and social changes. First, the accelerating rate of integration of the empire into the periphery of the capitalist world sys-tem hastened, albeit unevenly, the ongoing integration of local marketplace economies into a broader market economy. The salience of capitalist relations and associated institutions thus increased for many inhabitants of the empire, who now produced crops destined for regional and international markets, com-peted with workers overseas, sold their labor, loaned or borrowed money (often at usurious rates), and participated as middlemen and factors in foreign trade. The expansion of capitalist relations, along with its attendant leveling and ho-mogenizing effects, was facilitated by the second phenomenon: the attempts by the Ottoman government throughout the century to strengthen and rationalize central control. While the regulations promulgated in Istanbul often had desul-tory and even antithetic effects when applied in the provinces, over the course of the late nineteenth and early twentieth centuries they enabled government on all levels to expand substantially its role in society and its control over the citizenry.

Ottoman attempts to strengthen and rationalize central control were sparked both by conscious emulation of the European model of the nation-state, which Ottoman statesmen and politically involved intellectuals understood to provide a far more efficient foundation for imperial power, and by the exigencies ex-acted by a world system of nation-states, which imposed conditions governing the internal logic of each and every polity it incorporated. The world system of nation-states had created a world in which individual societies were conceived of as essential and autonomous entities with their own collective interest. It was a world in which the state had the responsibility to promote that interest by or-ganizing, regularizing, and advancing its citizenry for that end. Conversely, it was a world in which the citizenry had to internalize the notion of collective interest so that its activities would be directed toward the realization of that in-terest. Effecting these ends required the promulgation of official overt ideolo-gies that represented, and thus established, the collective interest of the integrated social unit and steered both the government and the citizenry toward their cor-porate responsibilities. During the period in question members of the Ottoman ruling elite, abetted by their compatriots outside official circles who also sought to compete on the playing field of imperial politics, did, indeed, promulgate such official ideologies.

Historians have commonly divided nineteenth-century Ottoman state responses to European economic, political, and military expansion into two periods, each corresponding to a different state-sponsored ideological formulation: the Tanzimat Period (1839–1876), which culminated in the promulgation of a constitution and the convocation of an Ottoman parliament; and the so-called Hamidian Period (1878–1909), when Sultan Abdülhamid II once again concentrated imperial power in the palace and imperial court. During the first period the Ottoman government followed (or, more accurately, was compelled to follow) prescriptions attuned to the dictates of the liberal economic and political dogmas associated with the empire's main European ally, Great Britain. In particular, historians point to two foundational documents promulgated by the Ottoman government as epitomizing this liberal strain: the *Hatt-i Sharif* of Gulhane (1839) and the *Islahat Fermani* (1856), the latter a reaffirmation of the first, purportedly dictated to the imperial chancellory by the British ambassador to the Ottoman court. The documents promised all Ottoman subjects "perfect security for life, honor, and property" and religious liberty and equality for the non-Muslim inhabitants of the empire.[11] In other words, the *Hatt-i Sharif* of Gulhane and the *Islahat Fermani* promoted a notion of Ottoman identity, *Osmanlilik,* which was analogous to what in a later period would be known as a civic form of nationalism—a community of equal citizens bound together by their residence in a common territory and their commitment to a common set of legal norms. While the thin stratum of Westernizers who aspired to infuse the empire with internationally recognized standards of civilization naturally supported the adoption of liberalism as official doctrine, few others were convinced. Within the latter category were political and cultural elites who accepted the same modernist assumptions that had spawned liberalism but who, like many state builders in non–core European states, found the specific precepts of Liberalism to be distasteful and/or an insufficient basis for imperial revival.

The policy that attempted to establish equality among Ottoman citizens satisfied few Muslims and Christians anyway. Political and social elites among the former resented a policy that highlighted European interference in Ottoman affairs (the protection of select minorities by European governments, the granting of special privileges to merchants from minority communities), that restricted Ottoman jurisdiction over its own territory (as in Lebanon, whose autonomy was guaranteed by the concert of European powers after those powers imposed the *Règlement organique* on the empire in 1861 and then reimposed it, with emendations, in 1864), and that prescribed numerical quotas for Christian political representation on all levels of governance. Many Christians, on the other hand, were not pleased that the notion of equality was applied in such areas as military conscription—a privilege of citizenship most Christians would have just as readily forgone. Their protests once again enabled Christians to avoid military service through the payment of a fee—an option not open to their increasingly resentful Muslim fellow citizens. Others, looking to developments in Bulgaria, Serbia, and Greece, preferred the path of nationalist separation rather than equality within a predominantly Muslim empire.[12] It is thus ironic that the policy of promising equality to all inhabitants of the empire regardless of religious affiliation hardened communal boundaries and precipitated instances of intercommunal violence. In the process, it created the distinctly modern phenomenon of sectarianism all too familiar to observers of the contemporary Middle East.[13] Thus, after Sultan Abdülhamid II suspended the Ottoman constitution and prorogued the Ottoman parliament (1878)—both of which had been imposed on him as a condition of his accession to the throne two years earlier—the sultan and court sought other means to guarantee the ideological unity of the empire.

Abdülhamid II and his inner circle retained the Osmanlilik concept but transformed its meaning. Instead of connoting the equality of Ottoman citizens regardless of religion, Osmanlilik came to connote an Ottoman-Islamic identity. Two conditions facilitated this transformation. First, a long list of intellectuals, belletrists, and activists from cultural centers exposed to the ideas and institutions associated with an expanding world economy and the colonial encounter had already formulated the ideological foundations for this transformation. Among this group were the Egyptian Rifaᶜa Rafiᶜ al-Tahtawi, who led the first Egyptian educational mission to Europe in 1826 and who was at the forefront of those who sought to translate European cultural constructs (civilization, *Kultur*) into an Arabic idiom; the Young Ottomans, an eclectic group of "reformers" who promoted an Islamic foundation for Ottoman patriotism; and the salafis (Islamic modernists), who sought accommodation with Western ideals and technical capabilities within the context of a reformed Islam and who included among their ranks religious scholars (ulama) who publicly championed a revived caliphate to inspire a united Islamic resistance to the West.[14] Middle Eastern intellectuals, belletrists, and activists such as these divided the world into distinct cultural units, asserted that the "East" and "West" represented two such units, and held that, in addition to whatever spiritual dimension it might bear, Islam functioned as a temporal cultural marker that distinguished the "East" from the "West."[15]

The second condition that facilitated the transformation of Osmanlilik was the steady retreat of the Ottoman Empire from Europe and the ensuing forced emigration of Muslims from Europe and the Caucasus into the empire. This set in motion two phenomena that reinforced and lent credence to the Hamidian reinterpretation of Osmanlilik: the proportion of Muslim to Christian citizens in the empire increased decidedly, and Muslim immigrants into the empire, who were compelled to flee their homes because, according to the precepts of southeastern European nationalisms and Russian imperial ideology, they represented an alien Islamic other, authenticated and disseminated the notion of an Islamic cultural identity referred to earlier.[16] Thus, while historians have commonly attributed obscurantism and religious fanaticism to Abdülhamid II, it should be apparent that the characterization of the Ottoman Empire as a Muslim empire and Ottoman identity as a Muslim identity was readily accessible to the sultan and his court, whatever their original propensities may have been.

Abdülhamid II not only asserted his caliphal role in a manner that was rare among Ottoman sultans; he also deployed an increasingly centralized and rationalized state apparatus for the purposes of standardizing Islamic belief and its supporting structures, in the process intermixing nineteenth-century state and religious institutions and fusing notions of loyalty to the state with loyalty to Islam—in effect ideologizing Islam. Thus, in the words of the semiofficial newspaper of the Ottoman government, *La Turquie,* "Islam is not only a religion, it is a nationality."[17] The Ottoman government attempted to achieve this goal during the Hamidian period through a number of activities.

1. *Missionary activity within the empire.* During the late nineteenth century the imperial center became increasingly anxious not only about foreign missionary activity but about the subversive potential of heterodox Muslim sects housed in the empire, particularly in the wake of large-scale tribal conversions in southern Iraq to Shiism (the branch of Islam identified with the Persian enemy) and the continuing threat posed by Wahhabism (a scripturalist-cum-puritanical sect) emanating from Arabia. Consciously modeling its efforts on the activities of Christian missionary societies whose actions both alarmed and fascinated the imperial center, the government in Istanbul dispatched missionaries throughout the empire to blunt the challenge posed by these various sects and to "convert" members of other Muslim sects considered heterodox—Yazidis in Iraq, Alawites in Syria, and select Sufi groups (i.e., the Bektashi, the Sanusiyya of North Africa) throughout the empire—to the officially recognized Hanafi legal school of Sunni Islam. Ironically, the imperial government frequently deployed members of pliant Sufi orders (such as the Qadariyya and Rifaᶜiyya) on these missions because it was assumed they would be more capable of speaking in a popular idiom.[18]

2. *Dissemination of propaganda and official Islamic texts.* In an attempt to secure religious consistency, the Ottoman state made the printing of the Quran a state monopoly and established a Commission for the Inspection of Qurans, which was overseen by the office of the highest imperial religious official, the *shaykh al-Islam* in Istanbul. In at least one case the cost of printing these Qurans was underwritten by the sultan himself from his personal funds, and the Qurans thus produced were distributed gratis at the request of a provincial governor.[19]

   The state supported the publication of a variety of other books as well—four thousand in the first fifteen years of Abdülhamid II's reign alone, according to one historian. These books included not only "classic" Islamic legal and religious texts but also texts that the state associated with "Islamic culture," that is, epics depicting the exploits of Muslim heroes such as Battal Ghazi and Saladin, who had fought the enemies of Islam.[20]

3. *Imperial patronage and employment of religious scholars.* In addition to expanded imperial patronage, ulama of all ranks from throughout the empire were
integrated into governing structures and imperial institutions, from municipal
and provincial councils to the network of imperial schools. Significantly, from
the beginning of the Tanzimat through the Young Turk period (1908–1918) religious scholars were enlisted into institutions and chancelleries associated with
the central government's modernizing effort: the Military Council, the Council
of Public Works, the Council of Finance, the Council of Agriculture, the Council of the Navy, the Council of Police, the Council of the Arsenal, and the Council
of State, the central legislative commission of the empire.[21]

4. *Support for religious endowments and infrastructure.* To bolster the Islamic credentials of the Ottoman government, and specifically the caliphal pretensions
of the Ottoman sultan, the imperial government undertook the construction and
restoration of Islamic monuments, such as the Umayyad Mosque in Damascus,
partly destroyed by fire in 1894. In addition, the state enlarged its commitment
to religious endowments from Syria and Palestine through the western Arabian
province of the Hijaz. These activities received extensive coverage in the official gazettes published in provincial capitals.

    The most famous building project during the Hamidian period was the
Hijaz Railroad, intended to connect Istanbul with the holy cities of Mecca and
Medina (it eventually reached the latter but not the former). Ostensibly built to
facilitate the annual pilgrimage (although the government was hardly unaware
of the assistance the project would provide to its centralizing goals), the railroad was conceived of as an *Islamic* railroad and was financed through sub-
scription by Muslims throughout the world.[22]

    As a result of what Charles Tilly calls the expanding influence of "mer-
chants and statemakers," the imperial government's attempts to standardize Islamic institutions and doctrine and spread them throughout the population were
often matched by initiatives from below. The central government placed great
stock, for example, in extirpating the domain of customary law (*ʿurf*) and in en-
larging the dominion of the religious courts. One governor in the Hijaz, for instance, proposed a strategy for "civilizing" the Bedouin of the province which
focused on their forced settlement and the granting to religious courts the sole
authority to handle disputes. But the same enlargement of the domain of the
religious courts took place from the other direction as well. As has been well
documented in the case of the Jabal Nablus region of Palestine, the spread of
commercialized agriculture and a cash-based economy undercut both the autarky
of the village economy and localized patronage networks and induced peasants
and middling merchants to abandon traditional legal remedies and seek justice
in urban-based religious courts. While each religious court maintained its
administrative autonomy, the spread of their authority marks a correspondent
spread of a congruent set of urban-based legal norms.[23]

Similarly, the transformation of Sufi *turuq* (networks or paths), through which popular religiosity was most commonly expressed, provides evidence for the increased standardization of religious convention and practice in the Ottoman Empire during the nineteenth century in a manner consistent with imperial imperatives. The two most prominent Sufi orders in the territory that now comprises Syria, for example, the Naqshbandiyya-Mujaddidiyya and the Khalwatiyya-Bakriyya, redefined themselves during this period by orienting to the legalist teachings, rationalist principles, and orthodox precepts of the Akbari school of thought. These precepts were, in the main, congruent with governmental efforts at centralization and defensive developmentalism. Significantly, one of the chief proponents of Akbari teachings in Syria was a recent immigrant to Damascus, the Qadariyya Sufi and military leader ʿAbd al-Qadir al-Jazaʾiri, who had determined that Muslims had to assimilate Western scientific and technological practices (within an Islamic framework) while leading the resistance against the French occupation of Algeria (1830–1847). While adherents of the aforementioned orders hardly made up the totality of those who belonged to Sufi orders—indeed, the increasingly reformist bent of the two orders sparked the emergence of what one scholar has called an "antinomian reaction" among the lower classes of some urban centers—they did include a significant number of religious scholars. Among them were those who belonged to or were associated with the most important urban notable families, whose inclusion in the tendency would have a profound effect on future religious orientation.[24]

Indeed, the efforts of the Ottoman government to effect a new religio-political synthesis during the Hamidian period were reflected convincingly in the realm of cultural production and, subsequently, throughout the expanding public sphere. This is amply demonstrated by the activities of a small but energetic group of "conservative" ulama in Damascus who, one year after the deposition of Abdülhamid II, adopted the title *mutadayyinun* (pious, devout) and disseminated their worldview through the journal *al-Haqaʾiq*.[25] The activities of these ulama and others like them kept alive the religio-political synthesis effected during the Hamidian Period—a synthesis that offered what might be called an alternative discourse of modernity to that derived from the unique historical experiences of Western Europe—even after the deposition of Abdülhamid II, the accession of an imperial government spearheaded by Young Turk military officers influenced by Comtean principles, and the eventual demise of the Ottoman Empire in the aftermath of World War I.[26]

The mutadayyinun who wrote for *al-Haqaʾiq* secured their self-definition by counterposing themselves to Westernizing intellectuals—the "overly Europeanized" (*mutafarnijun*)—who, according to the mutadayyinun, advocated the wholesale adoption of European customs. For the mutadayyinun the most egregious sin of their adversaries was the latter's attempt to separate politics from religion in the manner of the post-Reformation West. This complaint is, of course, what one would expect to hear from "conservative" ulama. On the other hand, the arguments they used to support their assertions defy expectations. The mutadayyinun based their formulations on a distinctive application of categories of thought that would not have appeared unfamiliar to their Damascene opponents or, for that matter, to intellectuals immersed in the dominant culture of Europe and North America. Thus, like their domestic and Western opponents (and like the salafis whom they also opposed), the mutadayyinun assumed the inevitability of and necessity for progress, the universal applicability of established "norms of civilization," and the distinctiveness of the individual cultural units that participated in, and contributed to, that universal civilization. Like their opponents, they readily accepted the new instrumentalities of governance demanded by the late-nineteenth-/early-twentieth-century empire-cum-nation-state—instrumentalities with which they, as urban dwellers, were intimately familiar—as well as the new configurations of power embodied in representative councils, corporate municipal governments, and mass-based political parties that had spread throughout the empire during the same period. Unlike their opponents, however, the mutadayyinun distinguished themselves by their defense of Islam and "traditional values" and by their incessant denunciations of the corruption of morals, which, they maintained, their opponents encouraged.

Ironically, the mutadayyinun based their defense of traditional values on the assertion that the Islamic nation, like any other nation in the modern world, could only progress if it remained true to the religion, customs, and mores (all of which they included under the rubric *Islamic*) which defined it and which provided the most powerful bonds of association for its citizens. The adoption of Western customs and mores and the separation of religion from politics advocated by their opponents would, they maintained, lead inevitably to the weakening of the Islamic nation and, ultimately, to the dissolution of the empire, which was the last bastion of its defense. The mutadayyinun thus called on the Ottoman government to safeguard the Ottoman polity's Islamic character, to protect the Islamic nation against European depredations by continuing Abdülhamid II's policies of defensive developmentalism, and to advance the nationalization of Islam by, for example, declaring the prophet's birthday an "official" national holiday and by using the monetary portion of religiously prescribed alms (*zakat*) to build an Ottoman/Islamic fleet.

The mutadayyinun and their like-minded counterparts in other cities of the Ottoman Empire were not the only groups engaged in the project of redefining religious structures and doctrines and reformulating the relationship between religion and state during this period. The salafis and so-called secular nationalists also engaged in similar projects. Nevertheless, the synthesis effected by the mutadayyinun has continued to have resonance in the region long after the demise of the Ottoman Empire and its replacement by the contemporary state system. Indeed, if one were to set aside the tendentious nationalist narrative that has guided most historical writing about the region, it might be argued that the efficacy of their project far surpassed that of the narrow (and elitist) band of salafis and has rivaled that of the secular nationalists.

In part this efficacy was the result of the political strategy adopted by the mutadayyinun and their heirs. Because they feared that their Islamic modernist rivals and those whom they identified as the overly Europeanized would impose their own religio-political synthesis on the empire after the deposition of Abdülhamid II and because they were ideologically committed to achieve progress through the moral reconstruction of society, the mutadayyinun advocated the organization of popular associations that would represent the purportedly traditional Islamic aspirations of the nation to the post-Hamidian state. Among the responsibilities to be assumed by these associations were those commonly shouldered by states, from approving the credentials of teachers and constructing schools to monitoring the activities of resident aliens and stimulating and guiding economic development. In addition, the popular associations were to be charged with safeguarding public morality.

While the cohort of mutadayyinun who wrote for *al-Haqa'iq* disbanded shortly before the onset of World War I, such associations were founded in the aftermath of the war, when the victorious Entente powers dismembered the Ottoman Empire and divided its Asiatic Arab territories among themselves as League of Nations mandates. For example, associations similar to those advocated by the mutadayyinun first emerged throughout Greater Syria during the interregnum period that intervened between the dismemberment of the Ottoman Empire and the imposition of the French mandate (1918–1920). During this brief and chaotic period popular committees, consisting of a diverse group of ulama, merchants, urban toughs, and lower-middle-class shopkeepers and articulating their objectives in an Islamic idiom, waged a guerrilla war against the French army positioned to their west while championing a nation-building program similar to that advocated by the mutadayyinun. The popular committees also struggled for political dominance against the heirs of the mutafarnijun, the secular nationalist elites of Syria. Not surprisingly, while the nationalist elites sought to win Entente approbation by adopting the slogan "Religion belongs to God, the nation to all," the tactic failed to convince the Entente powers that Syrians had reached a level of civilization commensurate with independence and therefore had no need for the mandates system's *mission civilisatrice.*[27]

The activity of Syrian associations whose doctrines might be traced back to the mutadayyinun did not end with the imposition of the French mandate, in spite of the efforts of the mandatory power and nationalist elites to marginalize or eliminate them. Throughout the mandate period overtly Islamic political associations counterposed themselves as an alternative to what would become the dominant nationalist tendency, finding a receptive audience for their ideas among the expanding population of lower- and middle-class urban dwellers, who were increasingly targeted by all political factions for mobilization.[28] While the state-building cards were clearly stacked in favor of their secular nationalist rivals for a number of reasons (not the least of which were the very terms of the covenant that sanctioned the mandates system),[29] the activism of Islamic political associations in Syria compelled nationalist elites to reach a strained modus vivendi with their Islamist competitors, the ramifications of which lasted well beyond the mandate period. Thus, while the states that emerged in the former Asiatic territories of the Ottoman Empire after World War I initially did so under the supervision of European imperial powers authorized to prepare them for the "strenuous conditions of the modern world,"[30] that preparation failed to produce, in Syria and elsewhere, a simple duplication of the public/private, religious/secular boundaries found in Western states—hence, for example, the exclusion of the state from many "personal status" matters (e.g., civil marriage, divorce) which Western states have appropriated for themselves as a matter of course.

While Syria was not, of course, the only state to emerge during this period, the evolution of its public sphere, the boundaries drawn between public and private and religious and secular realms, and the typology of players who participated in drawing those boundaries are emblematic of developments that took place elsewhere. Throughout the Arab Middle East, political ideologies similar to or derived from the religio-political synthesis of the Hamidian era were propagated through seasoned institutions and unconventional popular associations, providing their adherents with models of modernity and nation building that differed from those of secular nationalists with whom they competed or bargained. Thus, while the popularity of individual associations and the doctrines they advocated have, over the course of decades, waxed or waned, depending on a number of factors—levels of repression, the mobilization capabilities of the opposition, the successes or failures of secular nationalists to achieve the goals upon which their legitimacy rested—traces of the Hamidian religio-political synthesis not only found their way into the substructure of the independent states of the region; they continue to inform contemporary politics through movements of opposition which challenge the governments of those states.

Notes

I wish to thank the President's Research Fellowship in the Humanities of the University of California and the Woodrow Wilson International Center for Scholars, both of which provided generous assistance during the time this article was researched and written.

1. The list of academic histories and modernization literature that work within the framework of the secularization thesis is enormous. Perhaps the book that best exemplifies this approach is the appropriately named *The Development of Secularism in Turkey* by Niyazi Berkes. First published in 1964, Berkes's recently republished book has been a standard text for students studying not only Turkey but the Middle East as a whole. Berkes's take-no-prisoners approach to the question of secularization be-

gins with his first sentence: "A steady trend toward secularization in traditional institutions is a feature of Muslim societies facing the impact of modern civilization."
Even the electoral victories of the Democratic Party in Turkey during the 1950s—a
party that distanced itself from the official secularist line and wrapped itself in Islamic imagery—did not shake Berkes's confidence in the secularist future: "From
1945 until 1960 the religious, national, and civilizational principles of the secular
regime were overwhelmed by a wave of reaction that looked at times as if it were
sweeping the nation back to the days of Abdul-Hamid. The governments of the 1950s
gave free rein to all sorts of obscurantism under the guise of restoring the freedom
of religion and in the name of democracy. . . . It suffices to note here, however, that
Turkish secularism withstood all of the strains; it has come through its ordeal and is
still one of the guiding principles of modern Turkey" (Berkes, *The Development of
Secularism in Turkey* [New York: Routledge, 1998], 3, 503).

2. I am using the term *Islamist* here to refer to individuals and associations commonly
referred to as "Muslim" or "Islamic fundamentalist." I am avoiding the use of the
term *fundamentalist* because it implies a closer correlation between these individuals and associations and Protestant fundamentalists than actually exists.

3. See, for example, Bassam Tibi, *The Crisis of Modern Islam: A Preindustrial Culture
in the Scientific-Technological Age* (Salt Lake City: University of Utah Press, 1988);
David S. Landes, *The Wealth and Poverty of Nations: Why Some Are So Rich and
Some Are So Poor* (New York: W. W. Norton, 1999); Samuel P. Huntington, *The Clash
of Civilizations and the Remaking of the World Order* (New York: Simon and Schuster,
1996).

4. See, for example, Nikki R. Keddie, "Secularism and the State: Towards Clarity and
Global Comparison," *New Left Review* 226 (November–December 1997): 20–40.
According to Keddie, "In many societies, modernization has produced two major
cultures in each religion, roughly, that of the secular and that of the true believer. . . . In
Iran and the Middle East [*sic*] this split is largely tied to certain social classes—the
popular classes and the traditional bourgeoisie, on one side, and the new bourgeoisie and intellectuals, on the other." For a critique of the "sterile dialectic of popular
and elite culture," see *Les Intermédiares culturels: actes du colloque du Centre me-
ridional d'histoire sociale, des mentalités, et des cultures* (Aix-en-Provence, France:
Université de Provence, 1978).

5. Emmanuel Sivan, *Radical Islam: Medieval Theology and Modern Politics* (New Haven, Conn.: Yale University Press, 1985).

6. Olivier Roy, "Crisis of Religious Legitimacy in Iran," *Middle East Journal* 53 (spring
1999): 201–216.

7. See Karel Dobbelaere, "Some Trends in European Sociology of Religion: The Secularization Debate," *Sociological Analysis* 48 (1987): 107–137; Karel Dobbelaere,
"Secularization: A Multi-Dimensional Concept," *Current Sociology* 29 (summer
1981): 3–153. See also Bryan S. Turner, "Review and Commentary: Religion and
State Formation: A Commentary on Recent Debates," *Journal of Historical Sociology* 1 (September 1988): 322–333.

8. See Carlo Ginzburg, *The Cheese and the Worms: The Cosmos of a Sixteenth-Century
Miller,* trans. John and Anne Tedeschi (Baltimore: Johns Hopkins University Press,
1985).

9. Sufism might be defined as a popular form of Islamic spirituality in which adher-

ents, grouped in informal networks of like-minded devotees, follow teachings formulated by a pious forebear and maintained by his disciples. The beliefs held by various Sufi associations have varied widely. Probably the best analysis of Sufism from the eighteenth century to the present is in John Obert Voll, *Islam: Continuity and Change in the Modern World* (Boulder, Colo.: Westview Press, 1982).

10. Dobbelaere, "Some Trends," 117.

11. J. C. Hurewitz, *The Middle East and North Africa in World Politics: A Documentary Record,* 2 vols. (New Haven, Conn.: Yale University Press, 1975), 1:269–271, 315–318.

12. See Roderic H. Davison, "Turkish Attitudes Concerning Christian-Muslim Equality in the Nineteenth Century," *American Historical Review* 59 (July 1954): 844–864; Benjamin Braude and Bernard Lewis, "Introduction," in *Christians and Jews in the Ottoman Empire: The Functioning of a Plural Society,* ed. Braude and Lewis, 2 vols. (New York: Holmes and Meier, 1982), 2:1–34; Roderic H. Davison, *Reform in the Ottoman Empire, 1856–1876* (New York: Gordian Press, 1973), 132.

13. See Ussama Makdisi, *The Culture of Sectarianism: Community, History, and Violence in Nineteenth-Century Ottoman Lebanon* (Berkeley: University of California Press, 2000).

14. See, among other works, Rifaᶜ Rafiᶜa al-Tahtawi, *al-Aᶜmal al-Kamilah li-Rifaᶜa Rafiᶜ al-Tahtawi,* ed. Muhammad ᶜImara, vol. 1 (Beirut: al-Muʾasasa al-ᶜArabiyya lil Dirasat wal-Nashr, 1973); Serif Mardin, *The Genesis of Young Ottoman Thought: A Study in the Modernization of Turkish Political Ideas* (Princeton, N.J.: Princeton University Press, 1962).

15. See, for example, Jamal al-Din al-Afghani, *Aᶜmal al-kamila li-Jamal al-Din al-Afghani,* ed. Muhammad ᶜImara (Cairo: Dar al-katib al-ᶜarabi lil-tabaᶜa wal-nashr, 1968), 228–229, 295–296.

16. Kemal H. Karpat, "The *hijra* from Russia and the Balkans: The Process of Self-Definition in the Late Ottoman State," in *Muslim Travellers: Pilgrimage, Migration, and the Religious Imagination,* ed. Dale F. Eikelman and James Piscatori (Berkeley: University of California Press, 1990), 131–152.

17. Davison, *Reform in the Ottoman Empire,* 275. See also Selim Deringil, "The Invention of Tradition as Public Image in the Late Ottoman Empire, 1808 to 1908," *Comparative Studies in Society and History* 35 (1993): 5–6.

18. Selim Deringil, "Legitimacy Structures in the Ottoman State: The Reign of Abdulhamid II (1876–1909)," *International Journal of Middle East Studies* 23 (1991): 348–349; Selim Deringil, "The Struggle against Shi'ism in Hamidian Iraq: A Study in Ottoman Counter-Propaganda," *Die Welt des Islams* 30 (1990): 45–62; B. Abu-Manneh, "Sultan Abdulhamid II and Shaikh Abulhuda al-Sayyadi," *Middle Eastern Studies* 2 (May 1979): 131–153; Eugene L. Rogan, *Frontiers of State in the Late Ottoman Empire: Transjordan, 1850–1921* (Cambridge, U.K.: Cambridge University Press, 1999), 151–159.

19. Rogan, *Frontiers of the State,* 143.

20. Kemal H. Karpat, "The Mass Media: Turkey," in *Political Modernization in Japan and Turkey,* ed. Robert E. Ward and Dankwart A. Rustow (Princeton, N.J.: Princeton University Press, 1964), 265; Selim Deringil, "Invention of Tradition," 24.

21. David Kushner, "The Place of the Ulema in the Ottoman Empire during the Age of Reform (1839–1918)," *Turcica* 19 (1987): 51–74.

22. See, among other works, Vital Cuinet, *Syrie, Liban, et Palestine: Géographie ad-*

ministrative, statistique, descriptive, et raisonnée (Paris: Ernest Leroux, 1896); Deringil, "Invention of Tradition," 25; David Dean Commins, *Islamic Reform: Politics and Social Change in Late Ottoman Syria* (New York: Oxford University Press, 1990), 108; William Ochsenwald, *The Hijaz Railroad* (Charlottesville: University Press of Virginia, 1980).

23. Deringil, "Legitimacy Structures," 347; Beshara Doumani, *Rediscovering Palestine: Merchants and Peasants in Jabal Nablus, 1700–1900* (Berkeley: University of California Press, 1995), 165–171.

24. Itzchak Weismann, "External Influences and Inner Evolution among the Sufi Reformist Movements of Late Ottoman Syria" (paper delivered at the Third Conference on Bilad al-Sham: Processes of Identities and Ideologies from the 18th Century to the End of the Mandatory Period, Erlangen Germany, July 2000).

25. An overview of *al-Haqa'iq* and the mutadayyinun can be found in Commins, *Islamic Reform,* 118–121. For a more detailed account, see James L. Gelvin, "'Pious' Ulama, 'Overly-Europeanized' Falsifiers, and the Debate about the 'Woman Question' in Early Twentieth-Century Damascus" (MS, n.d.); James L. Gelvin, "Post Hoc Ergo Propter Hoc?: Reassessing the Lineages of Nationalism in Bilad al-Sham," in *Bilad al-Sham: Processes of Identities and Ideologies from the 18th Century to the End of the Mandatory Period,* ed. Thomas Philipp and Christoph Schumann (forthcoming).

26. For a detailed examination of the principles guiding the Young Turk movement, see M. Sukru Hanioglu, *The Young Turks in Opposition* (New York: Oxford University Press, 1995).

27. James L. Gelvin, *Divided Loyalties: Nationalism and Mass Politics in Syria at the Close of Empire* (Berkeley: University of California Press, 1998).

28. Elizabeth Thompson, *Colonial Citizens: Republican Rights, Paternal Privilege, and Gender in French Syria and Lebanon* (New York: Columbia University Press, 2000).

29. See James L. Gelvin, "The League of Nations and the Question of National Identity in the Fertile Crescent," *World Affairs* (summer 1995): 35–43.

30. Hurewitz, *Middle East,* 2:179.

PART III

CHAPTER 8

Tra(ve)ils of Secularism

ISLAM IN MUSEUMS FROM THE OTTOMAN EMPIRE TO THE TURKISH REPUBLIC

WENDY M. K. SHAW

*C*asually, Turkey is an Islamic country. Much like the United States, it is heavily invested in official policies of secularism while strongly tied to the religious traditions of its dominant population. The Ottoman Empire, which preceded it, was, in contrast, the seat of the caliphate and thus formally Islamic, in a manner indivisible from the concept of the state itself. In fact, one could argue that the dramatic shift to secularism undertaken with the institution of the republic in 1923 was not simply a move toward Westernization but a strategic move against the reemergence of the monarchy and the religious hierarchy that supported it. The concept of secularism in Turkey is therefore often associated with a posited historical rupture at the transition between the Ottoman and the Republican states. Yet, as the work of many contemporary Turkish historians indicates, the dramatic reforms of the early republic had precedents in the policies of the late Ottoman Empire. The changing relationship between Islam and the museums of the empire and the republic underscores the tenuous processes through which secularism has emerged as state policy in Turkey and has subsequently become submerged under the force of populist will and revivalist politics.

Although rarely thronged with visitors, the museums of the Ottoman Empire and Turkey trace out the shifts and uncertainties of identity politics across time. By choosing certain items to collect and by ordering these objects in certain ways, those in charge of museums reify the meta-narratives ·that order societies and their material culture. Objects displayed in museums expose the power to own as well as construct the narratives that link them within the format of exhibition. During the late nineteenth century, exhibitionary institutions, such as the museum and world fairs, increasingly displayed the bounties born of wealth and progress and put them on view for the world—primarily the Western world—to see.[1]

Birth child of the Enlightenment, the museum has often been described as a secular temple, where objects organized according to objective truths of time, geography, and style await the aesthetic and intellectual veneration of respectful visitors who, through viewing the objects, expect to gain the intangible benefits of cultural refinement, nationalistic pride, or universalist splendor, depending on the type of museum. Particularly in Europe and America, museums have often been housed in buildings resembling Greco-Roman temples designed to signify humanistic secularism through a vocabulary of pre–Christian (and thus popularly imagined as secular) religious references. Yet the mode of educational representation encouraged by museum display completely disassociates itself from religious practice. It precludes the act of prayer with objects—a cross, a relic, a triptych, a mihrab (niche indicating the direction of prayer in an Islamic structure), or a prayer rug—which were originally indivisible from faithful worship. It does so through the very practices that induce the respect toward material culture fostered by a museum: by distancing the viewer from the object through the use of glass cases, alarm systems, and cordoned sections; by replacing devotional wonder with labels that enlighten, define, and clarify; and by isolating the object from an original context that orchestrated its devotional function. Thus, as an institution, the museum raises questions about how a secular space devoted to material appreciation can function without automatically implicating much older religious spatial practices.

In response to dynamic political contingencies, the Ottoman Empire developed diverse and independent collections to display those aspects of its identity that became vital to its independence and survival. Of the museums and collections that developed in the last seventy years of empire, the smallest was devoted to the Islamic arts. The collection of Islamic arts emerged against a backdrop of already established European-style institutions of display. In 1846 the Ottomans began to collect and exhibit the seeds of what would become the Ottoman Imperial Museum. This fledgling museum took the form of two allied collections: one of archaeological and one of military antiquities.[2] The prodigious collections of antique sculptures helped to foster the empire's European aspirations by forging indigenous links to the Greco-Roman heritage, asserting the empire's territorial right to lands metaphorically claimed by European archaeologists. While at first glance these exhibitions mimicked the Greco-Roman collections of European museums, they did so in large part to question the exclusivity of the Greek heritage claimed by modern European nation-states.[3] As Homi Bhabha points out, such mimicry at once acts as a camouflage through which to fit into the model of dominant states and displaces that model as a defensive position from which to counteract its dominance.[4]

While the antiquities collections nimbly scratched at the boundaries of European heritage, the military collections redrew those of the Ottoman legacy. By including enemies and armies in the tale of Ottoman history, these exhibits reformulated the Ottoman perception of history from the dynastic to the populist. Much as the reforms of the *Tanzimat* had served to create a state designed to serve rather than to dominate the people, the new history displayed in the museum conceived of an empire that had emerged from the shared bravery and sacrifice of state and subjects alike, not simply as a succession of divinely sanctioned dynastic glories. Such displays replaced the projection of dynastic immortality with one that appreciated the martyrdom of soldiers for the Ottoman nation. Thus, it psychologically primed citizens and soldiers alike for the many wars that beleaguered the empire before its ultimate downfall: the Crimean, the Balkan, the Russo-Turkish, World War I, and finally the War for Turkish Independence.

These new museums did little to promote the Islamic identity of the empire, even though the reassertion of the caliphate was one of the primary interests of Sultan Abdülhamid II (r. 1876–1909). In the West, as the empire lost many European territories, the sultan tried to retain some control by maintaining governance over Muslim minorities through his role as caliph, which the sultanate had assumed in 1517.[5] In the East such assertions of caliphal power were equally important in the face of Arab nationalism, which emphatically called into question the Ottoman right to the caliphate, and in doing so implicitly questioned the link between the Islamic and the Ottoman.[6] As Kayali points out, "By emphasizing his role as caliph, Abdülhamid generated support from Arabs, as well as from other Muslims within and outside the Ottoman Empire, at a time when the world of Islam was under Christian imperialist domination."[7] During the reign of Abdülhamid the empire increasingly made use of Islamic symbolism to compete with secessionist nationalist symbols emerging throughout the empire.[8]

But, even as the empire promoted its political identity as the leader of the Islamic world, it chose not to include works of art and culture pertaining to its Ottoman or Islamic identity in its museum until 1889. It was only at this relatively late date that the Council of State set out a revised administrative program for the Ottoman Imperial Museum which included a department of Islamic arts as one of six branches of the growing institution.[9] As the empire weakened during the early twentieth century, the identification of Islamic works of art became increasingly important to the development of sense of an Ottoman national identity. Did this imply an increasing interest in religion or in the politics of religious cohesion? Was this an Islam that designated religiosity or politics? The collection of Islamic arts in the late Ottoman Empire marks a moment of transition from the sectarian to the national, from the religious toward the secular, and from the imperial against the colonial.

The belated interest in Islamic antiquities at first seems ironic: the objects most readily accessible to Ottoman collectors—those in common use in mosques and elite households around the empire—were among the last to be collected. This sharply contrasts with the nineteenth-century development of museums in Europe, where galleries and museums assembled both religious and secular artworks to foster national spirit. The Ottoman Empire learned the art of museum making from Europe, yet denied the progressive narrative espoused by most European national museums. For example, the Louvre in Paris had been transformed into a museum as one of the first outward symbols of the new order brought about by the French Revolution. Gathering the insignia of church and crown alike for the public gaze, it declared the formulation of a new state (at least in theory) dedicated to public service. Like other universal survey museums, the Louvre developed extensive collections of Greco-Roman antiquities that introduced an evolutionary narrative of Western heritage. Thus, during their tour of the museum, visitors first encountered ancient Egypt, ancient Greece, Rome, the Renaissance, the Enlightenment, and then the arts of modern Western Europe.[10] These categories of display established a temporal progression from the ancient to the modern coinciding with a geographic progression from the East to the West. Ottoman museums, in contrast, jumped from one autonomous collection to another, each displaying a single view of the new Ottoman identity, none promoting a model of cultural progress culminating in Ottoman modernity. Thus, the museum did not even try to include collections of Ottoman art to parallel the painting and sculpture galleries of the Louvre or the British National Gallery. Indeed, for many years Ottoman museums avoided the suggestion of a present moment for the empire, only multiple pasts from which to garner various aspects of a modern identity. This disavowal of developmental history coincided with a distrust in the belief of positivism as heretical to Islamic norms.[11]

The collection of Islamic arts in the Imperial Museum was the first to exhibit a contemporary identity. Unlike archaeological antiquities or military spolia, Islamic antiquities were not only part of a past conceived as part of the Ottoman legacy; they were also part of the Ottoman present. The shift in interest suggested by the establishment of an Islamic arts section for the museum near the end of the nineteenth century reflects a growing interest in the immediate past of the Islamic world as well as growing nationalistic implications for this past. Certainly, this shift was not unique in Istanbul: in 1883 the Museum of Arab Art opened in Cairo, and Islamic archaeology emerged for the first time in 1885, with the excavation of Samarqand. It was not until 1893, however, with the Exposition d'Art Musulman in Paris, that such arts became identified with religion rather than with region.[12]

Why is it that, in a taxonomic system obsessed with geography and history as the primary identifiers of communal identity, suddenly a religion emerged as a category? The designation of new Islamic collections allowed for the display of a new category of objects without disturbing the time/space progression established by the display pattern of universal survey museums. The positivist organization of such European museums relied on a unique and hierarchical model for progress which would have been challenged by the presentation of multiple cultures, parallel in space and time, differing yet not competing in aesthetics and values. For an object to be displayed as Egyptian, Iranian, or Ottoman would have connoted its use in a locale with a secular history that could theoretically compete with the evolutionary model presented in the main body of the museum. Redefined as Islamic, the value of such an object came to be equated with an aesthetic practice assumed to span a wide range of histories, languages, cultures, and customs—indeed, perhaps to exist outside of time and even geography. In effect, by calling these objects Islamic, museums could consider them outside of time and place. In their quest to import Western models of progress, colonial powers often favored such a perception of their newly acquired territories. Much as "Orientalism assumed an unchanging Orient," the idea of Islamic collections assumed a temporally static aesthetic for the Islamic world.[13] It displayed the arts of "Islam . . . as a 'cultural synthesis' . . . that could be studied apart from the economics, sociology, and politics of the Islamic peoples."[14] Moreover, through this designation the word *Islamic* came to denote an aesthetic value as much as a religious one. By identifying objects with religion rather than with region, such displays suggested two things: that all objects, even those designed for secular use, still somehow pertained to religion (perhaps because of the description of Islam as a way of life as well as a series of devotions); and/or that devotional objects should be moved from the metaphysical to the temporal realm for the sake of their protection and preservation in museums.

Perhaps in light of the Orientalist implications of the designation "Islamic," it is ironic that this new category served nationalist purposes when put into practice in the Ottoman Empire. It becomes less ironic in light of the constant slippage between European collections and their Ottoman counterparts, wherein Ottoman museums mimicked their European forebears only to subvert the assumptions of power implicit in them. Just as the archaeological collections redefined Hellenistic and Byzantine antiquities as part of the Ottoman heritage (as supplementary to its inclusion within European heritage), collections of Islamic antiquities reasserted the political affiliation between the Ottoman Empire and Islam. In order to promote Ottoman nationalism, the affinity between Muslim Ottoman citizens and Islam had to be harnessed as an identification with the Ottoman state. An emphasis on Islam as a national characteristic could mollify the many conservatives in the empire who worried that modernization would necessarily mean Westernization and, implicitly, Christianization. Moreover, by denying a national framework to the category of objects labeled as Islamic, the empire could avoid the problems of Arab nationalism plaguing its integrity in the real-life, political world outside of the museum. Within the Ottoman context Islamic collections provided a counterpoint to the growing association between Arabs and Islam. In effect, the neutralization of difference promoted by a category of art designated as Islamic supported the Ottoman cause as effectively as that of colonial European powers.

The Ottoman Imperial Museum designated an Islamic Arts Division in 1889, but the collection grew very slowly. While Hellenistic antiquities were housed in the lavish new Imperial Museum, a neoclassical building built for them on the grounds of the Topkapi Palace, the Islamic antiquities moved from site to site, first in an upstairs hall of the Imperial Museum and later into increasingly independent venues. Growing in the shadow of the antiquities collections, Islamic collections were never published in catalogs, nor were they extensively publicized in newspapers. The only early description of the collection comes from a short section of an extensive 1895 article about the museum authored by its assistant director, Halil (Edhem):

> At one time during the Middle Ages when in Europe and in Asia no trace of civilization remained and knowledge and science had become nearly completely extinct, Islam and the Arabs appeared as a vehicle for the formation of a new civilization. The advancement of knowledge and science and literature and art spread across the world and the Ottomans were the inheritors of this with their acquisition of the caliphate.
>
> Since today old Arab works and old Ottoman works are among quite desirable and rare antiquities, these are also now being collected in the Imperial Museum and are being arranged for display in a special hall. In this section, the most striking item is in the corner: an ornate tile mihrab from Karaman that is from the time of the Seljuk ruler Alaettin I. Stones with Kufic writing from the time of the Ahmed al-Malik of the Umayyad Caliphate; writing samples of famous calligraphers; book bindings, which are testimony to the fine handicraft of Ottoman artisans; Edirne-work cabinets; mother-of-pearl inlay bookstands; ringstones with Kufic writings; and quite breathtaking Persian carpets decorate this hall.[15]

In introducing the collection, Halil links its establishment with a reminder to the viewer that Europe's ascendancy depended on a history of Arab-Islamic science, a view often promoted by conservatives within the empire.[16] Thus he presents the desire to remember the Islamic past as more than a simple act of self-reflection or nationalist self-promotion. From the first display of Islamic arts, the presentation of artifacts still living in the Ottoman present was also an act of resistance to European cultural hegemony. It balanced, or perhaps even completed, the Ottoman usurpation of the foundations of Europe represented by the archaeological antiquities on exhibit in the rest of the museum. Just as the wide-scale Ottoman collection and display of Hellenistic antiquities exposed the shaky foundations of an exclusive pan-European Greek heritage, Halil sug-

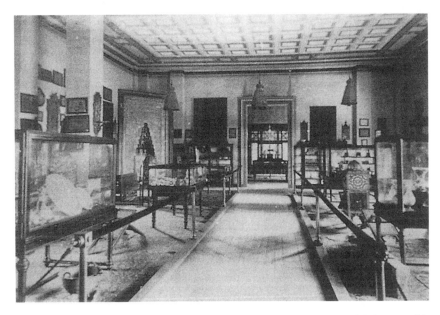

Fig. 8.1 Islamic collections in the Imperial Museum, c. 1903. Abdülhamid Photographic Collection. Courtesy of Nurhan Atasoy.

gests, the collection of Islamic arts underscored Europe's actual dependence on the Islamic world for its subsequent greatness. In these paragraphs Halil simultaneously exposes Europe's dependence on the Islamic world and the Islamic world's dependence on the Ottoman Empire in its role as protector of the caliphate. Thus, he conflates the Islamic with the Ottoman, producing a national, not a religious, identifier.

Like its European counterparts, the Ottoman museum used religious objects as national identifiers only by divesting them of their religious significance. The symmetrical organization of the display and the organization of the collection by material precluded its assessment in any sort of religious framework, in which disparate objects would be used together in an architectural setting for the purpose of worship. In the museum display only the lanterns hanging from the ceiling and the carpets covering the floor retain their original spatial function (see fig. 8.1). Unlike in the mosque or tomb from which they came, however, the carpets were roped off from the very people who would have prayed on them in religious settings. Much as the museum's primary collections enforced secular notions through the display of pre-Islamic arts, the hall devoted to Islamic arts subverted the religious content of mihrab and Quran alike, transforming them into objects for the aesthetic rather than the spiritual gaze. Carol Duncan refers to the museum as a space of secular ritual.[17] Indeed, while the architecture of the exterior—designed to recall a Greek temple, as the neoclassical tradition dictated for museum architecture—promoted a humanist, quasi-religious veneration of the antiquities within, the Islamic arts upstairs invited a new and secular ritual: that of impartial, categorical examination.

While the inclusion of Islamic arts in the museum acknowledged their cultural value in a way otherwise ignored by the Imperial Museum, the removal of objects from religious contexts to the secular halls of a museum itself had revolutionary implications. In mosques, tombs, and dervish lodges, the objects collected by the museum had nonmaterial value associated with their function and sometimes also with their venerable association with figures from the past. Often such objects acted as relics or gained local meanings because of the legends and histories surrounding their use. In the museum they exchanged such value for the secular equivalents of aesthetics and historical rarity and became signs of national eminence. By redefining objects from religious settings as works of art to collect and display, the Islamic Arts division of the Imperial Museum called into question the very identity of a devotional object.

Although never explicitly stated, the radical implications of Islamic collections in a museum setting were not far from the consciousness of the museum's administration. As the Imperial Museum developed as a project expressing the cultural aspirations of the empire, its florescence in the late nineteenth century depended heavily on the leadership of its director, Osman Hamdi (1842–1910). Educated as a lawyer and as an artist in France and known for his support of reformist politics, Osman Hamdi took on the roles of painter, educator, museum administrator, and archaeologist in his native land. Although neither his private nor his professional correspondence documents the motivations behind his curatorship of the museum, many of his paintings suggest his interpretations of and hopes for the collections.

It was no surprise to Osman Hamdi that the new collections promoted a radical shift in Ottoman modes of education. Whereas once Ottomans learned about religion by reading the Quran, in the museum, they would learn about the nation through the objects that once surrounded the transmission of religious knowledge. In his 1890 work, *In the Green Mosque of Bursa,* Osman Hamdi uses a Mamluk candleholder and a lamp from the Gebze Çoban Mustafa Pasha Mosque from the museum collections, and sets them in the quintessential early Ottoman Mosque, completed in 1424 (see fig. 8.2).[18] Here Osman Hamdi depicts himself seated, receiving the wisdom of a teacher, who reads aloud to him from a Quran, quite possibly one in the collection. Similarly, in the 1904 work *Fountain of Life,* he depicts himself reading the same Quran in front of a fountain in the Tiled Pavilion surrounded by objects from the museum's Islamic collection (see fig. 8.3).[19] As the curator of these collections, Osman Hamdi subsumed the age-old role of religious scholar to the modern role of a secular educator and suggests this relationship by depicting its inversion in his paintings. In such self-portraits he transposes his modern role into an anachronistic, timeless, and quintessentially Ottoman setting, emphasizing his aspirations more

Fig. 8.2 Osman Hamdi, *On the Green Mosque of Bursa*. Oil on canvas, 1890, 81 cm x 59 cm. Courtesy of Mustafa Cezar.

as an Ottoman citizen and innovator than as an aspiring European. One might even wonder whether the fountain of life in the title refers to the physical site behind him or to the activity of erudition in which he—and the museum—is engaged. Osman Hamdi's adoption of the Orientalist style of painting for his

Fig. 8.3 Osman Hamdi, *The Fountain of Life.* Oil on canvas, 1904, dimensions unavailable. Courtesy of Mustafa Cezar.

dissections of the museum, an organ of identity production, underscores both his and the museum's investment in the colonial art of mimicry.

Such strategies came at a high cultural cost, as suggested in the subtle symbolic drama of Osman Hamdi's 1901 work *Mihrab* (see fig. 8.4). In this painting a woman, modeled after Osman Hamdi's wife, sits on an inlaid Quran stand in front of the mihrab. She displaces many copies of the Quran, which lie disheveled at her feet. Although the incense at the foot of the mihrab continues to burn, the candle beside it stands extinguished. All of the objects in the picture—the Quran stand, the incense burner, the candleholder, and quite probably the

Fig. 8.4 Osman Hamdi, *Mihrab*. Oil on canvas, 1901, 210 cm x 108 cm. Collection of Demirbank. Courtesy of Mustafa Cezar.

Qurans as well—belonged to the growing collections of the Islamic section of the museum.[20] While the removal of the mihrab and the Quran stand to the museum preserved them as objects of fine art, this act simultaneously plundered their functions as aids to religious devotion. The museum saved devotional objects, but in doing so it secularized them.

Could any image be more shocking? As an allegorical representation of the museum, the painting implicates the Islamic collections in a secularist revolution that replaces religion in favor of art and the material world. In the museum an aesthetic appreciation of Islamic arts displaces the worship of the Quran, just as this figure sits directly between the viewer and the mihrab, precluding prayer. She, along with all that she represents, replaces the Quran on its stand and becomes the object of devotion. In one possible interpretation this figure, exposed in body and yet distant in her gaze, suggests the West: beautiful, alluring, distracting, and yet impassive and unattainable. Still, by placing a portrait of his own wife in front of the mihrab, Osman Hamdi made literal the classical metaphor between the beloved and the *qibla* (direction of prayer, indicating the direction toward the holy *Ka)beh* in Mecca) common in Persian poetry. Hafez writes, "Whoever comes to the ka)beh of your street/ Is like one praying before the qibla of your eyebrows."[21] Furthermore, during the late nineteenth century feminization of the national spirit (akin to the notion of the French la *patrie*) entered the Ottoman tradition. Thus, the painting implicates the museum in an act of national devotion akin to that of the personal beloved and also marked a moment of transition in the symbolism ascribed to the female form. With this tour de force of layered metaphor spanning several traditions, Osman Hamdi highlights the pivotal role of the museum in constructing a revolutionary bridge from the traditional into the modern sphere.

If the Islamic Arts Division of the Imperial Museum already served as a signpost for the secularization of the unborn Turkish Republic, then how radical was the reform that took place under the republic? During its first decade the republic turned monumental religious institutions such as the Mosque of Aya Sofya and the Tomb of Cellaleddin Rumi into museums. By doing so, it purposefully created potent exhibitionary symbols of the new order. These as well as other, more recently designated religious museums such as the Rooms of the Mantle of the Prophet at the Topkapi Palace Museum and the Tomb of Haci Bektashh in Central Anatolia serve as halfway houses between secular display and religious practice. They have provided reminders of sacred histories that undermine the notion of the museum as secular temple and question the secular frame that presents religion as cultural artifact. These museums beg certain questions concerning both the nature of secularism and the nature of museums: what is the dividing line between a museum object and an object of worship? Where is the boundary between religious faith and aesthetic appreciation? And, most important, as a secular state, what role has the Turkish government chosen in mediating between popular religious practice and historical sites?

As has often been pointed out, the centralized Turkish state formulated a laicist rather than a secularist ideal in which the government has attempted to channel religion, not replace it. The young republic attempted to transform Islam from a traditional devotional practice linked with the monarchy to a cultural practice bounded by national identity. From the first years of the republic the Ethnographic Museum in Ankara took on much of the task of preserving historical religious artifacts. In essence it took on the role of the Islamic Arts Museum while vocally espousing a politics of secularism which had always been implicit in the earlier institution. In addition to redefining local costumes and practices as historical and national by placing them behind glass, the museum gathered the devotional objects of historical mosques and dervish lodges across the country to redistribute them in the halls of secular display. Mannequins not only exposed the private customs of the dervishes in the frame of a cultural and ethnographic phenomenon; they also embodied the very recent death of these practices in notably non-Islamic effigy. Much as the dervishes had converted the Turkomen tribes people of Seljuk Anatolia to Islam, the abolition of the dervish orders twelve centuries later and their exposure in this exhibitionary fashion were designed to convert Turkish citizens to the new religion of secularism.

Yet this sharp break between display and religious practice was ephemeral. The Konya Museum of Antiquities, located at the Tomb of Mevlana Cellaleddin Rumi, established in 1926, merges the spatial elements of sites of worship and sites of exhibition in a deliberate attempt to confuse the boundaries of religious devotion and ethnographic value. According to the 1925 law that outlawed all dervish lodges along with the various titles and supernatural practices associated with them, all tombs and lodges were to be closed and their possessions appropriated by the state. In 1926, however, the government issued directives that recognized the value of their possessions. "Due to the architectural stylistic value and the ethnographic value of the works within it," the Division of Education asked the director of the Istanbul Archaeology Museum Halil (Edhem) to provide ideas about making the former lodge in Konya into a museum.[22] Such directives emphasized the secular value of the structure and its contents, shunning any reference to their devotional use except as a relic of the past. For example, Halil observed that the area of the dervish meditation, the *sema-hane,* had good light and thus would make a suitable exhibit space. How ironic that one sort of meditative peregrination would soon be replaced by another.

By defining the content of the museum as having stylistic and ethnographic significance, the administrators constructed two new frameworks for the objects: culturally Turkish and temporally Seljuk. They eschewed not only their religious devotional functions but also their identification as objects of Islamic art. The redesignation of Turkey's living material culture as objects of ethnographic interest served to contain and define traditional practices while distancing them from the modern practices encouraged by the urban elites. While the government staged the new museum as a secular institution within the architectural frame of a Sufi shrine, it also utilized the religious significance of the site in order to create a museum with a national significance. During his twelve visits to Konya, Mustafa Kemal Atatürk made many comments designed to frame Mevlana as a modernizing and Turkifying influence in Islam and to use this image of the popular Sufi saint as a model for the function of the tomb/museum.

> Mevlana was an important reformer who adapted Islam to the Turkish spirit. Islam is actually a tolerant and modern religion. . . . For Arabs, who live in a warm climate and spend their lives without moving, five prayers a day created a very active lifestyle. The prophet Mohammed led the people from inaction to action. For Turks, who washed in melted snow and raced horses on the high plateaus of the eastern mountains, ritual cleaning and prayer were quite natural. Being a Mevlevi was very natural to Turkish traditions. The idea of reaching God through turning on one's feet and in an active form is a very natural expression of the Turkish genius.[23]

Thus, Mevlana emerged not as a figure in the Persian-Islamic tradition but as an early national hero, almost akin to a modern athelete.

During his first visit in 1931, Atatürk transposed this image of Mevlana as modernizer to the physical space of the museum. While visiting the room of the museum director, which had previously been that of the leader of the Mevlevi order, he had one of his aids translate a Persian poem written on the wall. It said, "For the lonesome lovestricken [referring to the Sufi dervishes], all doors but [God's] were closed so that they wouldn't find another path, only yours [referring to the path of the Mevlevi order] was left open." "So," Atatürk interpreted, "even though all doors were closed, this door is open. The truth is that during my visit here in 1923, I suggested that we not close this lodge, but leave it open as a museum . . . I see that I brought the command of this poem to fruition. And you see what a fine museum it has become."[24]

Indeed, dramatic architectural changes to the structure of the lodge had transformed it from a place of one type of worship to another. Upon entry, a sign designated the structure as the Konya Museum of Antiquities, implicitly relegating all its contents to the past—including fragments of Seljuk city walls, Mevlevi tombs, and dioramic displays of dervish life. As already mentioned, the room reserved for the Çelebi, or dervish leader, became transformed into the room of the museum director, creating a palimpsest of secular over religious practices at the site. As proposed by Halil Edhem, dividing walls between former cells of the dervishes were knocked down in order to provide a well-lit display hall next to the primary tomb. Small rooms that had once fostered inward meditation gave way to public galleries for display and education. More radical changes erased the religious nature of the site with broader strokes. A group of graves in front of the entrance were removed—and thus desecrated—clearing out a public courtyard suitable for tourists. The ablutions fountain beside the graves was also removed, only to be reconstructed in the late 1980s, when the government was interested in promoting the Mevlevi order in an attempt to moderate the growth of the religious right wing. In planning for the conversion to a museum, Halil Edhem even suggested that the main hall—once a mosque—should become a library. Unlike the tomb that hitherto had housed the library, it received ample light. Thus, many of the attributes that made the building into a place of worship were forcibly erased in order to make it into a museum.

On the other hand, small gestures toward the religious integrity of the structure suggest that, even in this most radical period of secularist reform, the government did not expect to divest the museum of its religious significance. Halil Edhem emphasized that non-Islamic antiquities should not be moved to the museum. Accustomed to the detemporalization of the Islamic past in the Ottoman displays of Islamic arts which he had curated, he suggested removing European crystal chandeliers in an attempt to create an authentic atmosphere—even though the chandelier had certainly been in place only several years earlier when the site was in use as a dervish lodge. He suggested that the function of the internal *mescid* (small mosque) should be changed only in light of the existing mosque just outside of the lodge precincts. Perhaps most noteworthy, unlike any other museums to date in the country, the Konya museum was to preserve its original form in all of the tomb sections. Rather than placing most of the writings, candleholders, and tomb covers in glass cases, they were to remain as they had been in the dervish lodge. While on the one hand this mode of display created an ethnographic diorama, given the practice of visiting saints' tombs that remains common throughout Turkey, the government could not have been blind to the fact that the tombs would be used as a place of prayer. Indeed, during his visits to the tomb, even Atatürk participated in the reading of the most basic of Islamic prayers, the *Fatiha*—a practice that did not change even as the site became a secular museum.

This confusion between religious and ethnographic-historical value served Republican political goals, which utilized secularism not as a stance against religion per se but as a limit to monarchic sentiment fostered by earlier forms of official Islam. Folk Islam, as represented by dervish organizations, had been far more likely to support the nationalist cause during the war years. By incorporating this local version of Islam into nationalist, secular policies, Atatürk ensured a venue for religious practice under the wing of the secularist project of nationalist museums.

To this day the museum retains a bitextuality between the secular and the religious. While explanatory signs inform the nonreligious visitor of the identity of those buried in the tomb and the date of items displayed in glass cases, similar signs never elucidate the references to Mevlevi practice which pervade the museum in forms such as poetry *levhas* hanging on the walls, symbolic dervish hats in paintings and carvings, and inlaid tiles. In a museum attempting a complete ethnographic exposition of religious practices, one might expect all

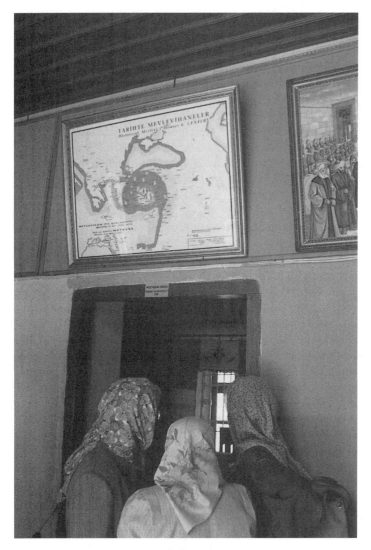

Fig. 8.5 Turkish women at the tomb/museum of Cellaleddin Rumi, with a map of Turkey overhead. Photo by Wendy M. K. Shaw.

of the religious mystery of the site to be defused in favor of scientific explanation. Instead, the museum allows—and today, with the mandatory removal of shoes and religiously modest dress, even fosters—the religious uses of the museum. At the same time, strategically placed maps emphatically link the Seljuk past with the Turkish present within an Islamic framework (see fig. 8.5). Here, above a diorama of a dervish in his cell, we see a map of modern Turkey with

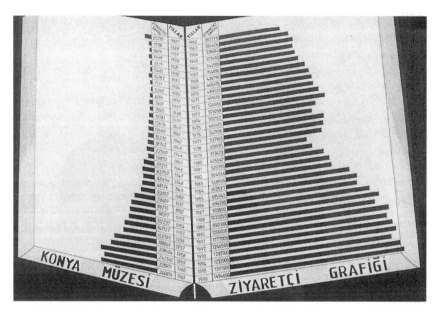

Fig. 8.6. Visitor chart in display case at the entrance to the tomb/museum of Cellaleddin Rumi. Photo by Wendy M. K. Shaw.

Konya at its center, suggesting this center of Anatolia not only as a site for religious growth but as a center point for the Turkish nation. The tomb/museum functions as a place of *ziyaret,* visitation, not only in the touristic sense but also in the sense of pilgrimage, uniting ancient and modern reasons for travel, exploration, and viewing in a single site (see fig. 8.6). One may easily wonder about the unintentional pun in this chart of visitors to the Konya museum on display in the glass case near the entrance to the museum—have they performed a ziyaret as a religious pilgrimage or as a secular visit to a museum of national heritage?

The tomb/museum of Cellaleddin Rumi is not alone in its production of a precarious balance between the museumlike and the religious. Much farther from the public and touristic gaze than the Tomb of Rumi, the Tomb of Haci Bektash near Cappadocia opened to the public as a museum in 1935. It operates as a Bektashi shrine under a thin veneer of museum practices. The museum charges admission, exposes the site by providing a museum plan, restricts access to valuables by placing them in glass cases, dictates ambulatory paths, and restricts visits to daytime hours. Like all museums, the site is marked as a modern, secular site with the prominent display of the bust of Atatürk, along with photographs of his visit to the shrine in 1919. As in Konya, Mustafa Kemal, the general, used his visits to popular folk shrines in order to reify the support of folk Islam behind the national cause. Despite the secular framework of the modern museum, the memory of his visit to the shrine—the visit of the personage that nationalist Turkish histories holds solely responsible for Turkish modernism and secularism—suggests an implicit ambivalence in the nature of the site.

An hour's drive from the nearest city of Nevsehir, this museum attracts people who are more interested in the museum as shrine than as cultural artifact. While the museum does not have its own gift shop, immediately outside the museum, amid the standard array of local touristic knickknacks, numerous salespeople offer keychains, *nazarliks* (blue glass charm decorations), posters, necklaces, and beaded souvenirs emblazoned with images not only of Haci Bektash but also of Ali and the twelve imams of Shiite Islam, with which the Bektashi order is closely associated.

Inside the museum labels produce a historical narrative of Bektashi practices. They inform the non-Bektashi visitor of how rooms were once used, of what objects on display are, and when they are from. Yet beyond this historical narrative that uses objects and spaces as material cultural remains, there is a second narrative constantly played out through the act of religious visitation going on within the museum. Numerous local and regional visitors respectfully bow through the low doorways in order to honor Haci Bektash, exiting the tombs backwards in order to never turn their backs on their spiritual leaders. Visitors drink the springwater that flows continually from the lion fountain. They believe that Haci Bektash chose this site of his lodge because of a prophecy that he would find an eternal spring in a dry land. While formal prayers are not held within the shrine, individuals pray at the several tombs at the site, ceremonially walking around the elaborate marble cenotaphs of the saints buried in the complex. People who would never visit a secular museum—old women from villages and young couples hoping for children—file through the museum spaces, praying in specific locations and tying fabric to the branches of trees believed to help bring spiritual aid from the saints.

If all this seems opaque to the chance urban or foreign tourist passing through the museum, the museum guards, all local townspeople and members of the order, can explain the invisible symbolism of spaces and movements to select Turkish visitors who appear curious but not too official. Beyond their official functions the rooms were often designed as illustrations of the Bektashi cosmology. The guards carefully explicate the symbolic significance and relationships between religious paintings on the walls and proudly read aloud and explain the significance of poetic *levhas* displayed on the walls. The sectarian knowledge that they informally narrate is completely absent from the formal museum labels, which try to reframe the spaces as a museum rather than as a religious shrine. Without a doubt, the museum has changed the functionality of the site, but it has done so selectively and has allowed it to retain much of its aura for believers. While Bektashis no longer perform their devotions within the complex, in recent years, since the relaxation of restrictions on Sufi orders, they perform them in private several miles away from the site.

Fig. 8.7. Interior to the Museum of Aya Sophia, view of Byzantine-era apsidal conch mosaic depicting Mother Mary and Christ and nearby Ottoman-era hanging plaque with the name of Mohammed. Photo by Wendy M. K. Shaw.

The commerce between the religious and the secular in museums has played itself out most prominently at the Museum of Aya Sofya in Istanbul. Much as the 1453 conversion of this monumental edifice to the primary mosque of the Ottoman Empire powerfully symbolized the transfer of power from one political and religious power to another, its closure in 1924 and its designation as a museum to open in 1935 symbolized the transfer of the state's allegiance from Islam to secularism. While the plaster that had covered the figural gold-and-glass mosaics throughout the structure since the mid-eighteenth century was removed to expose the Byzantine and Christian heritage of the site, the structures that had been laid over them in order to make the structure into a mosque—primarily the mihrab and the enormous *levha* with the names of God, the prophet, and the caliphs—remained in place (see fig. 8.7). While initially smaller exhibits were to join these architectural forms, the designers of the museum decided that this would interrupt the spatial integrity of the structure. Without any further exhibits, the juxtaposition of these two traditions in the monumental spaces of the religious structure suggests the equivalent demise of both. Side by side, the visitor sees a Christian altar and an Islamic mihrab; Islamic calligraphy and mosaics of Christ and the Virgin Mary. Already rendered inappropriate for Christian religious practice, the mosque has been equally rendered unusable for Muslim prayer because of the ubiquity of figural and iconic Christian representations.

It is no wonder, then, that in the 1990s the museum has served as a potent symbol for the Islamist cause. Not swayed by the deceptively practical argument that the Sultan Ahmet district has numerous large mosques, Islamists have argued that the use of Aya Sofya as a museum amounts to the desecration of a mosque for secular purposes. While no doubt numerous mosques have, in centuries past, been destroyed in various ways, the symbolic nature of Aya Sofya as a monument to secularism during the republican period has made it a prime target for the opponents of secularism. In response, its maintenance as a museum devoted to the rich Byzantine history of the city has become a passionate issue for secularists. As a temporary compromise in 1994, one side of the Aya Sofya structure was reopened for prayer, and the call to prayer began to compete with that from the nearby Mosque of Sultan Ahmet for the first time since the advent of loudspeakers and their ubiquitous cacophony.

Nearby, within the vast museum spaces of the Topkapi Palace, the Rooms of the Mantle of the Prophet raise similar issues about the interplay between the secular and the religious. Overall, the museum glorifies the classical age of the Ottoman Empire for the gaze of citizen and tourist alike. The vast majority of its visitors are foreign tourists, who visit in droves in the summer; most schoolchildren visit sometime on a school trip but rarely return. Yet, since the initial opening of the Rooms of the Mantle of the Prophet, the museum has begun to draw a new type of tourist: the religious pilgrim. Distinct from the throngs of sweaty visitors in shorts and sunglasses, religiously covered women and bearded men, often visiting from distant places in the country, file past the gaudy displays of the treasury and the harem toward the Rooms of the Holy Mantle, the primary objective of their trip.

Because the sultan visited every fifteenth of Ramazan, the Rooms of the Holy Mantle were among the only spaces of the Topkapi Palace in good repair. But they were not among the rooms opened to the public when the palace was opened as a museum, in 1926. As section after section of the dilapidated palace, in disuse since 1853, opened to the public, the Rooms of the Mantle of the Prophet only opened in 1953. In his introduction to the catalog of the newly opened section, the director of the museum, Tahsin Öz, writes:

> To date there has not been a clear examination of the historical and religious souvenirs known as the Holy Relics that have fascinated the Islamic world for centuries. Nor has there been any opportunity for such examination, for nearly all these works were under the locked and sealed safes of rulers. . . . When, following the Republic, the Topkapi Palace became a museum on April 3, 1924, while the administration of the palace was the charge of the Official of the Treasury, the Chamber of the Mantle of the Prophet was that of an independent official. In 1927 [understanding the significance of these works to the museum], the keys to this section were handed over to the museum administration. As the museum officials continued to clean the pieces in the collection, they also prepared their inventory and began to examine their value. . . . These holy works, although collected and kept out of love and appreciation of

their religious importance, each have artistic and historical value on a world-wide scale.[25]

While Öz implies that the display of the objects within the chamber was delayed because of the arduous process of preparing them for display, he does not mention the changing political climate that made the opening of the collection to the public possible. After nearly two decades of radically secularist policies, the republic's first election that was more than a referendum brought the populist Democratic Party to power in 1950. Restrictions against certain forms of religious expression relaxed; the official language of the call to prayer reverted from Turkish to Arabic. It was only under this government that religious expression of a form that had been associated with the Ottoman state became possible within the frame of republican national identity.

Like the Tomb of Mevlana Cellaleddin Rumi, the rooms of the Chamber of the Holy Mantle became defined by their history rather than their religious significance. In order to relegate their history to a more distant past, details of the structure were "corrected" to suit a pre-eighteenth-century vision of the Ottoman legacy. Thus, Öz points out that "the lovely mother of pearl inlay door [leading to the Chamber of the Holy Mantle] was made by the late Vasif, professor of inlay work at the Academy of Fine Arts. The previous door is a rococo work from the time of Mahmud II [c. 1830s] which has now been put into storage."[26] Architectural features and renovations from earlier periods remained untouched. While the newer door had been used throughout the nineteenth century under the republic, during the annual rituals of visiting the relics, these rituals had to be made more ancient. This was signified by the door itself, suggesting that the ritual belonged not to the present or even the recent past but to an Ottoman past that was safely distant in an indeterminate, atemporalized past.

After the military regime of 1980–1981, the rooms became a sign of the religious tolerance of the new civilian regime. For the first time ever, the Ministry of Culture hired reciters of the Quran (*hafiz*) to pray beside the mantle of the prophet behind a thick glass wall dividing the chamber from the public. A new catalog presented the collections in Turkish, English, and Arabic within a single booklet.[27] The cover featured an image of the hafiz praying beside the gold case of the mantle. Much like the government's investment at the Tomb of Mevlana, this hafiz acted as a sign for the religious populism of the government under President Turgut Özal. In 1995 the Ministry of Culture, in the hands of Prime Minister Erbakan's religious Welfare Party, extended the duties of the hafiz, who began to keep vigil over the relics twenty-four hours a day. In 1996 the Islamist government underscored the religious tenor of this section of the museum by opening a second room full of relics near the Chamber of the Mantle of the Prophet, in the ceremonial chamber beside it. This room included, among more footprints of the prophet in various materials and numerous flasks of dirt from the grave of the prophet, the begging bowl of the prophet Abraham and the well-polished crooked wooden walking stick of the prophet Moses. While these objects had been mentioned in earlier catalogues devoted to the chamber of the relics, never before had they been displayed. Religious visitors thronged to the museum.

During those years, I frequently worked at the Istanbul Archaeological Museum just down the hill from the Topkapi Palace. Often, a group of religiously conservative visitors, easily recognizable by the beards of the men or the covering of the women, accidentally wandered into the museum. They were appalled by the nude sculptures, and the guards, laughing genially, would direct them next door. Like them, the minister of culture was shocked that such sculptures were on display in an Islamic culture and went so far as to suggest the closure of the Istanbul Archaeology Museum—the first museum of the Ottoman Empire, which had, of course, been an Islamic state.

With the fall of the Welfare Party government in 1996, the extra display of relics was initially closed then reopened on a far smaller scale. A hafiz still prays during working hours but not day and night. According to one of the guards at the museum, the tradition of viewing the holy mantle has continued throughout the sixteen years he has worked there: the staff views the mantle in the middle of Ramazan, on a day when the museum is closed. All this to say that the museum, an institution that generally represents an idealized vision of reality and identity, perhaps functions with more honesty than one might expect. Turkey is a secular country, but its museums have found a balance, recognizing that secularism can exist without denying the very real demands of faith. If a museum represents society as an ideal, perhaps it is this reality that can spill out across the antagonism between Turkish laicite and religious politics.

Notes

1. Among the prodigious literature in museum studies which has recently emerged, the following are of particular interest to this discussion: Carol Duncan, *Civilizing Rituals: Inside Public Art Museums* (New York: Routledge, 1995); Gwendolyn Wright, ed., *The Formation of National Collections of Art and Archaeology* (Washington, D.C.: National Gallery of Art, 1996); Daniel Sherman and Irit Rogoff, *Museum Culture* (Minneapolis: University of Minnesota Press, 1994); and Eilean Hooper-Greenhill, *Museums and the Shaping of Knowledge* (New York: Routledge, 1992).
2. Wendy M. K. Shaw, *Possessors and Possessed: Objects, Museums and the Visualization of History in the late Ottoman Empire* (Berkeley: University of California Press, 2002).
3. Suzanne Marchand, *Down from Olympus: Archaeology and Philhellenism in Germany, 1750–1970* (Princeton, N.J.: Princeton University Press, 1996), 7–10.
4. Homi Bhabha discusses the mode of colonial mimicry at length in "Of Mimicry and Man," in *The Location of Culture* (New York: Routledge, 1994), 85–92.
5. Selim Deringil, *The Well-Protected Domains: Ideology and the Legitimation of Power in the Ottoman Empire, 1876–1909* (London: I. B. Taurus, 1998), 46–49.

6. Selim Deringil, "Legitimacy Structures in the Ottoman State: The Reign of Abdulhamid II," *International Journal of Middle East Studies* 23, no. 3 (August 1991): 345–359.

7. Hasan Kayali, *Arabs and Young Turks: Ottomanism, Arabism, and Islamism in the Ottoman Empire, 1908–1918* (Berkeley: University of California Press, 1997), 35.

8. Serif Mardin, *Religion and Social Change in Modern Turkey: The Case of Bediüzzaman Said Nursi* (Albany: State University of New York Press, 1989), 129.

9. Mustafa Cezar, *Sanatta Batiya Açilis ve Osman Hamdi II* (Istanbul: Erol Kerim Aksoy Kültür, Egitim, Spor ve Saglik Vakfi Yayini, 1995), 547.

10. Carol Duncan, "Art Museums and the Ritual of Citizenship," in *Exhibiting Cultures: The Poetics and Politics of Museum Display,* ed. Ivan Karp and Stephen D. Lavine (Washington, D.C.: Smithsonian Institution Press, 1991), 88.

11. Deringil, *Well-Protected Domains,* 45.

12. Stephen Vernoit, "Islamic Archaeology," *Muqarnas* 14 (1997): 3, 8.

13. Edward Said, *Orientalism* (New York: Vintage Books, 1978), 96.

14. Said, *Orientalism,* 105.

15. Halil (Edhem), "Müze-ye Hümayun," *Tercuman-i Hakikat / Serveti Funun* 1313 (special issue), 104.

16. Kayali, *Arabs and Young Turks,* 36.

17. Duncan, "Art Museums," 7–12.

18. V. Bilgin Demirsar, *Osman Hamdi Tablolarinda Gercekle Iliskiler* (Istanbul: Kültür Bakanligi Yayinlari, 1989), 107–108.

19. Demirsar, *Usman Hamdi,* 131–133. The first pavilion of the Topkapi Palace, the Tiled Pavilion is located directly across from the Imperial Museum building. At this time, it still housed part of the Hellenistic Antiquities collection.

20. Demirsar, *Usman Hamdi,* 119.

21. Parviz Khanlari, *Devan-e Hafez* (Tehran: Intisharat-i Bunyad-i Farhang-i Iran, 1359/ 1980), 98. Many thanks to Professor Richard Davis for providing this insight and example.

22. Prime Minister's Archives of the Republic, document 35:42, 24 Kanunevvel 1341 / 3 March 1926.

23. Mehmet Önder, *Atatürk Konya'da* (Ankara: Atatürk Kültür, Dil, ve Tarih Yüksek Kurumu Arastirma Merkezi, 1989), 2–3. The author is quoting a conversation that supposedly took place between Atatürk and the former Postnisin Veled Çelebi Izbudak, reported in a Konya newspaper in 1963.

24. Önder, *Atatürk,* 106.

25. Tahsin Öz, *Hirka-i Saadet Dairesi ve Emanat-i Mukaddese* (Istanbul: Ismail Akgün Matbaasi, 1953), 1–2.

26. Öz, *Hirka-i Saadet,* 14.

27. Erdem Yucel, *Hirka-i Saadet* (Istanbul: Yapi ve Kredi Bankasi, 1982).

CHAPTER 9

"These Hills Will Give You Great Treasure"

OZARK TOURISM AND THE COLLAPSE
OF SACRED AND SECULAR

AARON K. KETCHELL

*B*efore the twentieth century, the geographic region known as the Ozarks was virtually unknown to most Americans. While its pristine rivers and tree-covered mountains attracted urbanites from Kansas City and Saint Louis in search of an Arcadian myth of unspoiled nature, few outside of this immediate locale took note of the place. In 1896, however, a young religious seeker on the way to join family members in southern Missouri was forced to flee the floodwaters of the White River and sought refuge with J. K. and Anna Ross in their cabin atop Dewey Bald. Pastor-turned-author Harold Bell Wright's stay and return trips over each of the next eight summers were the fodder for his novel *The Shepherd of the Hills* (1907), a work that would eventually bring the Ozarks out of its seclusion and lay the groundwork for one of the United States' contemporary tourist meccas.

The Shepherd of the Hills, said to have been outsold only by the Bible in the early decades of the twentieth century, provides a meta-narrative for the subsequent growth and development of the Ozarks.[1] It tells the story of a messianic city dweller who moves to an isolated mountain village populated by simple country folk. Prior to his arrival, the community is in turmoil, with residents plagued by family misfortunes, by malaise about ever-encroaching elements of modernity, and an overall perception that traditional ethics and practices were rapidly decaying. After moving to a piece of land purportedly haunted by a malevolent spirit and proving to his superstitious neighbors that moral purity triumphs over even the nastiest demons in Moanin' Meadow, the Shepherd systematically heals all the ills of the Mutton Hollow residents. Most interesting about this seemingly patented narrative is the dual nature of the Shepherd's persona. Balancing the new and the old, he is able to adapt to the rugged life of the hills while still maintaining an air of urbanity, demonstrating to the Ozarkers that modern accretions such as industrial technology or a market economy need not destroy a community's virtue.

The Shepherd of the Hills describes a vital linkage between religiously grounded morality and materialism, a coupling of sacred and secular that still fuels the contemporary Ozark tourist industry. The book suggests that the infusion of a cosmopolitan spirit into a community does not have to result in moral degeneration and, in the realm of commerce, that one is not forced to choose between god and mammon. Mutton Hollow is morally rejuvenated, rather than transformed into a modernist Sodom, upon the arrival of the mysterious and economically endowed Shepherd. Instead of forcing unwanted cultural modifications on the residents of the hills, the hillbilly messiah enables a continuation of old ways—a refoundationalizing of the merits of family, locality, and the divine.

As Wright's text approaches its centennial celebration, his belief that folk tradition can utilize components of modernity while still resisting the inequities of contemporary change continues to undergird the region's ideology. With the vast success of the Ozarks as a tourist destination, the fusing of traditional values and Christian ethics with the modern is perhaps best exemplified by the area's most profitable vacation spots. Through an examination of the myriad variety shows in Branson, Missouri, and Precious Moments Chapel in Carthage, Missouri, one can discover a complex blending of god, amusement, and profiteering fueled by the evangelically oriented popular culture forms saturating the region.

In the closing pages of *The Shepherd of the Hills*, the protagonist speaks to a young painter who has arrived to sketch the Ozark landscape. The Shepherd vocalizes the proselytizing nature of the place and the Edenic qualities of the mountains: "They will give you great treasure, that you may give again to others, who have not your good strength to escape from the things that men make and do in the restless world over there. One of your noble craft could scarcely fail to find the good things God has written on this page of His great book."[2] While millions read this work, thousands arrived in the 1910s and 1920s to *meet* Wright's fictional subjects and partake of their simple, sanctified lifestyle, a body of visitors that inaugurated Ozark vacationing. At the turn of the twenty-first century, this gentle fusion of tourism and the divine still motivates millions to explore the Ozarks and its religiously based "treasures."

Seminal figures in the disciplines of sociology and religious studies have usually drawn a thick theoretical line between holy situations and practices and all else that is deemed unholy, suggesting that religion is bracketed and confined to explicitly sacred realms. From Émile Durkheim to Mircea Eliade to Bryan Wilson, such thinkers have demarcated faith as an entity uncompromisingly removed from a supposedly temporal arena such as leisure. Additionally, late-nineteenth-century anthropologists such as E. B. Tylor or James Frazer often situated religion as an entity distinct from all other social forms. By delineating religion as a bastion of belief removed from the conditions of everyday life, these authors laid the groundwork for a later religious studies venture that would primarily concern itself with institutional examples of spirituality. Undoubtedly, the slippery definitional issues surrounding the term *religion* are allayed through a methodological focus upon activities within church walls and the formal professions uttered by believers in explicitly demarcated sacred space. Such a focus, however, frequently overlooks the functional aspects of religious practice and their multifarious manifestations in social arenas marked as "profane."

French sociologist Émile Durkheim's work *The Elementary Forms of Religious Life* (1912) made the most conspicuous and heralded distinctions between that which is called religion and its juxtaposed profane world. Writing during an era that was witnessing an ever-increasing divide between public and private, a cleavage facilitated by the rapid proliferation of industrial technologies and the dawn of contemporary individualism, Durkheim utilized a functional definition of religion and marked faith as essential for the realization of social solidarity. For the author, sacred beliefs and practices possess the ability to bind individuals together into a "moral community" or "church," thus facilitating necessary public concord within an era of social and psychical fragmentation. In Durkheim's works, religion represented a hypostatized moral force, signified the ascendant nature of social realities too complex for most to grasp, and worked through collective representations to facilitate the creation of common consciousness. While he overturned earlier intellectualist notions by suggesting that faith served an eminently social function, he crafted a theoretical dualism that has implicitly driven much religious studies scholarship. Claiming that "sacred" and "profane" are "two categories of things so profoundly differentiated or so radically opposed to one another" that there is "nothing in common" between them, Durkheim proposed a theory that did not allow for the flexibility of sacredness or the complex intermingling of seemingly disparate value creating realms found within Ozark tourism.[3]

Durkheim's counterpart, Max Weber, was perhaps the first scholar to focus on the convergence between cultural value-creating realms rather than delimiting their unbroachable borders. By focusing on the complex connections between a Calvinist mind-set and the birth of the Industrial Revolution, Weber's much discussed 1904–1905 work *The Protestant Ethic and the Spirit of Capitalism* effectively blurred the line between sacred and secular. Noting that an "elective affinity" linked a mode of capitalist acquisition to Protestant convictions, Weber illuminated the permeation of religion into social arenas, disregarded by his predecessors and contemporaries. Intent upon describing the "moral justifications" that buttressed this-worldly activity instead of restricting them to the inherent status of Kantian philosophy, his arguments situated religiosity within the supposedly mundane sphere of labor. While many critics have labeled Weber an idealist, examination of *The Protestant Ethic* reveals a textured causal pluralism that points to both idea-oriented and material bases for the growth of Western industry. Nearly one hundred years of critique has generated a multiplicity of worthwhile rebuttals to Weber's historical claims. Yet *The Protestant Ethic,* as well as numerous other works within his corpus,[4] guides religion scholars in a direction that recognizes that "sacred" and "secular" are falsely dualistic. Ever cognizant of the "characteristic uniqueness of the reality in which we move,"[5] Weber was leery of speculative musing that posited staunch cultural or historical laws. Through methods that remained open to the unique melding of seemingly opposed spheres, such as religion and industry, he offered a heuristic vital to the analysis of the Ozark vacation enterprise.

American religious history, while not solely the intellectual child of the aforementioned anthropological and sociological traditions, can nevertheless be situated within their central methodological debates. Historiographical surveys of U.S. religion, beginning with Robert Baird's *Religion in America* (1843) up through Sidney Ahlstrom's contemporary classic *A Religious History of the American People* (1972), have continued to focus on sectarian machinations as the guiding principle of American religiosity. While commentators on this branch of religious studies often critique definitional divides between "mainstream" and "marginalized" groups or contest interpretive themes meant to synthesize American religious pluralism, little is made of the fact that such surveys often fail to examine the intricacies of *lived* religious experience and the multifarious appearances of the sacred within profane spheres.

The study of popular religion, relatively nascent within the field of religious studies, undertakes such a project through its focus upon Weberian "elective affinities" and, by doing so, offers a challenge to the methods of traditional American religious history. Peter Williams's definition of popular religion as "extra-ecclesiastical,"[6] outside of the structures of an authoritative clergy or formal church walls, seems appropriate for the examination of religion and tourism. Charles Lippy, confronting anti-institutional manifestations of religiosity, opts for a method that examines what ordinary people think and do when they are trying to understand and interpret their daily lives. He claims that a majority of Americans possess "a sense of the supernatural so lively that it cannot be contained in creed and doctrine."[7] Robert Orsi demands a reorganization of the analytic language of the field that creates polarities between the religious and the "profaned" realm and pleads for a consideration of the spiritual nature of lived experience.[8] Finally, Colleen McDannell, through her examination of the materiality of Christian belief, challenges a historical duality between the divine and matter and thus reiterates Lippy's call for an emphasis on what people do rather than what they are urged dogmatically to think.[9]

All of these scholars mark the complex relationships between American religion and other social spheres. The present essay, seeking to perpetuate this emphasis, considers a connection that was not alluded to in Weber's study of religiosity and production—the coupling of religion and consumption through the medium of tourism. Examination of the United States' tourism industry in general, and its Ozark variant in particular, yields a conclusion reached by Wright's Shepherd and still supported in the contemporary Ozarks. Reflecting upon his experiences in the hills, Wright's protagonist comments: "The unseen world is not so very far away. Strange forces, of which we know nothing, are about us everywhere."[10] Thus, locating the "unseen world" within observable worldly activity offers a way to mark the intricacies of lived religion within the region and to obscure further the sacred/secular dualism.

A brief glance at the development of tourism in the United States suggests that pious impulses have *foundationalized* the industry instead of standing in opposition to it. The nineteenth-century banner tourist destinations—Niagara Falls, Mammoth Cave, or the White Mountains—were heralded by visitors not only for their gigantic proportions or scenic attractiveness but also for affording a glimpse into the awesome nature of godliness. Often referring to themselves as "pilgrims," those who participated in the American Grand Tour claimed to discover the ethereal presence of the heavenly amid the consciously crafted consumer culture built around such locations. Reflecting this sentiment while writing in 1842, Niagara Falls guidebook author J. W. Orr stated: "Crowding emotions swell the bosom; thoughts that defy utterance, fill the mind. The power and presence of the Almighty seem fearfully manifest. You gaze, and tremble as you gaze!"[11] The sublimity of these organic sanctuaries sacralized leisure pursuits, granting otherworldly credence to the practices of vacationing and consumer fulfillment. Like medieval pilgrimage, an event that fused the reverence of saint tradition with socialization and consumption, nineteenth-century Americans found justification for their leisure through veiling seemingly secular activities in a language of religiously grounded reverence and wonder.[12]

While the aforementioned attractions employ religious imagery to sanctify the wilderness spectacles, the era also witnessed the dawn of American tourist sites specifically the products of sectarian impulses. Emerging out of the rural revivals of the Second Great Awakening, the Protestant camp meeting succeeded as an institution because, according to the words of historian R. Laurence Moore, it "satisfied the competing desires of piety and play."[13] The founding of the Chautauqua Association in 1873 marked not only an explicit entrance of religion into the realm of leisure but also furthered a blurring of the division between sacred and secular practices. Blending ocean bathing with sermons and lawn sports with Bible study, predominately Methodist sponsors of the camps assuaged historical animosities between Christianity and popular amusements through the invention of a unique tourist form. Moore, describing the functions of such gatherings in his text, *Selling God: American Religion in the Marketplace of Culture,* states: "They did not have to mention religion all the time. They could rely upon morality that was diffused through a light-hearted atmosphere. Consistent with their belief that it was wrong to divide the day into 'times for religion' and 'times for something else,' they did not find it necessary to remind people that everything they did was equivalent to worship. The best proof of a religious environment was when the formal symbols of religion could be left in the background. Saying that placed many of the activities of commercial culture within the reach of redemption."[14] Thus, pleasures were given religious justification, and all daily activities, candidly religious or otherwise, were imbued with an air of the divine.

An examination of the contemporary tourism industry in the Ozarks yields remarkable parallels with the much-discussed nineteenth-century Wesleyan Grove camp meeting on Martha's Vineyard. Wesleyan Grove originated as an alternative vacation destination for New Englanders seeking to avoid the elite enjoyments of Saratoga or Newport. These latter spots, replete with card playing, dancing, and champagne drinking, were not a viable choice for devout Methodists, who denounced luxury and vice. A modern-day visitor to Branson, Missouri, the heart of Ozark tourism, is met with a similar emphasis upon entertainments that cater to the nonelite and the abstinent. The city boasts scores of all-you-can-eat buffets and restaurants that welcome any attire, cheap but clean lodgings, and theatrical events for a price well below those of Las Vegas or even Nashville. The absence of drinking establishments is a matter of civic pride and attracted temperance advocates in the early twentieth century.

Branson also resembles its nineteenth century predecessor in its celebrated small-town atmosphere. Wesleyan Grove offered cottage-style vacationing in settings that resembled one's own neighborhood. Often individuals found themselves surrounded with family members or acquaintances and followed a social schedule that resembled the agenda of their day-to-day lives. Branson has recently adopted the slogan "America's Hometown," augmenting the also utilized moniker "The Family Entertainment Capital of the World." While vacationers may not lodge with a wide array of extended family members, local businesses and the chamber of commerce market the town as one in which intimacy and familiarity are guaranteed. Entertainers always mix and mingle with the crowd after shows, wholesomeness is promised at all attractions, and a similar sense of moral and physical security permeates every establishment. Charles Dudley Warner, discussing the allure of Wesleyan Grove and the nature of its visitors in an 1886 *Harper's* article entitled "Their Pilgrimage," wrote: "Most of the faces are of a grave and severe type, plain and good, of the sort of people ready to die for a notion. These people abandon themselves soberly to the pleasures of the sea and of this packed, gregarious life, and get solid enjoyment out of their recreation."[15] More than a century later, *sober* certainly could be used as a keynote descriptive term for Ozark tourism.

The region's attractions demonstrate a remarkable continuity with religiously sponsored camp meetings that initially reconciled theological tensions between worship and leisure.[16] While vacationers originally came to the Ozarks in the first two decades of the twentieth century to visit the sites documented in Wright's *Shepherd of the Hills,* they also came to stay at the region's first tourist community, the Southwest Presbyterian Assembly's Presbyterian Hill. Established in 1910 as the White River Chautauqua Ground, this site in Hollister, Missouri, attracted individuals who welcomed its ban on card playing and alcohol consumption. Boasting sermons, celebrations of democracy and patriotism, and staged recreations of Wright's novel, the family-oriented amusements available were characterized by an author in 1922 as "mother, home, and heaven lectures."[17] Branson, the progeny of this earlier mingling of sacred and profane, currently entices a multitude of visitors who come in search of this same clean, Bible-friendly fun. In the past few years Branson has become a premier vacation destination, with more tour buses pulling into this town of thirty-seven hundred than any other place in the United States. In addition, the city receives an enormous number of motor vacationers, with some sources claiming that it is the number one auto destination in the country and others listing it as a close runner-up to Orlando. This influx of tourists looking to spend their vacation dollars has turned Branson into a business community that generates multibillion dollar yearly revenues.[18]

The town's contemporary tourism is founded upon its country music and Broadway style variety shows. Beginning in 1959 with two weekly performances by the Bald Knobbers, a collection of members from the Mabe family who still provide traditional songs about god and country, the city witnessed the creation of roughly forty more theaters. With the arrival of Roy Clark in 1983, the town began to attract bigger names and to draw stars away from Nashville. Currently, country music giants such as Johnny Cash and Dolly Parton frequent venues along the city's Highway 76 "Strip," sharing space with a multifarious group of artists including Bobby Vinton, Mel Tillis, and Andy Williams.

What prompted Branson's increased popularity? The emergence of the Christian Right as a viable political force in the 1980s is well documented and prompts consideration of the connections between the rise of the national conservative movement and the development of a tourist region celebrating a similar sociocultural agenda. During Ronald Reagan's first term Jerry Falwell's Moral Majority exerted considerable influence and promoted a Christian Right agenda meant to combat perceived threats of homosexuality, abortion rights, and communism. Introducing the notion of "family values" into common parlance, evangelicals, such as Falwell, Pat Robertson, and Tim LaHaye, fiercely lobbied throughout the 1980s to revitalize the nation's ethical underpinnings, an effort that perhaps reached a crescendo with Robertson's 1988 presidential bid.

While obviously active on the political front, evangelicals in this era also made great inroads within the sphere of popular culture. Remarking upon the proliferation of conservative agendas in this arena, historian and American studies scholar Erling Jorstad writes, "Evangelicals are generally far more conscious of how they believe God works in all activities of their everyday lives; hence every part of that life, including popular culture, aims toward expressing that faith."[19] The emergence of Branson as a major tourist destination is concurrent with the ascendance of other evangelical popular culture forms such as Christian rock, romance novels, and performing arts fellowships, all meant to combat fears of increasing secularization. While the Ozark tourism industry has seldom engaged in overt political activity, it does present its entertainment offerings in a manner that witnesses to audience members and provides vacationers with a set of "traditional" messages consonant with many of the moral aims of the Christian Right. Thus, while direct links between conservative political initiatives of the 1980s and the birth of contemporary consumer culture in Branson are difficult to locate, it seems no accident that these forces developed in tandem. While millions claimed affiliation with a group such as the Moral Majority in that decade, millions also ventured to the Ozark hills to embrace popular culture offerings replete with themes of god, home, and country, welcoming expressions of faith and values in the realm of leisure which frequently mimicked those working their way into the political sphere.

While the entertainment provided in Branson has always been aimed at carefree fun for tourists of all ages, beneath the frivolity there does seem to be a monitoring of the various amusements offered. This ethical patrolling seems to support R. Laurence Moore's thesis that, in the industry of religiously based recreation, even seemingly "innocent pleasures" must be justified by a distinct and value-laden subject matter. Such moral policing, or "local editing," is evidenced, for instance, by the refusal of a donation by Wayne Newton to the College of the Ozarks because his act included "bawdy" jokes concerning senior citizens' sexuality or by the uproar surrounding John Denver's use of minor expletives during a performance in the 1980s.[20] While this type of monitoring might not be glaringly apparent to a casual observer, through my fieldwork I have come to believe that a core system of values underlies every production, thus making each venue into an evangelical site that preaches the merits of conservative Christian belief, unwavering devotion to family, rural sentimentality, and robust patriotism. Individuals are able to consume this cohesive ethical regiment, purchasing a sense of this- and otherworldly salvation through the disposal of tourist dollars.

Some sociologists of religion may qualify many Branson attractions as "quasi-religious," expressions of value lacking the ecclesiastical elements of liturgy, clergy, or sacrament. One may not instantly locate spiritual intentions, for instance, at the Silver Dollar City theme park on the outskirts of Branson. While nondenominational services are held at the Wilderness Chapel every Sunday, gospel music is piped throughout the park, and the venue's mission statement promotes the creation of memories "all in the manner of Christian values and ethics," Silver Dollar City lacks explicit iconography or traditional missionaries. The park can be fit, however, within the category of popular religion; as a recent article put it, the site offers "Christian fun without being preachy," a phrase that could be applied to all of Branson's marquee attractions.[21]

An observer in search of more distinct religious imagery will also not be at a loss. One of the town's most popular locales is the Promise Theater, which offers a musical based upon the life of Jesus and is listed among the top three destinations in the United States by the American Bus Association.[22] Numerous entertainers offer Sunday morning "services" that are a more direct encounter with religious themes than in their non-Sabbath shows. And no venue, on any day, would fail to include a segment devoted to hymns and pious anthems. This popular culture community is mediating the production of deep-seated values through its commodified experiences of moral awakening and distinctively crafted mode of cultural consumption.

The Internet site "Branson Church Group Getaway Planner" provides a resource for those seeking to take youth or adult church groups to the town or arrange religious conferences and retreats. Calling upon the popular religiosity of Branson to encourage pious tourism, the web page highlights the area's "wholesome atmosphere," one that is not "wild and crazy" and does not "attract the 'party' crowd." From the aforementioned theaters to the Shepherd of the Hills Outdoor Drama (a theatric recreation of the text) to Christian-friendly lodgings (see fig. 9.1), this site emphasizes the affordable, convenient, and friendly nature of the town and marks Branson as suitable for "the whole church family." Echoing themes and sentiments from Wright's novel, editor and publisher Richard Freihofer includes an essay to church leaders entitled "Can You Solve the Mystery?" Seeking to identify what draws millions of church members to the Ozarks on a yearly basis, he writes: "There is something about Branson that goes beyond the entertainment, the fishing, the attractions, or the leisure or even the opportunities. It is something deep inside of us that attracts us here. It is something that our hearts recognize, but that our minds can't quite put into words."[23] Alluding to an ineffable quality that pervades the town, an aura later described as a "mystery" produced by sacred plan and purpose, the author narrates an attitude found among a multitude of pilgrims to the region. In agreement with *The Shepherd of the Hills* Freihofer describes the allure and fascination of the Ozarks as no accident. The predominant fusing of sacred and secular is thus not only a product of theater owners and willing tourists but ultimately is said to find its roots in godly sanction and divine intention.

While the sentiments expressed through the town's attractions are meant

Fig. 9.1. Good Shepherd Inn, Branson, Missouri. Photo by Aaron Ketchell.

to have impact upon visitors while they reside in the region, they, like any missionizing attempt, also suggest ways in which a tourist can adapt his or her lifestyle upon return to a place of origin. Geographer Yi-Fu Tuan suggests that "an argument in favor of travel is that it increases awareness, not of exotic places, but of home as a place."[24] One is prompted to come back from a vacation with a newly invigorated sense of morality, induced to rejuvenate the simple merits extolled by the site within one's own vicinity. Thus, while merging sacred and profane through popular culture forms permeated with value-laden messages, the Branson industry also prompts tourists to note social and cultural elements outside the Ozark setting which are in need of sacralization. Linda Purvis, a frequent visitor to the region, commented, for instance, upon the imminent harms to the town if gambling were to become part of its offerings:

> Gambling would be a disaster in Branson! I live an hour and a half from the Gulf Coast in Mississippi and the casinos have ruined the coast! Not to mention many lives and families! I have been to Branson many times . . . and I love the CLEAN entertainment and FAMILY atmosphere! There aren't many places to take a family and be completely at ease with the surroundings and what's going to be seen or heard! Please don't take this family vacation spot away. There is enough of the distasteful things in life all around us, every day!"[25]

For some individuals the Ozark vacation setting facilitates the demarcation of good and bad culture in the United States and serves as an oasis of propriety in

Fig. 9.2. Billboard for the Precious Moments Chapel, Carthage, Missouri. Photo by Aaron Ketchell.

a nation viewed as spiraling downward toward degeneracy, a viewpoint that seemingly rigidifies sacred/profane boundaries. The Branson enterprise also actively seeks to allay this cultural bifurcation, however, by disseminating a homogeneous ethos. Attesting to the view that tourism can serve as a proselytizing impulse that is meant to have repercussions upon the non-vacation lives of visitors and can therefore sanctify realms beyond the Ozark hills, Jay Scribner, pastor of Branson's First Church, writes that "God has commissioned us to take the city— meaning we're trying to do everything we possibly can to make it extremely difficult to go to hell from Branson, Missouri."[26]

Although Branson may be the most heralded of the Ozark region's tourist havens, the Precious Moments Chapel in Carthage, Missouri, a two-hour drive away, also deserves discussion as a site that buckles distinctions between sacred and secular through its blending of religion and consumer or popular culture (see fig. 9.2). Precious Moments, the world's most popular collectible items,[27] are porcelain figurines of angelic children which play upon the ideologies seen in Branson and through *The Shepherd of the Hills*. Each figurine is inscribed with a saying that promotes family, religion, or basic moral tropes such as honesty, frugality, or modest behavior. Sam Butcher, the creator of the figurines, describes his journey to Carthage as one that was divinely inspired, echoing the themes represented by the protagonist in Wright's novel. Rising from humble roots to become a Christian at the age of twenty-five, Butcher and friend Bill Beil formed Jonathan and David, Inc. in 1967 and began the production of his now-famous figurines. At a convention in 1977, his art was noticed by Eugene Freedman, president of the giftware company Enesco. Precious Moments skyrocketed from its original forty-dollar investment to a multimillion-dollar undertaking within the first three years of the Butcher-Freedman partnership.[28]

While Butcher's rise to prominence in the giftware industry is certainly an extraordinary story, the narrative surrounding the formation of the chapel in Carthage is perhaps even more astonishing. In the early 1980s, traveling from a business meeting in Arizona to his home in Grand Rapids, Michigan, the artist decided to deviate from his intended route and, as he put it, "go where the Lord led me." Ending up in Joplin, Missouri, he went to a real estate office and drew his idealized homestead for an agent. The drawing included a house on a hill surrounded by trees and adjacent to a river. Both Butcher and the agent doubted that such a site existed, but a man then entered the agency and claimed that he knew of a place that fit the criteria. Upon seeing the thirty-two acres he would eventually purchase, Butcher recounts that there was no doubt in his mind that the Lord led him to this hilltop.[29]

On average 500,000 to 750,000 visitors per year take the free tour of the Precious Moments Chapel. Butcher decorated the chapel with murals of his collectibles in biblical scenes, depicting stories from both the Hebrew Bible and New Testament with the aid of his wide-eyed children. The ceiling is painted on the style of the Sistine Chapel, with Michelangelo's subjects supplanted by his own. Perhaps the most visited area of this tourist attraction/pilgrimage destination is the gift shop, densely populated during my numerous visits by throngs of collectors purchasing hard-to-find figurines that sell from twenty dollars upwards.

While Butcher's creation may seem to be an essentially economic endeavor thinly veiled in religious representations, pilgrims to the site often claim to have received divine aid during their visits and describe the figurines' creator as a superbly righteous individual who possesses the ability to heal mental and spiritual woes through his product and his constant physical presence in the chapel. In the spring 1998 edition of the site's official magazine, *Chapel Bells,* collector Joan Frankhauser recounted her own transformation, facilitated by a visit to the chapel. She first visited Carthage in May 1996. Sixteen months before, her husband of forty-two years, Fred, had died from a heart attack while she and her daughter attempted to administer CPR. Upon entering the sanctuary, Joan expected to find a modest space adorned with a few paintings of Precious Moments figurines. As she opened the doors, she discovered a shrine laden with dozens of murals and highlighted by the multistory piece named *Hallelujah Square.* This work, which represents the unique vision of heaven crafted by Butcher, was especially pertinent to Joan, as she had purchased a print and hung it beside Fred's photograph shortly after his death as a testimony to his afterworldly existence. Averting her eyes from that mural, Joan saw on her left a representation of the "Jacob's Ladder" narrative, with Jacob lying on the ground and a band of angels descending from above. Once again allying the art with her own personal experience, she wondered whether "Fred might have seen a similar scene as he lay there that morning." Determined to purchase Jacob's Ladder prints for herself and her three children, Joan discovered, to her dismay, that the picture was part of a retired series and unavailable through the gift shop.

The next morning, while eating at one of the dining establishments on the grounds of the chapel, Joan noticed Sam Butcher at an adjacent table with some business associates. After telling him her story, the artist told her to remain at the restaurant while he went to his house to search for the elusive prints. When he returned with a leather portfolio, Joan pondered what she would say if he asked her to purchase the series selling for five hundred dollars before retirement and hundreds more in the current secondary market. She was never confronted with such an uncomfortable situation, however, because Butcher offered the series as a gift, an act of benevolence that, as Joan claims, "ministered to our whole family" and prompted an amazing six visits to the chapel from Seattle over the next year. At the close of her reminiscence Joan echoed the sentiments of many pilgrims: "Thank you, Mr. Butcher, for creating that atmosphere, for being sensitive to the Holy Spirit, and showing compassion to so many hurting people."[30]

Purchasers of the figurines often use them to render a changeable human existence intelligible. Sheryl Williams of Minnesota, a collector for thirteen years who possesses nine hundred pieces, which she values at "close to $100,000," writes, "I'm a Christian, and there's something there for every little moment, a little testimony for every little piece on the shelf."[31] Butcher's creations seem to function in different ways for different people, yet the therapeutic nature of his wares comes through in almost all reminiscences. Deann Eastirn, of Tulsa, Oklahoma, grieving over the death of her daughter, claims to have found comfort in a Butcher figurine of a child holding a sign reading, "There are no tears in heaven." Lisa Cottman, another Oklahoma native, turned to the sculpture *No Tears Past the Gate* for help in dealing with the death of her father. Purchased for her by work mates, Cottman claims, "Every time I get to missing my daddy, I look at the figurine and remember that there aren't any tears of pain anymore."[32] Shirley Fox, of Denver, Colorado, had a husband who was a lifelong alcoholic. In 1987 she and her five children intervened. While Bob was in a rehabilitation program, Shirley purchased *My Love Will Never Let You Go*, a figurine that displays a boy holding a tiny fish—appropriate for her husband, an avid fisherman. Recalling the event, Shirley described the way in which she believes a Precious Moments piece can speak to those in need: "I don't believe he would have accepted the message from me, but the figurine was able to say what I couldn't." When Bob died one year later from a cerebral hemorrhage, a friend gave Shirley *This Too Shall Pass*, a piece that she keeps next to the fisherman sculpture in her display case. The figurines thus provide a narrative that details both the pain and the spiritual reconciliation that have shaped her life.[33]

The chapel is a place where such individual religiosity is practiced. It also provides a space for the furtherance of *communitas* and a shrine for ritual purification, dispelling anxieties and fears about both this life and the promised hereafter. *Hallelujah Square* is a constant work in progress. The painting depicts the entrance into heaven as well as the myriad of angelic children who have already gained admittance. The majority of these figures represent people who have died over the past thirteen years. The guide provides a narrative for each child, telling of both the horrible deaths suffered by the person who is represented as well as the joys loved ones have achieved by seeing heaven portrayed in such a benign and innocent fashion. By infantilizing visions of the Christian afterlife, the artist offers viewers who may have also lost loved ones, adults or children, a squeaky-clean representation of the world to come.

Ultimately, Butcher is offering a new interpretation of Scripture, one that divests the Bible of any element that hints at suffering. His Adam and Eve bear no signs of shame or transgression. The naked boy Adam sits near a stream, his girlish other submerged neck deep in the water and the tempting serpent nowhere to be found. In *Daniel and the Lion's Den*, Butcher adapts the Hebrew Bible account and strikes any reference to apocalyptic visions or the devouring of the hero by hungry beasts. Instead, the viewer is treated to two smiling lions, complete with the jovial wide eyes that all his characters possess. Paradoxically, the site offers a theology undergirded by the suffering of a great number of individuals, memorialized through paintings of innocent children. Visitors are urged to recall the losses and tribulations they have undergone and buttress their suffering against the stories told by the tour guide. While the site might affirm that life is riddled with purposeless pain, it offers a pilgrim the chance to contemplate a world in which all people revert to a state of childlike credulity, one that does not know of illness and where all is tearless. The combination of a spiritual message that reaches millions and a product that makes millions grants Sam Butcher and his chapel a unique place within the Ozarks and the American religious scene. In a 1984 interview the artist stated: "Precious Moments is the pulpit that I preach behind. People who won't go to church to hear the same message will go to the store and buy it."[34] This quote seems to strike at the heart of popular religion in the region, reflecting its extra-ecclesiastical nature, its alliance with lived experience, and its partnership with consumer culture. While Butcher's creation may appear to many detractors as exploitive kitsch, the testimonies of pilgrims and collectors problematize such an easy explanation and further muddle distinctions between sacred and profane in Ozark tourism.

The analysis of the Ozarks religiously based tourist attractions certainly cannot end with discussions of Branson's value-laden theaters or the Precious Moments Chapel's collectible iconography. A lengthier exposition of the subject could, for instance, comment upon the entertainment complex situated in Eureka Springs, Arkansas. A visitor to this town, roughly an hour south of Branson, finds the city overseen by an eight-story-tall Christ of the Ozarks monument, a

Fig. 9.3. Christ of the Ozarks, Eureka Springs, Arkansas. Photo by Aaron Ketchell.

statue erected in 1966 which peers out over the hills and sanctifies the land-scape (see fig. 9.3). Eureka Springs is also home to the Great Passion Play, Ar-kansas' most popular tourist attraction and a venue that offers theatrical enactments of Jesus' trial, death, and resurrection for millions of visitors per year. Other sacred projects surround the statue and the theater, among them the Christ Only Art Museum, the Bible Museum, and the New Holy Land, a twenty-

Fig. 9.4. *Praying Hands Memorial,* Webb City, Missouri. Photo by Aaron Ketchell.

five-exhibit tram tour that offers "accurate archaeological replications" of Moses' Tabernacle in the Wilderness, the setting of the Nativity, Golgotha, Jesus' tomb, and a host of other scriptural recreations. If Christian statuary is one's desire, Webb City, Missouri, augments the region's offerings with its giant *Praying Hands Memorial* (see fig. 9.4), a pair that rivals the more illustrious set erected by Oral Roberts. Finally, the region is peppered with motels catering to religious families, Christian-theme bakeries, and a multiplicity of outlets peddling Bibles, pious T-shirts, and other souvenirs for believers.

While some might view the proliferation of these religious commodities as only a sign of the ever-increasing corruptions of secularization, the words of Ozark tourists and their lived experiences in the region suggest a reconciliation of the dichotomous sacred/profane categories. Rather than viewing commodification and profanation as synonymous, the people I encounter during my field-work instead frequently label the Ozarks as "one of the few good places left." Capitalism with a religious twist seems fully acceptable to most, though a profit-generating enterprise such as gambling, divested of sacred intentions, is frequently denounced as an evil threat to regional purity and piety. Like the camp meetings of an earlier day, the Ozark enterprise prides itself on balancing impulses often falsely construed as competitive, those of leisure and devotion. While this recreational piety may not always be explicit, its effectiveness as an evangelistic mechanism seems to lie in its subtle and gentle reminders of the religiosity that underlies the region's touristic successes.

Vance Randolph, collector of Ozark folklore, recorded a story entitled "The

Devil's Pretty Daughter" in a 1955 anthology. In this tale a farmer's daughter named Ruthie and her sweetheart flee from a spiteful and covetous father, called "old Devil," who forbids the marriage of his child. As the couple attempts to escape from old Devil, who chases them throughout the Ozark hills, the two engage in a mythological process of creation that speaks to the contemporary tourist enterprise. Pulling bramble briars out of her pocket, Ruthie casts them on the road, and they magically grow to fill the valley with thousands of miles of briar patch. The persistent father rides around the impediment, however, and continues his chase. Throwing gravel on the trail, Ruthie creates long chat piles and fifty-foot-deep quicksand, but old Devil once again skirts the two thousand mile–long gravel bar. Pouring a bottle of water on the route, the daughter creates the region's heralded creeks and lakes, but her father prevails by circumventing the flood. Finally, in a moment of desperation, a Bible is taken out of Ruthie's pocket and hurled to the ground. At that moment, according to the story, "the little Bible took root and growed a mile a minute; the whole country was full of paper with holy words on it, and everybody knows the old Devil can't stand Bibles. He couldn't get through and he couldn't go round, so finally he just gave up and went back home."[35]

Once the Devil is deterred by Scripture, the couple goes on to live happily ever after. Thus, according to the tale, it is not the region's mountains or bodies of water that provide it with character and foundation but, rather, its "holy words." In a place that has historically lacked significant industries other than tourism, religious sentiments have indeed been responsible for cultural creation and continue to provide Ozark consumer culture with the ability to produce pious commodities that mitigate sacred and secular tensions, collapsing the distinctions between such categories through a unified experience of leisure and spirituality.

Notes

1. According to Asa Don Dickinson, Wright was the third most popular American writer between 1895 and 1926 and the first in popularity between 1909 and 1921 (*The Best Books of Our Time, 1901–1925* [New York: H. W. Wilson, 1928], 201).
2. Harold Bell Wright, *The Shepherd of the Hills* (Gretna, La.: Pelican, 1994), 301–302.
3. Émile Durkheim, *The Elementary Forms of Religious Life* (New York: Free Press, 1965), 53–54. Despite the shortcomings of Durkheim's sacred/profane distinction, works such as *The Elementary Forms of Religious Life, The Division of Labor in Society* (1893), and "Individual and Collective Representations" (1898) are still of great use when analyzing the religiosity of the Ozark tourism industry.
4. Besides *The Protestant Ethic and the Spirit of Capitalism* (Upper Saddle River, N.J.: Prentice-Hall, 1958), Weber broaches the relationship between religion and other social spheres within his historical studies of world religions: *The Religion of China* (1916), *The Religion of India* (1916–1917), and *Ancient Judaism* (1917–1919). Ad-

ditionally, *The Sociology of Religion,* originally a monograph in *Economy and Society* (1922), points to the intricate relationships between issues such as class status, soteriology, and differing types of asceticism by tracing religious development from its supposed primal roots through modernity. Perhaps the best example of Weber's concern with the linkage of religion and worldly activity, however, is his 1916 essay, "Religious Rejections of the World and Their Directions." By examining the ways that religion both supports and contests the economic, political, aesthetic, erotic, and intellectual spheres, Weber outlines sacred/secular convergences while resisting a normative stance that decries such intersections as indicative of institutional depreciation or individual moral decline.

5. Max Weber, "'Objectivity' in Social Science and Social Policy," in *Methodology of the Social Sciences,* trans. Edward A. Shils and Henry A. Finch (Glencoe, Ill.: Free Press, 1949), 72.
6. Peter Williams, *Popular Religion in America: Symbolic Change and the Modernization Process in Historical Perspective* (Englewood Cliffs, N.J.: Prentice-Hall, 1980), 7.
7. Charles Lippy, *Being Religious American Style: A History of Popular Religiosity in the United States* (Westport, Conn.: Greenwood, 1994), 18.
8. Robert Orsi, "Everyday Miracles: The Study of Lived Religion," in *Lived Religion in America: Toward a History of Practice,* ed. David D. Hall (Princeton, N.J.: Princeton University Press, 1997), 11.
9. Colleen McDannell, *Material Christianity: Religion and Popular Culture in America* (New Haven, Conn.: Yale University Press, 1995), 4.
10. Wright, *Shepherd,* 101.
11. J. W. Orr, *Pictorial Guide to the Falls of Niagara: A Manual for Visitors* (Buffalo, N.Y.: Salisbury and Clapp, 1842), 155.
12. For further information on the religious nature of nineteenth century tourism, see John F. Sears, *Sacred Places: American Tourist Attractions in the Nineteenth Century* (New York and Oxford, U.K.: Oxford University Press, 1989).
13. R. Laurence Moore, *Selling God: American Religion in the Marketplace of Culture* (New York: Oxford University Press, 1994), 149.
14. Moore, *Selling God,* 155.
15. Charles Dudley Warner, "Their Pilgrimage," *Harper's New Monthly Magazine* 73 (July 1886): 172.
16. For a further discussion of the Wesleyan Grove camp meeting and the evolution of tourism on Martha's Vineyard, see Dona Brown, *Inventing New England: Regional Tourism in the Nineteenth Century* (Washington, D.C.: Smithsonian Institution Press, 1995), 75–104.
17. Allen Albert, "The Tents of the Conservative," *Scribners* 72 (July 1922): 59. See also Lynn Morrow and Linda Myers-Phinney, *Shepherd of the Hills Country: Tourism Transforms the Ozarks, 1880s–1930s* (Fayetteville: University of Arkansas Press, 1999), 155–161.
18. For statistics concerning tour bus traffic, motor vacationers, and yearly revenues in Branson as well as writing that reflects the utopian views and representations of the place, see: Bob Sipchen, "Two Cities Moving to Different Beats," *Los Angeles Times,* 10 July 1997, E1; Peter Applebome, "Miles from Anywhere Flocks of Tourists Descend," *New York Times,* 1 June 1993, B1; Jan Biles, "Branson Beyond Boom," *Lawrence (Kans.) Journal-World,* 4 June 1997: extra sec., 1; and Damien Francaviglia,

"Branson, Missouri: Regional Identity and the Emergence of a Popular Culture Community," *Journal of American Culture* 18, no. 2 (summer 1995): 57–74.

19. Erling Jorstad, *Holding Fast / Pressing On: Religion in America in the 1980s* (New York: Greenwood, 1990), 113. See also Robert Elwood, *The History and Future of Faith: Religion Past, Present, and to Come* (New York: Crossroad, 1988).

20. See Courtney Leatherman, "Abolition of Tenure Rattles Faculty at College of the Ozarks," *Chronicle of Higher Education,* 26 January 1994, A18; Francaviglia, "Branson, Missouri," 65. Over the past several years I have corresponded with many Ozark vacationers and gathered their thoughts on the region and its performers. An examination of their comments demonstrates that visitors are attracted to the Ozarks because it offers entertainments viewed as "safe," "friendly," and "moral" (with the later term constructed in a manner that reflects the conservative Christian makeup of the Branson tourist demographic). For instance, "Donnie" writes: "I feel at peace. In the middle of the busiest place I feel comfortable. The Ozarks offer a simple way for most people." "Sue" writes, "We enjoy the nice, courteous people, and we feel safe there; we don't have to worry about being robbed." In addition, visitors offer resounding critiques of theaters which fail to fulfill their vision of discrete amusement, thus harking back to the ways in which vacationing was ethically justified in its camp meeting variety. A frequent traveler to the region, writing about her trip to a venue called the Legends Theater which offers impersonations of bygone stars, writes: "We wanted to see the Blues Brothers and Elvis mostly. We didn't see Elvis at all and the Blues Brothers didn't perform long. What we mostly saw were showgirls in sexy costumes flaunting their bodies in our faces!! All consisted of low-cut, midriff bare tops, and high cut or short short bottoms. I will never go back there and I have told everyone I know not to go unless they want to hear and see a bunch of naked women and husbands and boyfriends drooling and acting stupid. This show should be driven out of town or cleaned up." Examples of backlash against productions deemed "racy," "vulgar," or "Las Vegas oriented" are legion. Tony Orlando and Wayne Newton have been frequent objects of attack in this regard. One tourist, summing up the animosity toward Newton expressed by many, states, "It is time for Wayne Newton to pack his bags and get out of Branson." Currently, Newton has done just that and returned to Las Vegas, a tourist site more amenable to his flashy style and his desire to mix and mingle with audiences on a less frequent basis. (All quotations are drawn from posts by Branson tourists to the Branson Show Discussion Board located at the Branson Live website, <http://www.bransonlive.com>).

21. "Silver Dollar City Park Sets Gold Standard for Family Fun," *Lawrence (Kans.) Journal-World,* 16 April 2000, 8B.

22. Promotional brochure from the Promise Theater.

23. Richard Freihofer, "Can You Solve the Mystery?" *Branson Church Group Getaway Planner,* 2000, <http://www.bransonchurchgroups.com>.

24. Yi-Fu Tuan, "Space and Place: Humanistic Perspectives," *Progress in Geography* 6 (1974): 236.

25. Linda Purvis, "Re: Gambling," *Branson Courier,* 17 April 1997, <http://www.bransoncourier.com>

26. Stacey Hamby, "God in Branson," *Word and Way,* 30 April 1998, 6.

27. According to the National Association of Limited Edition Dealers, the umbrella organization for most American giftware retailers, the Precious Moments figurines

have been "unquestionably" the world's number one collectible for the past twelve years. See Lynn Van Matre, "1,400 'Moments' Later . . . Itasca Firm's Figurines Still Going Strong," *Chicago Tribune,* 22 May 1998, sec. 2D, 1.

28. For additional information about Butcher's early life and the founding of his Precious Moments empire, see Marti Attoun, "Ministry Reaps Blessings for Artist," *Joplin (Mo.) Globe,* 23 December 1984, D1; Janet Hughes, "The Story Behind 'Precious Moments' Figurines," *Saturday Evening Post,* 19 November 1993, 38–39; and Mary Daniels, "Hot Pursuit," *Chicago Tribune,* 24 June 1990, sec. 15, 1.

29. Dallie Miessner, "Creator of 'Precious Moments' Moves to Carthage," *Carthage (Mo.) Press*, 13 June 1984, 3.

30. Joan Frankhauser, "My Chapel Experience," *Chapel Bells* (spring 1998): 31.

31. Beverly Beyette, "Moments to Remember," *Los Angeles Times,* 9 October 1991, E9.

32. John Rogers, "Precious Moments, A Prayer Answered," *Kansas City Star,* 24 January 1998, E12.

33. Hughes, "'Precious Moments' Figurines," 38, 40.

34. Attoun, "Ministry," D1.

35. Vance Randolph, *Stiff as a Poker and Other Ozark Folk Tales* (New York: Columbia University Press, 1955), 5.

CONCLUSIONS

CHAPTER 10

World Religions and Secularization from a Postcolonial and Anti-Eurocentric Perspective

※･⋙◎⋘･※

ENRIQUE DUSSEL

$\mathcal{T}$hirty years ago, we examined this subject for the first time; now we will renew our reflection in an anti-Eurocentric, postcolonial critique.[1] One must begin by distinguishing *secularism* from *secularization.* Secularism is a Eurocentric, metropolitan ideology belonging to colonial expansion. It is the fruit of the Enlightenment and liberalism (which is the ideology of the Second Modernity).[2] Secularization, on the other hand, is a process that began at least twenty centuries ago with Christianity itself and even earlier in Chinese culture (with its secularized Mandarin bureaucracy in the third century B.C.E.) and Islamic culture (in which philosophy had an autonomous place with regard to the faith of the Quran). Secularization is a requirement for a healthy autonomy of reason and for political, economic, and sexual freedoms. Thus, we will affirm the need for secularization, for the purpose of creating an atmosphere of freedom, but not secularism.

Second, one must distinguish religion as a mytho-ethico-ontological nucleus from religion as fundamentalism. The mytho-ethico-ontological nucleus generated by universal religions (such as the Taoist and Confucian components of Chinese religions; the Egypto-Mesopotamian component of Judaism, Christianity, and Islam; or the ontology and ethics of Hinduism and Buddhism) originated from their respective universal cultures.[3] In this first sense religion has a solid mytho-critical nucleus, a collection of rites, symbolic narratives, and a community institutionalized and organized in time and space. But religion also has a second dimension: structured as fundamentalisms, religions that had been central to the origin of their cultures are transformed in times of decadence (although frequently also in cultural splendor) into ideological rationales that justify the dominating expansion of the cultures from which they came. These dogmatized, bureaucratic, and decadent forms include, among others, Chinese Mandarin Confucianism, the antiprophetic Judaism of Jerusalem, Christiandoms since Constantine,[4] Buddhism in Thailand, and Islam since the Caliphate of Baghdad. These are the fundamentalist forms of religion which secularism would oppose in Europe (confronting the modern Catholic, Anglican, Lutheran, Evangelical, and other Christiandoms) and which would be transformed into secular ideologies, inadvertently colonialist, opposing all non-European religions and cultures in the name of enlightened Reason. This process (of religious redefinition) runs concurrently with the capitalistic imperial expansion against more ancient and profound religious expressions of humankind, which still live and continue to expand among the great masses of humanity at the periphery at the beginning of the twenty-first century.

The Unilinear View of the Progress of History: From Religion to Secularism

A certain view of history, that of the romantics such as Johann Winckelmann, Johann Wolfgang von Goethe, Johann Gottfried von Herder, Georg Friedrich Hegel, Friedrich von Schlegel, and Wilhelm von Humboldt in Germany, but equally that of Auguste Comte in France, tries to explain the development of mankind as a progression from primitivism to secularism. Beginning with a mythical, irrational, infantile time of primitive cultures, history in this view continues to reach superior levels of humanization, from the Orient (from China, Hindustan, and Persia) to the "Classic Age" par excellence of the West (through the Greeks and Romans), passing from antiquity through the "Dark Ages" of medieval Christiandom. Through this world history of religions final and universal maturity is reached in Latin-Germanic Modern Europe, where self-conscious rational individuality is discovered and expressed in reasoned Enlightenment, knower of its own content. Religion, say the secularists, has given way to the "Absolute Knowledge" of reason (this is the movement from religion to the philosophy of the *Encyclopedia* and Hegelian *Logic,* from myth to Logos, from belief to science, from traditional feudalism to modern innovative capitalism). With Émile Littré in France, this secularism of institutions, systems, beliefs, theories, and daily life arrives (as a natural development of the Jacobin position) at its most developed point. The only thing missing is for this antireligious laity to reach the uttermost parts of the earth, from the "barbaric" cultures of Africa to the "despotism" of Asia or to the "primitivism" of Latin America, so that the "false consciousness" of religion (a concept that is still shared with the militant leftists of the second Enlightenment, of bureaucratic Marxism) or fanaticism (for the liberals) may be replaced by a utopia of pure scientific rationality and liberal freedom in daily and political life. This is the vision of the second Modernity, the Enlightenment: Eurocentric, colonialistic, and reductive of other types of rationality which nonetheless have not been exhausted, despite such definitive judgment hurled at them by modern secularism.[5] The problem is more complex than that and very relevant today.

A Non-Eurocentric, Postcolonial Vision: Religion and Secularization

Religion (as I defined it in the first sense, as a mythical-ethical core) and secularization (as tending to the autonomy of reason) are not only not opposed to each other, they actually rely on each other. In fact, by making rationality autonomous, some universal religions have produced the conditions that made secularity possible. In Western culture it is impossible to think of secularization without Christianity (but not fundamentalist Christianity). The great historian of science Pierre Duhem writes:

> Modern science will be born, it can be said, on the day that it has reached this truth, that it is the same mechanisms, the same rules, which regulate the celestial and sublunar movements, the circulation of the sun, the rise and fall of the seas, the fall of bodies. So that it was possible to conceive of such movement, it was necessary that the stars be divested of their divine status, where Greco-Roman Antiquity had placed them. It was necessary that a technological revolution be produced. This revolution will be the work of Christian theology. Modern science has been ignited by the spark produced in the clash of pagan and Christian theology.[6]

This is not only true for science but for politics and social action as well. In *La Philosophie de la misére,* Proudhon wrote: "As I study in the silence of my heart and far from all human consideration, the mystery of social revolutions, God, the great Unknown, has been transformed for me into a hypothesis: that is to say, into a necessary dialectic instrument."[7] To what does this socialist so criticized by Marx refer? As I have explained in my works,[8] Proudhon shows that the social transformation of the entire social and economic system presupposes the fact of its nondivinity. But how could a divine, eternal social structure, loved wholly by God, be transformed in a revolutionary way? All social transformation presupposes that God, the great Unknown, the creator, is neither the cosmos nor historical social systems. Creationism says the Absolute is creator. The cosmos is created; it is not God. Thus both the cosmos and the political-social world are secularized. Creationism is the metaphysical and ethical basis for the secularity of the created, of everything that surrounds us, since the Divine is transcendental exteriority. Marx understood that unfetishized atheizing of social structures was a condition for revolutionary praxis. But well before him were

Isaiah, Jeremiah, and Jesus, all of whom affirm that "the origin of all criticism is the criticism of (fetishist) religion."

A non-Eurocentric view of world history understands that European hegemony has existed for just over two centuries (to give it a date: 1789, for both the industrial and political revolutions). In only two centuries, Europe has been able to impose its definitive domination on the periphery.[9] It was never the center of history, nor was it history's necessary reference point, contrary to what Hegel imagined. Instead, the neolithic process of the urban revolution passes from Mesopotamia and Egypt, through the Indus Valley, the Yellow River, and later appears in Mesoamerica, where it culminates in the world of the Mayas and Aztecs and in Tiahuanaco in Bolivia (later the Incas of Peru).[10]

These great civilizations have symbolic macro-stories, and ethical systems, of long history and influence. Within the cultures of the eastern Mediterranean, this is clearly expressed by the founding ethical macro-story of the god Osiris, a story more influential in the so-called Eastern culture than the myths of Prometheus or Adam, so well interpreted by Paul Ricoeur in *The Symbolism of Evil*. Osiris, perhaps a historical king later converted into a god, judges the dead, becoming their personal Ra (a sort of *principium individuationis*) in the Great Universal and Final Judgment in the hall of Maat (goddess of Order and Justice). Osiris is represented in Egyptian hieroglyphics by an eye, a figure still present on the Masonic pyramid found on the U.S. one dollar bill because he sees all human works, even the most secret. His is a founding myth of the Mediterranean, Jewish, Christian, and Muslim cultures and through them the Western secularized culture. The dead in all their physical flesh (not the soul nor the body, for there are no such dualistic beginnings) are judged by the ethical criteria of life: "I gave bread to the hungry," declare the deceased in the *Book of the Dead,* chapter 125. The most private acts are seen by their perpetrator as they would be judged by the universal intersubjectivity of the justice of Osiris. Upon performing that intimate, secret act in private, the actor experienced in advance the judging presence of humanity and thus should offer up some argument before the invisible but present god: a discursive moment of consensual rationality (an intersubjective ethical discourse of the "have-mores" from five thousand years ago!). The Osiris narrative deals with nothing less than the birth of the personal ethical conscience, responsible before others and before the community for the consequences of all personal, individual acts, seen *sub lumen aeternitatis.* This ethical tradition, which is so much a part of Judaic, Christian, and Muslim thought, is found in the Egyptian Osiris story. Had Charles Taylor known of it, this is where he would have found "the sources of Self."[11]

The founding religious myths of cultures continue until today to feed the sense (or the "common sense," as Alasdair MacIntyre or Taylor would say) even of postconventional, secularized, modern, globalized ethics. The experience of liberty, of personal responsibility, of moral argumentation[12] as justification for individual personality, of "remorse for blame" (is Freud's *Über-Ich* not still

Osiris?), is explicitly explained in that Egyptian mythical macro-story born more than two thousand years before the "Pivotal Agĕ" of Jaspers. The urban revolution was then founded in the East.

Similarly, Indo-European cultures, beginning with the invaders from the Gobi into China, or from Kabul toward Hindustan, would expand toward the south. Originating in the Euroasiatic steppes, these Indo-European cultures domesticated the horse, used iron, and worshiped the God of the day.[13] Like the Medes and the Persians, like the Greeks, Latins, and Germans, these invaders left their mark on the Promethean macro narrative in the mytho-ethical nucleus of later cultures, as valued everyday contents present in secularized form until today.

The spread of the universal religions born in the first millennium B.C.E.—among others, the pre-Socratics, the prophets of Israel, the Zoroastrian Iranian Manichaean movement, and the definitive books of the Hindu, Buddhist, Taoist, and Confucian traditions—produced a planetwide religious geography enduring almost up to the present. If we were to go back to approximately 300 C.E., we would observe the following panorama: in China the Confucian-Taoist dynasty of the western Tsin Dynasty ruled (265–317 C.E.), dominating the "Silk Route" toward the west; Asoka imposed Buddhism on the entire Hindu continent in 232 C.E.; the Sanssanid Persian Empire was organized by Sapor II (309–379 C.E.); a corrupt Rome, which had united the Greek empire with the Latin, declined under Diocletian, and was surrounded by hostile Germanic tribes; and the Bantu kingdoms expanded from south of the Roman Empire into the south of Africa. Thus, we can observe perfectly organized "cultural blocs" (with their mythic macronarratives of original religions, always in self and mutual transformation), which still remain and which mimic each other beneath a superficial clothing of secularist and instrumental globalization.[14]

During the period following 300 C.E., the Semitic tradition reappeared amid the Hellenistic empires (not so much in the East with the Seleucids but, rather, in the Ptolomaic center and the Byzantine West) and expanded through the Germanic-Latin region thanks first to the Jewish Diaspora and later to the phenomenon of Christianity. With Heraclitus this Semitic tradition was established in a territory spanning Mesopotamia in the East to the Latin Empire in the West, to Portugal, England, and the Scandanavian countries. Even greater expansion can be seen in the development of Semitic Islam, built on the decadent Byzantine and Persian empires (returning in part to its pre-Hellenic traditions). At the commercial center of an "old system and world," stretching from China, Hindustan, and Southeast Asia to Europe and North Africa, was Bagdad. The Muslim world extended from the Atlantic at Morocco to the Pacific at Mindinao in the Philippines, passing through Melaka, center of the eastern market. The Hellenistic or Roman world, and to a greater extent western Latin-Germanic Europe, did not become the center of the "old system" until the end of the eighteenth century.

The First Spanish-Portuguese (and later Dutch) expansion, prior to the

Industrial Revolution (1492–1789), was Latin Europe's attempt to open itself through the western Atlantic, subsequent to the Renaissance powers' (Venice, Genoa, Amalfi) attempt to penetrate the East (the "Holy Land" of the Crusades). The Portuguese domination from Africa to India and China and Spain's breaking through the "fence" of the Muslim-Turkish world, annexed to the "old world" an unknown one-fourth of the planet (the known portions were Asia, Africa, and Europe). The "world system" was thus born as a new structuring of the "old" and "new" world. But, in contrast to what Eurocentric historiography would seem to suggest, Europe (from 1492 to 1789) never had a hegemony in the new world system, which originated in Spain. Europe was completely peripheral and secondary to the productive, demographic, and cultural center found in China, holding sway over the Southeast Asian market as far as Hindustan. The commercial connecting belt of this old system was the Muslim world uniting China with Hindustan and through Baghdad, the commercial center for five hundred years, to Byzantium until the Turks destroyed the caliphate in the eighth century.

The Iberian expansion (Spanish and Portuguese) into America in the sixteenth century allowed Europe, principally with Mexican and Peruvian gold and silver, to purchase in Asian markets and to begin the theoretical-technological accumulation and development that bore fruit in the eighteenth century as the Industrial Revolution. This revolution was spurred by a crisis in the eastern market that created a vacuum for high-demand products. England rushed to fill this demand. Instead of handcrafted production of porcelain or silk cloth by the numerous and badly paid popular masses of China, cotton cloth, produced by new machinery that revolutionized the production process, reduced the proportion of world value (salary) while increasing earnings. Thus was born capitalism, properly speaking.

The ideology underlying this European-capitalist, colonialist hegemony, through the annexation first of new colonies in Asia and later in Africa, is the Enlightenment (Aufklärung). In this generational, philosophical, theoretical-ideological current, secularism imposed itself rapidly as one of the central aspects of "the coming out of self-blaming immaturity" as illustrated by Kant's definition of Aufklärung. It is thus necessary to remember that it has not been more than two hundred years (1789–1989) that this Eurocentric religious position we call secularism has been expanding into the political field as liberalism, into the economic field as capitalism, and into the philosophical field as the Enlightenment. In the same way, the negative attitude toward other religions, which has been a constituting ideology of colonial politics since the first modernity, is not more than two centuries old.

With the rise of metropolitan Europe as the center of the peripheral colonial world, the mythic-ethical-ontology of secular common sense (secular according to MacIntyre or Taylor but inevitably Christian) will be opposed to cultures of the periphery and most of all against its religions. These religions came to be seen as expressions of sorcery, magic, witchcraft, barbarity, savagery, primitivism, error, unenlightened positions, or fanaticism. Through the secularist argument that religion is an expression of irrationality and underdevelopment, appropriate to non-European peoples, all the cultures of the periphery are negated. And at the same time, the internal struggle in Europe by the Jacobin secularists (in an ultramontanist France) will be extended inadvertently to the periphery as a sign of humanization: "The English assumed the huge responsibility of being the missionaries of *Civilization* in all the world," Hegel would say in his *Lessons in the Philosophy of History*.[15] Religion comes to be seen as a remnant of superstition and irrational mythology, a mark of a primitive age in history which has necessarily been superseded by the scientific development of humanity. On this both the bourgeois Jacobins and the revolutionary socialists of the Enlightenment agree.

Religion, Secularity, and Liberation

Presently, 85 percent of the world's population lives in the southern part of the globe, the postcolonial peripheral world, whose popular masses, and even its elites, manage secularized theoretical, technical, economic, and political instruments. Yet in their daily lives (and even publicly) people refer to the universal religious, mythical macro-stories that originated in universal cultures. I say "universal" in both cases because, for example, Islam and its cultures of origin are the result of a complex meta-process, spanning many centuries, of development of a tradition that rejuvenated and assimilated a variety of existing cultures. This process involved, among others, the Berbers of North Africa, the Asian Filipinos of Mindanao, the cultures of Indonesia, the multiplicity of Hindustanic and Iranic cultures, the steppe and desert culture of the Gobi, Chinese Turkestan or Tarim, and the Coptic Egyptian, Libyan, Turkish, or Balkan world. Islam and other religions are universal religions whose founding myths have inspired diverse texts, rituals, and institutions and which fostered the use of complex instrumental systems (from agricultural technique, navigation, astronomy, engineering, and mathematics to law, philosophy, theology, history, and politics). These religions have been globalized through a far-reaching geographical-cultural regional expansion and are regional only with reference to the modern planetary globalization, beginning in 1492 and reaching its end at the beginning of the twenty-first century. These religions have adequate capacity for dialogue and to assimilate contemporary technology.[16]

The question is this: has the secularist process, with its clear scorn for religions and cultures in the postcolonial periphery as well as in its own popular culture (in Europe, the United States, and Japan) imposed on contemporary humanity the rational scientific-technological vision without the presence of symbolic interpretations belonging to the traditional religious macro-stories? Has this vision become the ultimate valuing authority in the face of the realities of the existence of the universe or of the human being in life and death? Can it be said that postcolonial popular religions have disappeared or are in danger of disappearing? Has the scientific-technical world managed to replace the everyday explicative power of the old mythic-religious stories?

In Nairobi, Kenya, I sat in the home of Odera Oruka, doctor of philosophy from Uppsala (Sweden), president of the Association of African Philosophers, who was later assassinated by the dictatorship of his nation. While I waited to speak with him, I lifted a small tablecloth on a little table. To my surprise I discovered a large drum: the heart of every African home. The doctor of western philosophy never ceased to refer back to his ethic-mythic nucleus, woven into the drum's rhythm, the dance, the ritual movement of the body, the community, and the living cosmos. Western instrumental and hermeneutic rationality coexists with ancestral symbolism. Paul Ricoeur called this instrumental and hermeneutic rationality a "universal civilization," a system of instruments (though still rational and scientific-technical and today globalized). Ancestral symbolism he called "regional culture": the ethical-mythical nucleus that is ultimately religious and found in all postcolonial, peripheral, and popular cultures.

Have two hundred years of superficial European secularizing capitalistic and imperialistic hegemony been able to destroy those profound, unconscious, symbolic, ritualistic, festive, popular worlds, so full of history and daily sense? I do not believe so. Nor do I believe such a thing would be adequate for the development of those peoples, of their cultures, of the concrete subjectivity of each participant in those worlds full of sense and celebration, despite poverty, exploitation, and alienation on other levels. If secularism were effective, religious and symbolic alienation would destroy traditional religion, leaving in its place a destructive senseless emptiness.

Is some connection possible between postcolonial peripheral cultures with their traditional religions and secularity? Could there be some connection that would go beyond the necessary confrontation of secularism and religions in their fundamentalist forms (e.g., as in the Muslim world)? Is a critically creative dialectic possible? This has been the project of the so-called Liberation Theology in Latin America since the end of the 1960s.

In Latin America, after the 1959 Cuban Revolution, a revolutionary air swept the continent. Marxism won the will of the youth, even within the church youth movements. If the first bourgeois Enlightenment was secularist, the second (Marxistic) Enlightenment[17] was social, critical, socialist, and in this case atheistic, at least in its best-known doctrine since the Second International.[18] Its objection to religion was not, as in the first Enlightenment, that it was irrational but, rather, that it was alienating, justifying the domination of classes, nationals, and oppressed cultures. Latin American Christian thinkers who were committed to social struggle had to separate themselves from this objection. So it is that since 1968 an entire sociopolitical, practical, massive, and theoretical movement of Christians has been produced which has tried to show that Christianity was not the fundamentalist Christiandom. Rather, this movement has shown that the solid ethical-mythical nucleus of the message of Jesus of Nazareth in the Roman Empire and Palestine of its day was directed in favor of victims, the poor, and the excluded. Jesus' religious criticism was leveled at the temple of the priests, who had turned their backs on the "people of the land" (*ham ha'aretz*) and who had reintepreted the foundational text of Judaic tradition, the macronarrative of the liberation of the slaves from the Pharoah's Egyptian domination under the prophetic leadership of Moses. It was not difficult for Latin American theologians to demonstrate a similarity between Latin American revolutionary processes and the "flight from Egypt."

It is a clearly defined, methodical, and political process not in line with secularism. Secularism had insisted that to be revolutionary and for the revolution to triumph one had to be an atheist and be done with popular religion. On the contrary, the methodology of Liberation Theology began with the religion of the people, taking it as an ancient symbolic production by that same oppressed people. Elaborating on a basis of this religiosity, Liberation Theology began a critical work, discerning that which alienated and dominated and which justified oppressive structures. It then developed to the maximum the liberating aspects of that most ancient and long-lasting message of Christianity: "Blessed are the poor, for theirs is the Kingdom of Heaven!" "I was hungry and you fed me!"

The simple oppressed people, submerged in their popular religion and culture, heard these suggestions not as something coming from a foreign ideological horizon but, rather, as emerging in a coherent form from their own tradition, which they had jealously guarded, even against the oppressive Christianity of the elite. They could now, in the name of those original religious symbols and from the solid ethical-mythical nucleus of their own popular religiosity, rise up against the oppressive order. This happened in the year 2000 in Chiapas, Mexico, where the secularity of the practices of Subcommandante Marcos did not contradict the critical-popular or prophetic religiosity of Bishop Samuel Ruiz but, instead, articulated itself in the actions of the popular community. The secularized rationality of the revolutionary agenda was thus united with the symbolism of the revitalized, clarified traditional mythic story. Christianity was made again (as in its origin) a criticism against the dominators, just as when Jesus of Nazareth rose up against the Roman Empire or criticized the Hebrew elite who collaborated with the empire, the ossified bureaucratic priesthood of the temple with their rites that had lost their meaning, the moralizing hypocritical leaders who in the name of the law opposed life. Liberation Theology brought up to date in revolutionary Latin America the critical capacity of religion while still being respectful of political, economical, and rational autonomy. It is not hard to understand that in the decades since then this post–secularist theology has extended itself through Africa and Asia and among the minorities in those countries that are central to capitalism. It did likewise in those feminist, antirational, ecological movements in cultures that were indigenous prior to the European invasion of 1492.

This movement is a critical affirmation of religion and a mature affirmation of secularity. In Nicaragua, during the time of the Sandinista Revolution, there could be heard all over the Plaza de la Revolución, "Entre cristianismo y revolución no hay contradicción!" ("Between Christianity and Revolution there is no contradiction!") The same could be repeated: between a critical-liberating religion and the secularization of political, economical, educational, and other institutions, there is no contradiction. On the contrary, one demands the other.

Thus we have gone beyond the necessary opposition between fundamentalist religion (as an alienating and irrational myth) and secularism (a Eurocentric, colonialist, and dominating ideology) to arrive at a mature, healthy relation between critical-liberating religion and the necessary secularization of political, economic, and other institutions, which are part of the contemporary development of history in this age of globalism.

Notes

Translated by Stephen L. Bishop, department of modern languages, the College of New Jersey.

1. See "From Secularization to Secularism: Science from the Renaissance to the Enlightenment," *Concilium* 47 (1968): 93–119.
2. Second Modernity refers to the period of European global and intellectual dominance following the late eighteenth century. The First Modernity was the period in world history during which China was the center of the world system, with the Spanish and Portuguese empires as peripheral centers of power. See André Gunder Frank, *ReORIENT: Global Economy in the Asian Age* (Berkeley: University of California Press, 1998).—Eds.
3. The "mythic-ethico-ontological" nuclei of religions originated in a continuous dialogue with their own cultures: cultures are the fruit but at the same time the seeds of religions; religions are also the fruit and yet at the same time the seeds of culture. See my work *A History of the Church in Latin America: Colonialism to Liberation (1492–1979)* (Grand Rapids, Mich.: William B. Eerdmans, 1981).
4. We have expounded at great length in numerous works of history about the Hispanoamerican Christianity (1492–1992) as a prolongation of the history of Greek Christianity (Oriental, tied to Jerusalem, Antioch, Alexandria, and Constantinople) and Latin Christianity (Western Roman, which makes up European, Germanic-Latin Christian culture at least since the sacred Roman Germanic Empire). See my work *History and the Theology of Liberation. A Latin American Perspective* (New York: Orbis Books, 1976); and especially "The Christiandoms," in *Historia General de la Iglesia en América Latina,* ed. CEHILA (Salamanca: Ediciones Sígueme, 1983), 1:173–205.
5. Dussel here advances an argument that has been central to his work: that modernity was not conceived prior to Europe's colonial expansion but was, rather, a way that

an expanding, capitalist Europe differentiated itself from religious others. As he puts it in another essay: "European Modernity is not an independent, autopoietic, self-referencing system, rather it is a part of the world system: its center. Modernity, then, is a phenomenon that globalizes itself" (Enrique Dussel, *Etica de la liberación en la edad de la globalización y de la exclusión* [Madrid: Editorial Trotta, 1998], 68; trans. in Roberto Goizueta, "Locating the Absolutely Absolute Other," in *Thinking from the Underside of History: Enrique Dussel's Philosophy of Liberation,* ed. Linda Martin Alcoff and Eduardo Mendieta [Oxford, U.K.: Rowman and Littlefield, 2000], 181–193).—Eds.

6. Pierre Duhen, *Le système du monde. Histoire des doctrines cosmologiques de Platun à Copernic* (Paris: Hermann, 1954), 2:453. See also my work *El humanismo semita* (Buenos Aires: EUDEBA, 1969), 118ff.

7. P. J. Proudhon, *Système des contradictions économiques ou la philosophie de la misére* (Paris: Union Générale d'Editions, 1964), 25. See also Henri de Lubac, *Proudhon et le Christianisme* (Paris: Editions du Seuil, 1945).

8. See my book *Filosofía ética latinoamericana: Política,* vol. 4 (Bogotá: USTA, 1979).

9. See the controversial work of A. G. Frank, *ReOrient.*

10. See my recent work *Etica de la liberación,* 24ff.

11. Dussel engages with Taylor at greater length in Eduardo Mendieta, ed. and trans., *The Underside of Modernity: Apel, Ricoeur, Rorty, Taylor, and the Philosophy of Liberation* (Atlantic Highlands, N.J.: Humanities, 1996).—Eds.

12. The dead one had to "justify" his justice before Osiris in a true court. For this his good deeds were carefully recorded (on papyrus for the poor, texts sculpted into the pyramids for the Pharaohs) so as not to forget them before the judge. He should then argue his goodness rationally in order to show he deserved resurrection. There is thus a denial of the immortality of a noncorporeal soul; there is a valuable affirmation of the living embodiment, which could merit eternal life or not. This stamps its character on future Judaic, Christian, Muslim, and modern Western European ethics, becoming worldwide secularity today. An originating myth—one of many—which is behind and continues valid in present-day secularized rationality.

13. *Dios* (God) and *dia* (day) have the same etymology.

14. The history of ethnicities has been of long-standing interest for Dussel; see *Etica de la liberación.*—Eds.

15. As Hegel wrote, "Die Engländer haben die grosse Bestimmung übernommen die Missionarien der *Zivilisation* in der ganzen Welt zu sein" (*Vorlesungen über die Philosophie der Geschichte* [Frankfurt: Theorie Werkausgabe, 1970], 538.)

16. It is said that (Bill) Gates has indicated that the best Microsoft research team is found in China. This should not be surprising to those familiar with the high level of analytic rationalization Chinese reading and writing require.

17. The "second Enlightenment" to which Dussel refers is the ongoing dialogue in Latin America over Marxist social theory and praxis.—Eds.

18. See my work *La Teología metafórica de Marx* (Estella [Navarre, Spain]: El Verbo Divino, 1994).

CHAPTER 11

Literacy in the Eye of the Conversion Storm

GAURI VISWANATHAN

*I*n an otherwise cheerless and desultory year, euphoria seized India as it celebrated the award of the 1998 Nobel Prize to Amartya Sen for his work on welfare economics. The distinctiveness of this work lay in Sen's commitment to a concept of human development aimed at realizing social and political processes for the betterment of human life. In insisting that all forms of human deprivation such as hunger, malnutrition, and illiteracy should be brought within the purview of public policy, Sen transformed economics into a moral science, challenging the direction of a discipline focused primarily on those social aspects that are only instrumentally useful for human life. Among the deprivations he targets as most ignored by public policy is the citizenry's right to education, full access to which is still an unrealized goal in postcolonial India, despite the professed commitments to universal literacy. On hearing the news that Sen had won the Nobel Prize, even those on both the left and the right in India who had long questioned the pragmatic usefulness of his work suspended their skepticism and joined the rest of the country in lauding his achievement.

There was, however, a lone voice of dissent and disapproval, and it came from the Vishwa Hindu Parishad (VHP), the right-wing Hindu religious organization currently backing the ruling Bharatiya Janata Party (BJP) government. VHP president Ashok Singhal gave a sinister turn to Sen's economic program, darkly interpreting his Nobel award as a Western conspiracy to promote literacy in developing societies in order to bring them within the ultimate pale of a global Christian order and thus "wipe out Hinduism from this country."[1] "Despite the accuracy of Prof. Amartya Sen's conclusions," he charged, "the same could prove harmful to Hindu society as Christians would be bringing in more money ostensibly for promoting education, but actually proselytization would increase and everything in India would be undermined."[2]

Incidentally, Ashok Singhal had earlier launched a scathing attack on Mother Teresa's Nobel Prize as well. Then, too, he accused the Nobel committee of rewarding only those who promoted the work of Christian charity. Skeptical of Mother Teresa's work as properly deserving to be called social service, he insisted that the driving aim behind all the activities of the Missionaries of Charity was to convert poor and ignorant Hindus to Christianity. At that time, unlike the occasion of Sen's prize, Singhal's voice was joined by others, though admittedly not in huge numbers. Publicly at least, few cared to endorse his views on Sen, as a result of which he was isolated from other hard-liners in his own party. Even the prime minister of the BJP-led government, Atal BehariVajpayee, denounced such provocations as churlish, intemperate, and irresponsible.[3]

Yet, even as he refused to participate in Singhal's denunciation of Sen's award, the prime minister simultaneously urged that there be a "national debate on conversion" following the attacks on Christians and their places of worship since December 1998. As if in repetition of the horrendous violence of 6 December 1992, which resulted in the destruction of the Babri Masjid in Ayodhya by Hindu extremists, Christian churches were razed to the ground, and in a series of particularly gruesome events, a Christian missionary and his sons were burned alive; most recently, in September 1999, a nun was stripped and forced to drink the urine of her would-be rapists.[4] Ostensibly a response to Christian proselytization, the violence began in the western state of Gujarat but spread to other states as well, including the eastern state of Orissa, which witnessed not only the burning alive of the Australian missionary Graham Staines but also the murder of a Roman Catholic priest, Arul Das, in September 1999. To a country that had come to expect communal clashes as a conflict involving Hindus and Muslims primarily, the sudden surge of hostility toward Christians took many Indians by surprise, accustomed as they had become to the central role of Christian mission schools and hospitals in Indian life. In this context Vajpayee's appeal sounds innocuous enough, outwardly a sincere attempt to engage in serious dialogue and discussion about the motivating force behind the violence.

The Constitution and Conversion

The call for a debate was clearly intended to reopen the discussions that had taken place at the time of Indian independence, when the constitution was framed. In the Constituent Assembly discussions that were held between 1946 and 1950, there was a strong move by powerful Hindu lobbies to ban conversions altogether. The call for constitutional provisions against conversion was made in response to the widespread fear that Hinduism, typically described as a nonproselytizing religion, would be under threat and its numerical strength diminished if conversions to other religions were allowed. While all religious groups may theoretically disseminate their beliefs, it has been a long-standing belief among Hindus that only Christians and Muslims actively proselytize, placing Hinduism at a disadvantage. This conviction lay behind the attempt by the Hindu lobby to bar conversions altogether and achieve a level playing field among the various religions. Furthermore, Gandhi's famous distrust of Christian missionaries and Christian conversions offered a screen behind which the anti-Christian lobby could conveniently hide.[5] The fear of conversion produced a strange marriage between Gandhi and the Hindu nationalists, who in all other instances denounced him for making concessions to Muslims but nonetheless heralded him as the voice of reason when he opposed Christian proselytization. In his deep skepticism about the work of missionization, Gandhi imbued Indian nationalism with a Hindu ethos that laid the groundwork for an identitarian notion of Indianness. His resistance to Christian conversions simultaneously affirmed a Hindu past that had the power to assimilate different communities and produce a sense of oneness. Of course, the vital difference between Gandhi's position and that of Hindu nationalists was that, while he believed Christian conversions were the instrument of British colonialism and therefore must be resisted as vigorously as British rule, Hindu groups had no such larger aim and remained trapped within their own self-interests.

The final draft of the Indian constitution effectively resisted all such attempts to outlaw conversions and instead made the propagation of religion permissible under the law. Article 25 (1) of the constitution gives everyone the fundamental right to "profess, practice, or propagate religion," a right that is only circumscribed by considerations of "public order, morality, and health."[6] Whereas the constitutional freedom of conscience is described as a mental process, the right to propagate religion externalizes the mental freedom of conscience, rendering active propagation a field of open and lawful endeavor.[7] Freedom of conscience was thus broadly interpreted to mean the right not only to choose one's religious views but also to disseminate them. Not until 1977 was this provision modified in an Indian Supreme Court ruling that specified that the right to propagate religion did not necessarily extend to the right to convert. The ruling further allowed states to legislate "Freedom of Religion" bills forbidding the conversion of minors as well as requiring Hindus converting to Christianity to provide magistrates an affidavit. Such forms of legislation brought civil officials directly into the administration of spiritual affairs, a move that seriously qualified the secular conception of the modern state and challenged the tacitly accepted divisions between religious faith and law.

The impetus for the Supreme Court judgment came from a series of rulings set in motion by the findings and recommendations of a pivotal commission chaired by Justice Niyogi. Set up in 1954 to investigate the role of foreign missionaries in the state of Madhya Pradesh, located in the geographical center of India, the Niyogi Commission produced a report that, in the eyes of many missionaries, was intended to regulate Christian conversions and drive foreign missions out of the country.[8] Noting that the term *propagation* was originally intended to refer to freedom of expression and conscience, Niyogi's report implied that conversion militates against such freedom and therefore cannot be regarded as a disinterested dissemination of religious knowledge. By calling for a constitutional amendment reserving the right to propagate religion to Indian citizens, the report was clearly generated in a climate of chauvinism and ultranationalism.

But the report went further than merely reopening the constitutional debates on conversion, just as Prime Minister Vajpayee, in calling for a national debate on conversion, had more than an academic exchange in mind. The Niyogi report introduced a new argument by highlighting loss of control over free will through weakness, ignorance, and poverty as a reason for outlawing conversion altogether, since it left the economically deprived sectors of Indian society particularly vulnerable to the inducements of converting to another religion. Such a view was possible only by representing India's economically weaker sections as essentially disabled, incapable of distinguishing motives and inexperienced in the exercise of their own judgment. The report painted a picture of conversion as a form of exploitation threatening the integrity of the Indian state, an assault so heinous that it justified the state's curbing of missionary activities on the grounds that they posed a danger to national unity. Conversion is construed as a form of mental violence, no less severe than bodily assault. The Niyogi Commission's landmark report set the lines of an argument that have continued to the present day, blurring the lines between force and consent and giving very little credence to the possibility that converts change over to another religion because they choose to. Interestingly, in charging that Christian missionaries take advantage of the weakened will of the poor and the disenfranchised, the report confirmed an elitist view of free will and autonomy as a privilege of the economically advantaged classes. As in the fiery age-of-consent debates over prepubertal marriages of females, "consent" is not allowed as an option among the poor, and the missionaries' promise of new religious possibilities is construed entirely as a violation akin to the rape of women.

Over the years the ambiguity in the semantic distinctions between *propagation* and *conversion* went a long way in creating a charged environment culminating in such incidents as the fractious ones in Gujarat in December 1998, when scores of Christians and Christian places of worship were attacked. Indeed, the mounting violence against Christians since late 1998 replays an ongoing battle between Christian missionization and Hindu nationalism which was often fought in the houses of the Indian Parliament to introduce legislation banning conversion. So-called Freedom of Religion bills were routinely proposed seeking extension of state protection to those being wooed away from their religion. Freedom of religion came to be a euphemism for freedom *from* religion.

Ostensibly secular in motivation, the bills to ensure freedom of religious conscience were primarily intended to protect Hinduism against the incursions of other proselytizing religions, revealing the collusion of the state in the preservation of Hinduism. *Conversion* implies force, a radical takeover of people's will, whereas *propagation* acquires a more intransitive connotation, a middle term between force and instruction. Slipping from one meaning to another in the recent debate on conversion, the VHP general secretary Praveen Togadia invoked comparative history in order to argue that no other society gave a free rein to conversion, which has never been able to escape the connotations of force and disruption. Seeking a universalist point of reference, he linked economic well-being with free will to argue that "if these are the views of even the developed countries, how can we allow conversion in India where a large section of the society is poor and illiterate?"[9]

Here again is the evocation of poverty as mental disability, leaving the masses peculiarly vulnerable to religious manipulation. In rehearsing the earlier constitutional debates on conversion, Togadia failed to mention that the constitutional framers invoked Western precedent, particularly that of American freedom of conscience, when they decided to include provisions to permit propagation of religion. Selectively calling up the West as a reference point to argue against conversion, Togadia's comparative perspective evidently breaks down in its inability to deal with the multiple genealogies of religious freedom comprising the constitutional debates. These genealogies make room for the notion of conversion as a matter of individual choice and conscience, which the constitution was obliged to protect.

Conversion and the Historical Legacy of Conquest

Yet, despite such constitutional protection of religious conscience, nationalist discourse has turned conversion into a threat, a challenge to the cohesiveness of tightly woven communities. This is not difficult to understand, given that nationalism's recourse to concepts of ethnicity, race, religion, and language is precisely what conversion contests. Conversion's interest for a postnationalist culture is its resistance to positivist ways of conceptualizing difference through such essentializing markers as race, religion, color, ethnicity, and nationality. When identity is destabilized by boundaries that are so porous that movement from one worldview to another can take place with the regularity of actual border crossings, a challenge is posed to the fixed categories that act as an empirical grid to interpret human behavior and actions. While terms like *hybridity* are offered as an alternative to essentializing identities, *hybridity* does not capture the dynamism of movement signified by conversion, which regards crossovers of identity not merely as items of exchange or even fusion but as a remaking of the categories that define identity. Nor is *syncretism* a satisfactory term to describe the overlapping of identities, since, as its etymology and historical usage indicate, it constitutes a blurring rather than a negotiation of differences.[10] Moreover, *syncretism* is as much a construct as are terms like *tradition* and *modernity*.

In destabilizing the determinants of race, religion, gender, and so on, conversion unsettles the understanding of difference through purely essentialist categories. It shifts the focus away from visible markers of difference (such as race or gender) to the distance in viewpoints emerging from the pragmatics of communication. Such gaps in communication are the starting point for conversion's reconstructive role in initiating movement between opposing viewpoints. The fact that neither origin nor destination is finite and determinate allows the convert to be critical of the religion to which she converts, even as she seeks to reform the religion she has repudiated. This sense of critical distance and fluidity gives conversion its peculiar power—the power to destabilize which belongs to the individual who moves incessantly between disparate viewpoints.

I am therefore suggesting that *conversion* performs the epistemological function of negotiating differences in viewpoints. Yet historically the term has been associated with violence and erasure rather than mobility and communication. To those who patrol the barriers around religion, conversion rudely shuts down communication and is forcible by definition; it is "a colonization of consciousness."[11] Violence is at its core, as it tears away the secure lineaments of identity and orders the extinction of an individual's most innate beliefs and understandings. Even when conversion works by persuasion, it is no less coercive in that it leaves the individual vulnerable to alluring promises. This is violence of the most hateful kind, because it induces assent by planting the seeds of hope for a better life. The legacy of historical conquest has made this notion of conversion a palpable and uncontestable one, even though violence does not inhere in conversion but, rather, in the historical moment in which conversion occurs. Indeed, when examined as a form of intersubjective communication, conversion can be understood as the outcome of a process whose alternative endpoint is violence, especially when the differences between parties remain unresolved.[12]

Coercion, erasure of identity, and forced assimilation are embedded in colonial desire, which has assigned conversion a set of meanings rooted in violence. Yet the fact remains that conversion becomes violent only when shifts to another worldview turn into a desire to make it prevail. This, of course, is Matthew Arnold's classic definition of culture, which is deeply rooted in the logic of conversion by virtue of its ambition to be expansive and all-embracing. Translating the spread of culture into the terms of religious expansion, Robert Hefner describes conversion as a "great transformation" that assimilates local cults into world religions. This description, however, can be parsed further to reveal an inherent tension in conversion between being a break in the continuity of knowledge and at the same time representing a prelude to the institutionalization of new knowledge systems. What appears as a violent erasure of identity— "epistemic violence," in Gayatri Spivak's term—is more precisely an effect of discontinuous knowledge. But while, on one hand, discontinuity of knowledge makes universalist propositions more difficult to sustain, on the other hand, the very presence of competing systems creates a different set of compulsions leading toward violence. In the first instance discontinuity prevents false universalisms, but in the second the desire to make the new system prevail reintroduces universalism. Violence is contingent upon the latter, but it also signifies the implacable opposition of claims. Not only does violence symbolize the disruptive power of difference, but it also preserves and reproduces it. The history of religious transformations cannot be written outside the framework of these dual impulses: of knowledge interrupted and then transformed from dissent into assent.[13]

Discontinuity and radical pluralism make culture vulnerable to what Habermas terms "legitimation crises." Such crises reveal the need for a theory of religious communication which moves beyond relativism, even as it repudiates universalism in values. Some critics prefer to look toward notions of faith as the "establishment of a ground or foundation immune to the relativizing powers of Enlightenment and providing, thereby, a basis for the legitimation of belief."[14] Conversion's proactive nature, combined with its maneuvering between discrepant belief systems, makes it a powerful epistemological tool to face the broad challenges of a pluralistic society. If pluralism is not to be reduced to a slogan of "live and let live" but imagined as the groundwork of community, communication between disparate groups on lines other than the assertion of their separate identities is the first step toward that goal. Conversion highlights the crisis of pluralism as the absence of a point of reference for religious groups to negotiate their differences and conflicting needs. Religious absolutism sets up a single center of values as the ultimate arbiter in conflicts, overriding individual self-definitions. On the other hand, while constitutional provisions for freedom of religion relativize religious difference and thus repudiate the exclusionary force of doctrine, they leave nothing in its place to enable religious communication between groups.

To a large extent, this is the dilemma of secularizing societies. The failure of relativism enables the return of conversion in postemancipation society, not as forcible assimilation but as intersubjective communication.[15] In its challenge to thwart the violence that results when groups interact as equal but competing members of civil society, pluralism's real test is to find new philosophical ways of conceiving relationality, particularly to heal the wounds inflicted by restrictive laws on communities in the colonial past of societies. Kept out of full civic participation in the past, communities are robbed of the conditions to relate effectively with one another, especially when consensus in civil decision making is thwarted by the historical baggage of colonialism, which includes the perception that colonial rule was intended to obliterate indigenous religions. Yet, other than to sanction freedom of religious conscience, the constitutional protection of the right to propagate religions does nothing to establish new conditions for communication or promote the proactive exercise of tolerance, even though civil pluralism forces communities to rethink their relations with one another on principles other than that of religious difference.

The Role of the Mission Schools

The perceived threat posed by conversion reminds one that, for formerly colonized societies, the history of colonial education is also the founding moment of violence. This conviction underwrites Indian prime minister Vajpayee's call for a national debate on conversion. In so doing, he insists on revisiting the role of missionary institutions in India: to ask, in other words, whether their aim was to propagate religion—which could also broadly include morality, civic virtue, and character—or convert people to Christianity. Without attacking the constitution itself, Vajpayee asserted that, while the right of religious propagation was constitutionally guaranteed, "the country must ensure that it is not misused."[16] This statement is no less than a dire warning to those who would use constitutional provisions as a license to apply force. "Poverty cannot be a reason for conversion," warned Vajpayee, firmly dissociating economic circumstances from the imperatives of religious change. Regardless of his own disapproval of Singhal's attack on Amartya Sen, Vajpayee kept the two issues of Christianization and welfare economics squarely within the same frame of reference, however much he may have denied that there was any connection between the two. It is thus no coincidence that Amartya Sen is denounced for advocating basic education, and religious conversion by extension, at the same time that Christianity is under siege in south Gujarat for promoting tribal conversions. In being forcibly linked with conversion, literacy is disengaged from development issues and relocated as an exclusively religious issue. In an effort to reclaim literacy from Christian uses, Sen's critics pointed to what is now a consistent thematics of antimissionary resistance: literacy has legitimacy only when it is a marker of indigenous cultural identity. Either way, the development issue drops out of the picture.

The public repudiation of Singhal's viewpoint, however, does not mean that his is an aberrant one, the voice of the lunatic fringe unable to make a dent on mainstream opinion. On the contrary, India's history of colonial education provided a real context for the deep suspicion cast upon the Nobel Prize committee's recommendations. That this context was exploited to detach literacy from issues of social reform is perhaps one of the dimensions of the conversion controversy which needs more analysis and clarification than it has received. Views such as those held by Ashok Singhal have been sustained over time and buttressed by references to India's colonial history. The deep distrust of missionary institutions has a colonial past providing Hindu nationalists a much-needed moral stance to defend Indian religion and culture. (The collapsing of *Hinduism* and *India* is not the least of the rhetorical slippages.) It is well known that Christian missionaries were attacked long before the BJP and the VHP came on the scene. Hinduism put up a stiff resistance to Christianity on both an organizational and a theological level.[17] Richard Fox Young has meticulously documented the development of a whole tradition of anti-Christian polemics in nineteenth-century India focused on a refutation of Christian doctrine, point by point.[18]

There is nothing new in the Hindu antagonism to missionary schools as hotbeds of conversion activity ("wolf in sheep's clothing," as they were often called).[19] Opposition to literacy reform has long been motivated by fear that its ultimate intent is religious change. On the other hand, why Sen's research would benefit Christians more than any other group is never clear in the VHP attacks on him. But it is telling that one of their chief complaints is that the Nobel Prize was never awarded to social activists such as Gandhi or Baba Amte, who had both worked tirelessly for the uplift of the poor and other marginalized sections of society.[20] Yet social activism in India, even that practiced by someone like Gandhi or Amte, has never been totally removed from a related compulsive desire to contest the reach of Christian missionaries, particularly in tribal and outlying areas. In regions where lower castes and outcastes were denied the educational facilities open to higher-caste groups, missionaries often stepped in to fill a social vacuum.[21] In the light of caste tensions it is easy to see why social reform has been as strongly contested as conversion itself. Neither can be separated from a colonial history that continues to inform attitudes to an ethics of improvement, the content of which, to many today, is still indistinguishable from the *mission civilisatrice*. This is by no means to justify the crudest premises of cultural nationalism, but we are obliged to acknowledge the complex historical formations driving nationalists to the depths of paranoia and suspicion.

Historically, missionary schools opened their doors to socially excluded groups, while the schools run by the colonial government had as their main clientele students from the upper castes. Yet this division so heavily reinforced the caste structure that it appeared as if the very form and spirit of colonial education was driven by caste feeling. There was more complacency than truth in colonial administrators' belief that English studies altered attitudes to caste. The Serampore missionary John Marshman wryly observed, "I am not certain that a man's being able to read Milton and Shakespeare, or understand Dr. Johnson, would make him less susceptible of the honour of being a Brahmin."[22] The association of missionary schools with vernacular education and the government schools with English education marked the differential development of languages and literary instruction.[23] Yet precisely because missionary schools were so closely identified with lower-caste education, missionaries found their aims compromised by their desire to lure the upper castes to their schools, if only to extend the range of Christian influence. Partly this was motivated by their fear that, by attracting only "the most despised and least numerous of society," they were creating a new virulent strain in Indian society, "a new class superior to the rest in useful knowledge, but hated and despised by the castes to whom their new attainments would always induce us to prefer them."[24] Caste lines being as implacable as they were, missionaries dreaded that the huge efforts they expended on the education of the lower castes would remain confined to these groups and not spread farther. Recognizing that the reform of Hindu society was impossible without involving all castes, they modified their instructional objectives, expanding their curricular offerings to include English literature alongside the vernaculars. In time the lines between missionary and government schools blurred as both types of institutions competed for students from the upper castes.

Interestingly, the work of vernacular education started by missionaries was taken up by Hindu reformist organizations, such as the Ramakrishna Mission and the Arya Samaj. The linguistic stratification was so rigid that the vernacular schools produced a militant brand of youth who pledged themselves to the preservation of Hindu culture, religion, and language against the encroachments of an English-educated, Westernized elite. So it is somewhat ironic that this form of cultural nationalism developed as a consequence of the vernacular missionary schools and the so-called government schools switching their linguistic orientation, with the former increasingly moving toward English instruction primarily and the latter now having virtually become vernacular-medium schools. The development has also inspired the defenders of Hinduism to view the English press, which has extensively covered the atrocities against Christians in the past year, as a key player in the drama of linguistic, religious, and caste stratification, its corps of writers having themselves often been educated in Christian mission schools. Therefore, while the English-language newspapers have gone a long way in bringing the violence against Christians to public attention, they have also been attacked by Hindu nationalists as complicit in the work of Christian missionaries in propagating an alien culture.

Historically, in seeking to break out of narrow caste identification, the missionary schools set in motion a number of significant developments. The original objectives of imparting basic literacy skills were considerably qualified by the new infusion of literary content. If missionary schools initially sought to remedy the exclusionary effects of caste prejudice by offering educational opportunities denied to lower castes, their turn to an English course of studies took them in a markedly different direction. That conversion rather than caste or poverty relief more often engaged their interest is evident from the perfection of certain pedagogical techniques to produce belief, catechism and hermeneutics prominent among them. The Word offered access to the world, but it also opened up access to faith through the power of imagination. Education in imagery supplemented, and in time surpassed, instruction in the fundamentals of literacy. In all its clarity and brilliance imagery pointed the way to the Bible, to the power of arguments, reasons, and demonstrations vividly impressing themselves on the mind, to an experience of truth that could only be known when seen and felt. To missionaries aware of the hostility that direct Christian instruction might produce, there was no better way to convey the deep swell of religious feeling than through the rich tapestry of images, sensations, and impressions found in the best of English Romantic writers such as Wordsworth, Cowper, and Young.

These alternating instructional objectives in missionary institutions kept the pendulum swinging between poverty and caste relief, on the one hand, and conversion, on the other. Let us recall Vajpayee's admonition that "poverty cannot be a reason for conversion." He was far closer to the course of colonial history than he may have realized, for institutional developments suggest a complex evolution of conversion motives not always directly related to economic circumstances. The violence against Christians in Gujarat and elsewhere since late 1998 was caused by the perception that missionaries were targeting poor tribals to convert them to Christianity, often by imparting literacy skills to them. Radical Hindu groups interpret Christian conversion as an inducement, an enticing avenue of escape from grinding poverty. But conversion is just as significantly involved in the constructions of new selves, and it is this shift from the ground of economics to that of culture which continues to alarm Hindu opponents, perhaps even more than the threat of religious change. Their will is steeled, therefore, to reclaim culture as the ultimate goal of all future attempts at literacy reform.

Religions assign different functions for reading and writing. In religions of revelation the word is the Word. Hinduism's self-description as a nonproselytizing religion has also meant that it conceives of reading and writing in different ways. One point of difference is the creation and affirmation of community. This does not necessarily mean an interpretive community, however, but a community marked by systems of inclusion and exclusion, which are in turn determined by criteria of purity and pollution. Verbal acts are modes of community affirmation as much as they are forms of communication. But where the use of language signals the expression of faith in a supreme being, religions that employ such language open up the new possibility that language can cause changes in one's conceptions of divinity. Are these, then, proselytizing religions? It can be argued that Hinduism establishes a relation between literacy and faith different from that of Christianity and Islam. If, as is maintained about Hinduism, faith does not lie in words, then a Hindu can have access to the world without the mediation of language. Language, however, is threatening when it is tied to faith. Literacy arouses suspicion because it can alter faith by providing a different form of access to the world. Access to language is essential for economic betterment, yet it also contains the potential to introduce worldviews at variance with those affirmed by the community. The conflicting perspectives on literacy throw open the divide between economics and culture, which further translates into artificial distinctions between religions on the basis of whether they proselytize or not.

Ironically, the VHP leaders who attacked the Christian conversions of illiterate tribals do not accept that literacy can also be a defense against forcible conversions of any kind—Christian, Hindu, Muslim, or any other religion. Their unquestioned assumption is that illiteracy is gullibility. But if its opposite is also true—that literacy is skepticism and critical judgment—then the threat posed by the lure of other faiths should be diminished. The Word may be the source of faith, but it is also the maker of selfhood and independent judgment. Yet the rhetoric of the VHP suppresses this fundamental understanding of literacy's role, which, in offering the tools of knowledge, discrimination, and evaluation, shapes the modern self. We are led to inquire whether literacy as self making, independence, and private judgment poses the real threat, an unnamed one perhaps, acknowledged only as a tool of Christianization but not of Hindu modernity.

Literacy, Economics, and the Culture of Conversion

At this point I want to return to Amartya Sen and his Nobel Prize for economics. We may now place Ashok Singhal's diatribe in the framework of a perceived shift in literacy's address from economics to culture. That is why no matter how much of a non sequitur his comments may appear, his view that Sen's mass literacy would benefit only Christians reflects how definitively culture, not economics, has become the contested ground for discussions of development issues. In part this shift has strategic uses for a government seeking to deflect attention from the dismal failure of *swadeshi* (self-sufficient) economics, despite the BJP's campaigning for power on this issue. And, as its economic policies have met with one disaster after another, the BJP has needed to keep economics out of public discussion. Religion has always been its surrogate theme, and it is not surprising that turning even literacy into a conversion issue offsets the government's dismal showing on the economic front. But, apart from turning the focus away from a string of economic failures, the perception that mass literacy is a tool of cultural imperialism undermines the developmental rhetoric of secular progress that literacy reform, on the other hand, also tends to generate. Singhal's denunciation of Amartya Sen reflects attitudes toward literacy which are part of an ongoing tension between development priorities and cultural purity.

By objecting to literacy as a missionary-inspired practice, do Hindus really want to say they object to the introduction of social benefits to the people? Most would probably say no, but the ethics of social reform has been challenged in the mounting anti-Christian rhetoric since the BJP assumed power in early 1998. It can and should be argued that if missionaries give people services they would otherwise not have had, no one has a right to restrict their activities, particularly when there are no other state-supported or private initiatives. After all, missionaries do not have a monopoly on the opening of new schools and hospitals, and there is nothing to stop Hindus or any other group from doing likewise. But the cumulative effect of the attack on Christianity has been a fierce questioning of whether social benefits can ensue at the cost of religious and cultural integrity. This is nothing less than an anti-Orientalist response to a condition sewn into Indian history through the reformist ideology of British colonialism. But its corollary is that social reform has, and always will be, politicized in postcolonial India. The view that social service has a national or a religious identity suggests that no act of reform or service can take place in postcolonial India without its being measured against a corresponding degradation of Hindu customs and rituals in the process.

But I think there is something fundamentally more worrying in the antiliteracy, anticonversion posture of the VHP. The numbers of Hindus who actually converted to Christianity are far less than the numbers of those who detached themselves from Hinduism over time and affiliated themselves to more secular conceptions of modernity. Today we call the latter group "secular Indians," though that term has its own problems. The main difference between these two groups of Hindus is that the former have converted to Christianity and the latter to modernity. The mechanism is the same, even though the characterization may be different. Critics will argue this was the effect of mission-school education on the middle classes. But there are deeper issues involved. Hinduism is once again at the crossroads of change. Instead of attending to the problems of overwhelming illiteracy, caste and gender discrimination, and poverty, the most extreme among the Hindu nationalists have narrowed their agenda to attack other groups—notably Muslims and Christians—for the erosion of cultural traditions. India's struggle to keep pace with a changing world is most pronounced in a stagnant educational system that, while professing secularism, is still caught up in the forms and practices of a religious culture. Is the desire to interrogate mass literacy ultimately a desire to renounce the modern world altogether? Is the quest for cultural integrity so supreme that it creates a longing in Hindus to supplant modernity with a more reassuring past in which their traditions are uncorrupted? These are difficult questions, but they go to the heart of the resistance to literacy as a development issue and the antagonism toward conversion in general.

Significantly, even as some Hindus recoil from the demands of modernity, at another level they are reclaiming literacy as a hallmark of Hinduism's cultural past. Indeed, when literacy performs the work of culture in Hinduism, it is assigned an economic role denied in the work of missionary schools. In the context of an ancient past literacy extends beyond reading and writing to encompass a range of technical and vocational skills. This is illustrated in the comments of Vajpayee and other government figures on indigenous technical education. On a trip to the southern city of Mysore, Vajpayee lauded the work of Basaveshwara, a social reformer who made significant efforts in educating the masses while also promoting women's education. Vajpayee pointed to the Veerashaiva *mutts* as ideal service institutions providing training for literacy— training that the government ought to provide but did not. The Veerashaiva *mutts,* he further added, were the only institutions serving society for a long period of time with the same missionary zeal as that of Christian educational institutions.[25] As if on cue in a musical duet, the state chief minister who hosted him glorified the work of institutions such as the JSS Mahavidhyapeetha, saying they were providing opportunities for the disabled and the disenfranchised to become useful citizens. Significantly, both political figures consider the indigenous schools important because they are first and foremost technical training institutes. The vocational training offered in these indigenous institutions becomes that site of difference turning basic literacy into a colonized space, a zone of foreign domination.

Conflicting approaches to developmentalism underscore a deep ambivalence about literacy which has remained unresolved since the framing of the Indian constitution. Amartya Sen reopened the old debates about rights versus directives when he released the Public Report on Basic Education (PROBE) on 1 January 1999. The PROBE report is described as "a people's report" on school education. Prepared by a team of independent academics and social activists, it set out to counter the prevalent official myths about Indian schooling. The report claims to be the first attempt of its kind to examine the condition of India's elementary education from the standpoint of the underprivileged. It demolishes a set of ruling myths that have guided Indian education since the country's independence, among which are, first, that poor parents are not interested in sending their children to school, as is conventionally believed; second, that child labor is the main obstacle to school attendance and therefore to universal literacy; and, third, that elementary education is free. Most important, the report attempts to clarify the links between child labor and schooling by showing that, far from being unable to go to school because they have to work, full-time child laborers often work because they have dropped out of school, typically for family reasons.[26] Amartya Sen had argued against this form of educational deprivation for a long time, noting with chagrin that "child labour is considered perfectly acceptable for the boys and girls of poor families, while the privileged classes enjoy a massively subsidized system of higher education."[27]

Encouraged by the report's conclusion that, contrary to popular perception, education remains sought after even by the most economically disadvantaged sections of society, Sen declared that the time for demanding elementary education as a fundamental right had arrived. Simultaneously, he unveiled his plans to set up a charity trust with the Nobel money for development of education and health in India and Bangladesh.[28] Stressing the West's economic progress as a function of its planned development of human resources, Sen persuasively spoke of how the general availability of elementary education would enhance a sense of citizens' participation in India's overall economic expansion. He sounded a theme that placed the economic imperatives of educational growth in the perspective of social choice theory. Economic advantages, he appeared to suggest, were the fruit of participatory democracy whose foundations rested on basic literacy.[29]

Education as a Right

If, then, literacy is the chief basis of economic development and social change, education as a fundamental right has still remained largely undefined in the Indian constitution. On the other hand, articles 25 and 26 of the constitution, constituting the section on fundamental rights, were careful to give "every religious denomination" the right to propagate religion and maintain religious institutions. Constituent Assembly discussions struggled to untangle the contradiction between the secular goals of Indian democracy and the permission granted to religious groups to practice (and preach) their religious philosophies in their own institutions. Article 30 addresses educational rights, but it is less interested in universalizing education than in providing for the rights of minorities to maintain their own educational institutions and have full control over curricular content.

The right-to-education needs of citizens still remain largely undefined. Vajpayee acknowledged the continued failure of his own government to address educational needs, uttering in a moment of complete candor, "We pray to Saraswati (the Hindu goddess of learning) but make no arrangements to educate our children."[30] Hence his admiration for the efforts of nongovernmental institutions such as the Veerashaiva *mutts* or the Mahavidhyapeeta for doing what the government was obliged to do but failed. Unable to invest adequately in education, the Indian government has appeared to be resigned to the possibility of nongovernmental organizations (NGOs) taking the initiative. Yet social strife results when religious groups (operating as parallel NGOs) undertake the work of education, often work that is considered disruptive of another religious tradition. And in order to resolve conflicts of this nature, the state is required to intervene, even though it prefers to leave educational initiatives to nongovernmental organizations. This contradiction remains at the core of the state's fraught relation with the education of its citizens.

By proposing universal education as a fundamental right, Amartya Sen has called for alternative ways to rethink "inconsistencies of means and ends," by which he means the present arbitrary distribution of resources and the uncertain division of labor between government and nongovernmental (minority) agencies.[31] To be sure, he is less forthcoming about the sources of investment in education, for it is never entirely clear whether he would be willing to settle for an education funded by nongovernmental agencies to supplement government funding. To some extent this uncertainty has augmented the deep anxiety of his opponents that groups seeking to propagate their own beliefs—such as Christian missionaries—would seize the momentum for educational change. But Sen's most important intervention is in shifting freedom away from a concept that denotes a community's right to practice and propagate its beliefs. Rather, freedom for him is the creation of conditions for the wholesome participation of citizens in the democratic process. Universal literacy is the key to this process. As the instrument for securing the representation of people belonging to the unorganized sector, universal primary education is more than an entrée into people's participation in their economic advancement. By enacting democracy, it confers a reality on participatory processes which Indian democracy still lacks, despite its adult suffrage.

At the same time Amartya Sen has been careful not to make freedom an all-encompassing category overriding goals of equality, such that one person's freedom becomes another's unfreedom. His suspicion of *freedom* as an unqualified term leads him to argue that the freedom accruing from a market economy is attended by far too many dangers of inequality and poverty stemming from the market.[32] Instead, he proposes five kinds of freedom: (1) enabling freedom, which signifies that each individual is able to participate in social and economic activities and that the quality of life is improved through education and health facilities; (2) political freedom, which invariably involves democracy and civil rights; (3) economic freedom, which involves transactions and the market and could thus promote efficiency and equity; (4) transparency freedom, which encompasses a person's right to know that he or she was not being cheated in a transaction; and (5) protective freedom, which is freedom from droughts, floods, famine. These freedoms are important insofar as they constitute the legitimate end of development.[33]

Thus, for Sen literacy is not exclusively an economic issue, as some commentators believe. His notion of freedom encompasses culture—the kind of life we would like to lead—as an essential goal of development.[34] What his critic Ashok Singhal evidently feared was that culture would be made synonymous with social choice, and to that extent Amartya Sen's notion of freedom uncannily confirmed his anxiety that development had a Christian trajectory.[35] Singhal obviously got the story wrong in most of the particulars. But on the subject of choice Sen offered a new set of questions that could potentially have more bearing on how individuals construe selfhood, as opposed to being affirmed by their community, and it is this move that set alarm bells ringing for Singhal. Instead of asking the old question, "Is it possible to have socially rational decisions based on the interests and preferences of the members of the society?" Sen proposed asking, "Which of the various ways of equity and justice are most relevant?" The choice, he suggests, is between different ways of evaluation whose ultimate validity is that they draw upon foundational notions of justice and fairness. Even the apparently scientific subject of choosing a suitable measure of poverty for a nation or a state can be approached in terms of the competing values reflected in different ways by distinct statistical measures. Because welfare economics and social choice theory link knowledge with practice, their operative premise is that self-construction is national construction. So, even though economic development has merged into an issue of culture in the rhetoric of the postcolonial state, driven by its own sense of cultural nationalism, the question of choice is deliberately suspended. Where it does appear, it is turned into proof of forcible conversion.

Notes

1. This article was first published as "Literacy and conversion in the discourse of Hindu nationalism," *Race and Class* 42 (2000):1–20.

2. "Sangh Parivar Comes under Fire," *The Hindu* (Madras, India), 29 December 1998, 13.

3. "Singhal Statement on Amartya Sen Misquoted," *The Hindu*, 3 January 1999, 7.

4. "Vajpayee Criticises VHP Remarks on Christians," *The Hindu*, 31 December 1998, 1.

5. The nun claimed, in her police report, that her assailants questioned her about the number of conversions her convent brought about, while also warning her that the killings, rapes, and kidnappings would continue as long as the Christian missions engaged in proselytizing ("Nun's Assailants Untraced," *The Hindu*, 25 September 1999, 1). Three weeks earlier a Roman Catholic priest had been murdered in Orissa.

6. See M. K. Gandhi, *My Experiments with Truth* (Boston: Beacon Press, 1957), 122–125.

7. Ministry of Law, Justice and Company Affairs, Government of India, *The Constitution of India* (as modified up to 1 August 1977), 14.

8. M.M. Singh, *The Constitution of India: Studies in Perspective* (Calcutta: The World Press, 1975), 480.

9. Andrew Wingate, *The Church and Conversion* (Delhi: Indian Society for Promoting Christian Knowledge, 1997), 35.

10. "VHP Charge against Sonia Gandhi," *The Hindu*, 9 January 1999, 13.

11. Gauri Viswanathan,""Beyond Orientalism: Syncretism and the Politics of Knowledge," *Stanford Humanities Review* 5 (1995):18–32.

12. Robert W. Hefner, "World Building and the Rationality of Conversion," in *Conversion to Christianity: Historical and Anthropological Perspectives on a Great Transformation*, Robert W. Hefner, ed. (Berkeley: University of California Press, 1993), 5.

13. David J. Krieger, "Conversion: On the Possibility of Global Thinking in an Age of Particularism," *Journal of the American Academy of Religion* 63 (1990):238.

14. It was John Henry Newman's special contribution to reverse the institutionalization of assent and to produce a grammar of dissent. His major philosophical treatise, *A Grammar of Assent*, bears an ironic title in that, in order to arrive at an affirmation of faith, the knowing believer must proceed through successive stages of dissent from accepted premises. See Gauri Viswanathan, *Outside the Fold: Conversion, Modernity, and Belief* (Princeton, N. J.: Princeton University Press, 1998), 44–72.

15. Alan Olson, "Postmodernity and Faith," *Journal of the American Academy of Religion* 58 (spring 1990): 44.

16. By emancipation, I mean the series of bills passed in early nineteenth-century England enfranchising Jews, Catholics, Dissenters, and other non-Anglican groups and bringing them into the national fold. The price of such emancipation was, as I argue in *Outside the Fold*, that religious groups were often asked to forego the specificity of their religious beliefs in order to become citizens of the state.

17. "PM Calls for National Debate on Conversion," *The Hindu*, 11 January 1999, 1.

18. See Antony Copley, *Religions in Conflict: Ideology, Cultural Contact, and Conversion in Late Colonial India* (Delhi: Oxford University Press, 1997).

19. Richard Fox Young, *Resistant Hinduism: Sanskrit Sources on Anti-Christian Apologetics in Early Nineteenth-Century India* (Vienna: Roberto Nobili Institute, 1981).

20. Copley, *Religions in Conflict*. See also my *Outside the Fold*, particularly chapter 3, "Rights of Passage," for a discussion of the antagonism felt by Hindu parents to-

ward Christian missionaries, whom they blamed for the Christian conversions of their young children. Deprived of their rights to inheritance on conversion, converts were often assisted by missionaries in bringing their cases to court so that their rights would be restored.

21. "Singhal Statement on Amartya Sen Misquoted," *The Hindu*, 3 January 1999, 7.
22. Sathianathan Clarke, *Dalits and Christianity: Subaltern Religion and Liberation Theology in India* (Delhi: Oxford University Press, 1998).
23. Great Britain, *Parliamentary Papers*, 1852–1853, Evidence of J. C. Marshman, 32:119.
24. See Gauri Viswanathan, *Masks of Conquest: Literary Study and British Rule in India* (New York: Columbia University, 1989), 151–152.
25. Great Britain, *Parliamentary Papers*, 1831–1832, Minutes by M. Elphinstone, 13 December 1823, 9:519.
26. "Poverty Hingering Spread of Literacy: PM," *The Hindu*, 4 January 1999, 10.
27. The Probe Team, *Public Report on Basic Education in India* (Delhi: Oxford University Press, 1999), 14–17. On child labor, the report is not entirely convincing, as it tries to distinguish between family and hired labor and in so doing vacillates between empathy for family needs and condemnation of capitalist exploitation.
28. Amartya Sen, "Basic Education as a Political Issue," in *The Amartya Sen and Jean Dreze Omnibus* (Delhi: Oxford University Press, 1999), 120.
29. "Sen to Set up Charity with Prize Money," *The Hindu*, 28 December 1998, 14.
30. Sen's research in Indian villages consistently pointed to the special value of basic education as a tool of social affirmation. As the *Probe Report* later confirmed, even among the most socially and economically disadvantaged groups, education was strongly valued for enabling upward mobility. Sen punctures the myth propagated by upper castes that the lower castes did not place much importance in literacy because they view education as an instrument of uppercaste domination. On the contrary, as the *Probe Report* also affirms, education remains highly desirable to lowcaste groups.
31. "Poverty Hindering Spread of Literacy: PM," *The Hindu*, 4 January 1999, 6.
32. Sen, "Basic Education as a Political Issue," 117.
33. See Amartya Sen, *Inequality Examined* (Delhi: Oxford University Press, 1992), in which Sen trenchantly shifts the question economists typically ask ("should there be equality?") to the more important one: "equality of what?" Sen forces the discussion to concentrate on the diversity of human populations, which inevitably involves different standards of equality; in other words, what is equal to one group of people might be deemed inequality to another. The heterogeneity of social groups requires one constantly to rethink how a range of human capabilities might be harnessed to achieve specific goals, from which standpoint questions of rights and equality can be raised more profitably.
34. See Amartya Sen, "Well beyond Liberalization," for an exploration of these themes, as well as an assessment of India's recent economic reforms. His conclusion that "the 'uncaging of the tiger' has not—at least not yet—led to any dynamic animal springing out and sprinting ahead" draws attention to the still unfulfilled promises of participatory growth, evident in the alarming illiteracy rates and social deprivations

("Well beyond Liberalization," in *The Amartya Sen and Jean Dreze Omnibus*, [Delhi: Oxford University Press, 1999], 180).

35. See particularly Sen's essay "Freedom, Agency and Well-Being," in *Inequality Re-examined*, which describes freedom as our right to set goals for ourselves and our ability to get what we value and want; in short, to lead a life we would choose to live.

SELECTED REFERENCES

Almond, Philip. *The British Discovery of Buddhism.* Cambridge, U.K.: Cambridge University Press, 1988.

Anderson, Benedict. *Imagined Communities: Reflections on the Origin and Spread of Nationalism.* London: Verso, 1983.

Appadurai, Arjun. *Worship and Conflict under Colonial Rule.* Cambridge, U.K.: Cambridge University Press, 1981.

Asad, Talal. *Genealogies of Religion: Discipline and Reasons of Power in Christianity and Islam.* Baltimore: Johns Hopkins University Press, 1993.

Bacon, Gershon. *The Politics of Tradition: Agudat Yisrael in Poland, 1916–1939.* Jerusalem: Magnes Press, 1996.

Banerjee, Partha. *In the Belly of the Beast: The Hindu Supremacist RSS and BJP of India, an Insider's Story.* Delhi: Ajanta Press, 1998.

Bayly, Susan. *Saints, Goddesses, and Kings: Muslims and Christians in South Indian Society, 1700–1900.* Cambridge, U.K.: Cambridge University Press, 1989.

Berkes, Niyazi. *The Development of Secularism in Turkey.* New York: Routledge, 1998.

Bhabha, Homi. *The Location of Culture.* New York: Routledge, 1994.

Casanova, Jose. *Public Religion in the Modern World.* Chicago: University of Chicago Press, 1994.

Chatterjee, Partha. *Our Modernity.* Rotterdam, Neth., and Dakar, Senegal: SEPHIS and CODESRIA, 1997.

———. The *Nation and Its Fragments: Colonial and Postcolonial Histories.* Princeton, N.J.: Princeton University Press, 1993.

Chidester, David. *Savage Systems: Colonialism and Comparative Religion in Southern Africa.* Charlottesville: University Press of Virginia, 1996.

Clarke, Sathianathan. *Dalits and Christianity: Subaltern Religion and Liberation Theology in India.* Delhi: Oxford University Press, 1998.

Cohen, Richard S. "Kinsmen of the Son: Śākyabhikṣus and the Institutionalization of the Bodhisattva Ideal." *History of Religions* 40 (August 2000): 1–31.

Cohn, Bernard. *An Anthropologist among the Historians and Other Essays.* Delhi: Oxford University Press, 1987.

Commins, David Dean. *Islamic Reform: Politics and Social Change in Late Ottoman Syria.* New York: Oxford University Press, 1990.

Copley, Antony. *Religions in Conflict: Ideology, Cultural Contact, and Conversion in Late Colonial India.* Delhi: Oxford University Press, 1997.

Dalmia, Vasudha, and Heinrich von Stietencron, eds. *Representing Hinduism: The Construction of Religious Traditions and National Identity.* New Delhi: Sage Publications, 1995.

Davison, Roderic H. *Reform in the Ottoman Empire, 1856–1876.* New York: Gordian Press, 1973.

Deringil, Selim. *The Well-Protected Domains: Ideology and the Legitimation of Power in the Ottoman Empire, 1876–1909.* London: I. B. Taurus, 1998.

Dobbelaere, Karel. "Some Trends in European Sociology of Religion: The Secularization Debate." *Sociological Analysis* 48 (1987): 107–137.

Duara, Prasenjit. *Rescuing History from the Nation: Questioning Narratives of Modern China.* Chicago: University of Chicago Press, 1995.

Duncan, Carol. *Civilizing Rituals: Inside Public Art Museums.* New York: Routledge, 1995.

Durkheim, Emile. *The Elementary Forms of Religious Life.* New York: Free Press, 1965.

Dussel, Enrique. "From Secularization to Secularism: Science from the Renaissance to the Enlightenment." *Concilium* 47 (1968): 93–119.

———. *History and the Theology of Liberation: A Latin American Perspective.* New York: Orbis Books, 1976.

———. *A History of the Church in Latin America: Colonialism to Liberation (1492–1979).* Grand Rapids, Mich.: William B. Eerdmans, 1981.

———. *The Invention of the Americas: Eclipse of "the Other" and the Myth of Modernity.* New York: Continuum, 1995.

———. *The Underside of Modernity: Apel, Riceour, Rorty, Taylor, and the Philosophy of Liberation.* Ed. and trans. Eduardo Mendieta. Atlantic Highlands, N.J.: Humanities, 1996.

Elwood, Robert. *The History and Future of Faith: Religion Past, Present, and to Come.* New York: Crossroad, 1988.

Frank, Andre Gunder. *ReORIENT: Global Economy in the Asian Age.* Berkeley: University of California Press, 1998.

Geertz, Clifford. "Common Sense as a Cultural System." *Antioch Review* 33 (1975): 5–26.

Gelvin, James L. *Divided Loyalties: Nationalism and Mass Politics in Syria at the Close of Empire.* Berkeley: University of California Press, 1998.

Gluck, Carol. *Japan's Modern Myths: Ideology in the Late Meiji Period.* Princeton, N.J.: Princeton University Press, 1985.

Gombrich, Richard. *Theravāda Buddhism: A Social History from Ancient Benares to Modern Colombo.* London: Routledge and Kegan Paul, 1988.

Hall, David D., ed. *Lived Religion in America: Toward a History of Practice.* Princeton, N.J.: Princeton University Press, 1997.

Hardacre, Helen. *Shintō and the State, 1868–1988.* Princeton, N.J.: Princeton University Press, 1989.

Hastings, Adrian. *The Construction of Nationhood: Ethnicity, Religion and Nationalism.* New York: Cambridge University Press, 1997.

Hefner, Robert W., ed. *Conversion to Christianity: Historical and Anthropological Perspectives on a Great Transformation.* Berkeley: University of California Press, 1993.

Hobsbawm, Eric. *Nations and Nationalism since 1780: Programme, Myth, Reality.* New York: Cambridge University Press, 1990.

Hobsbawm, Eric, and Terrence Ranger. *The Invention of Tradition.* New York: Cambridge University Press, 1983.

Hooper-Greenhill, Eileen. *Museums and the Shaping of Knowledge.* New York: Routledge, 1992.

Huntington, Samuel P. *The Clash of Civilizations and the Remaking of the World Order.* New York: Simon and Schuster, 1996.

Inden, Ronald B. *Imagining India.* Cambridge, Mass.: Basil Blackwell, 1992.

Jorstad, Erling. *Holding Fast / Pressing On: Religion in America in the 1980s.* New York: Greenwood, 1990.

Joshi, Sanjay. *Fractured Modernity: The Making of a Middle Class in Colonial North India.* Delhi: Oxford University Press, 2001.

Karp, Ivan, and Stephen D. Lavine, eds. *Exhibiting Cultures: The Poetics and Politics of Museum Display.* Washington D.C.: Smithsonian Institution Press, 1991.

Kayali, Hayali. *Arabs and Young Turks: Ottomanism, Arabism, and Islamism in the Ottoman Empire, 1908–1918.* Berkeley: University of California Press, 1997.

Ketelaar, James Edward. *Of Heretics and Martyrs in Meiji Japan.* Princeton, N.J.: Princeton University Press, 1990.

Kuroda, Toshio. "Shintō in the History of Japanese Religion." *Journal of Japanese Studies* 7 (winter 1981): 1–21.

Landau, Paul. "Explaining Surgical Evangelism in Colonial Southern Africa: Teeth, Pain and Faith." *Journal of African History* 37 (1996): 261–281.

———. "'Religion' and Christian Conversion in African History: A New Model." *Journal of Religious History* 23 (1999): 8–30.

Lippy, Charles. *Being Religious American Style: A History of Popular Religiosity in the United States.* Westport, Conn.: Greenwood, 1994.

Lopez, Donald S., ed. *Curators of the Buddha: The Study of Buddhism under Colonialism.* Chicago: University of Chicago Press, 1995.

Makdisi, Ussama. *The Culture of Sectarianism: Community, History, and Violence in Nineteenth-Century Ottoman Lebanon.* Berkeley: University of California Press, 2000.

Mamdani, Mahmood. *Citizen and Subject: Contemporary Africa and the Legacy of Late Colonialism.* Princeton, N.J.: Princeton University Press, 1996.

Mani, Lata. *Contentious Traditions: The Debate on Sati in Colonial India.* Berkeley: University of California Press, 1998.

Mardin, Serif. *Religion and Social Change in Modern Turkey: The Case of Bediüzzaman Said Nursi.* Albany: State University of New York Press, 1989.

———. *The Genesis of Young Ottoman Thought: A Study in the Modernization of Turkish Political Ideas.* Princeton, N.J.: Princeton University Press, 1962.

Mbiti, John. *African Religions and Philosophy.* New York: Praeger, 1969.

———. *Introduction to African Religion.* Portsmouth: Heinemann, 1975.

McCutcheon, Russell T. *Manufacturing Religion: The Discourse on Sui Generis Religion and the Politics of Nostalgia.* New York: Oxford University Press, 1997.

———, ed. *The Insider/Outsider Problem in the Study of Religion: A Reader.* London: Cassell Press, 1999.

McDannell, Colleen. *Material Christianity: Religion and Popular Culture in America.* New Haven, Conn.: Yale University Press, 1995.

Minault, Gail. *Secluded Scholars: Women's Education and Muslim Social Reform in Colonial India.* Delhi, Oxford University Press, 1998.

Mitchell, Timothy. *Colonising Egypt.* Berkeley: University of California Press, 1991.

Mittelman, Alan L. *The Politics of Torah: The Jewish Political Tradition and the Founding of Agudat Israel.* Albany: State University of New York Press, 1996.

Moore, R. Laurence. *Selling God: American Religion in the Marketplace of Culture.* New York: Oxford University Press, 1994.

Nandy, Ashis. "The Politics of Secularism and the Recovery of Religious Tolerance." In *Mirrors of Violence: Communities, Riots, and Survivors in South Asia.* Ed. Veena Das. Delhi: Oxford University Press, 1990.

———. "The Twilight of Certitudes: Secularism, Hindu Nationalism, and Other Masks of Deculturation." *Alternatives* 22 (1997): 157–176.

Pandey, Gyanendra. *The Construction of Communalism in Colonial North India.* Delhi: Oxford University Press, 1990.

Prakash, Gyan. *Another Reason: Science and the Imagination of Modern India.* Princeton, N.J.: Princeton University Press, 1999.

Reader, Ian. *Religion in Contemporary Japan.* Honolulu: University of Hawaii Press, 1991.

Reader, Ian, and George J. Tanabe Jr. *Practically Religious: Worldly Benefits and the Common Religion of Japan.* Honolulu: University of Hawaii Press, 1998.

Ruel, Malcolm. *Belief, Ritual and the Securing of Life: Reflexive Essays on a Bantu Religion.* Leiden: Brill Academic Publishers, 1997.

Said, Edward. *Orientalism.* New York: Vintage Books, 1978.

Sarkar, Sumit. *Writing Social History.* Delhi: Oxford University Press, 1997.

Sears, John F. *Sacred Places: American Tourist Attractions in the Nineteenth Century.* New York: Oxford University Press, 1989.

Shaw, Rosalind. "The Invention of 'African Traditional Religion.'" *Religion* 20 (1990): 339–353.

Shaw, Wendy M. K. *Possessors and Possessed: Objects, Museums and the Visualization of History in the Late Ottoman Empire.* Berkeley: University of California Press, forthcoming.

Silberstein, Lawrence J., ed. *Jewish Fundamentalism in Comparative Perspective: Religion, Ideology, and the Crisis of Modernity.* New York: New York University Press, 1993.

Sivan, Emmanuel. *Radical Islam: Medieval Theology and Modern Politics.* New Haven, Conn.: Yale University Press, 1985.

Smith, Jonathon Z. "'Religion' and 'Religious Studies': No Difference at All." *Soundings* 71 (1988): 231–244.

Sontheimer, Gunther-Dietz, and Hermann Kulke, eds. *Hinduism Reconsidered.* Delhi: Manohar, 1997.

Taylor, Mark C., ed. *Critical Terms for Religious Studies.* Chicago: University of Chicago Press, 1998.

Thapar, Romila. "Imagined Religious Communities? Ancient History and the Search for a Hindu Identity." *Modern Asian Studies* 23 (1989).

Thelle, Notto R. *Buddhism and Christianity in Japan.* Honolulu: University of Hawaii Press, 1987.

Tibi, Bassam. *The Crisis of Modern Islam: A Preindustrial Culture in the Scientific-Technological Age.* Salt Lake City: University of Utah Press, 1988.

Turner, Bryan S. "Religion and State Formation: A Commentary on Recent Debates." *Journal of Historical Sociology* 1 (September 1988): 322–333.

van der Veer, Peter. *Imperial Encounters: Religion and Modernity in India and Britain.* Princeton, N.J.: Princeton University Press, 2001.

———. *Religious Nationalism: Hindus and Muslims in India.* Berkeley: University of California Press, 1994.

van der Veer, Peter, and Hartmut Lehmann, eds. *Nation and Religion: Perspectives on Europe and Asia.* Princeton, N.J.: Princeton University Press, 1999.

Viswanathan, Gauri. "Beyond Orientalism: Syncretism and the Politics of Knowledge." *Stanford Humanities Review* 5 (1995): 1–32.

———. *Masks of Conquest: Literary Study and British Rule in India.* New York: Columbia University Press, 1989.

———. *Outside the Fold: Conversion, Modernity, and Belief.* Princeton, N.J.: Princeton University Press, 1998.

Voll, John Obert. *Islam: Continuity and Change in the Modern World.* Boulder, Colo.: Westview Press, 1982.

Weber, Max. *The Protestant Ethic and the Spirit of Capitalism.* Upper Saddle River, N.J.: Prentice Hall, 1958.

Williams, Peter. *Popular Religion in America: Symbolic Change and the Modernization Process in Historical Perspective.* Englewood Cliffs, N.J.: Prentice Hall, 1980.

ABOUT THE CONTRIBUTORS

RICHARD S. COHEN is assistant professor of South Asian religious literatures at the University of California, San Diego. His work on the social history of Indian Buddhism has appeared in *History of Religions,* the *Journal of the American Academy of Religion,* and the *Indo-Iranian Journal.* He is currently writing a book-length study of ancient Indian Buddhism as a modern artifact.

ENRIQUE DUSSEL is professor of philosophy at the Universidad Autonoma Metropolitana in Mexico. He is the author of numerous works in philosophy, theology, and history, including *Etica de la liberación en la edad de la globalización y de la exclusión* and *The Invention of the Americas: Eclipse of "the Other" and the Myth of Modernity.*

JAMES L. GELVIN is associate professor of history at the University of California, Los Angeles. He is author of *Divided Loyalties: Nationalism and Mass Politics in Syria at the Close of Empire.* He has written numerous articles and book chapters on the social and cultural history of the modern Middle East, particularly on Greater Syria during the late nineteenth and early twentieth centuries.

SANJAY JOSHI is assistant professor of history at Northern Arizona University, Flagstaff. His research deals with power, culture, and identity in modern South Asia. He is the author of *Fractured Modernity: The Making of a Middle Class in Colonial North India.*

AARON K. KETCHELL is a doctoral candidate in the American Studies Program at the University of Kansas. His research concerns the relationship between American religion and leisure, especially in the Ozarks. He has recently published a more extensive study of the Precious Moments Chapel in the *Journal of American Culture.*

DEREK R. PETERSON is assistant professor of history at the College of New Jersey. His work on the history of language, religion, and ethnicity in colonial central Kenya has appeared in the *Journal of African History,* the *Journal of Religious History,* and in three edited books.

WENDY M. K. SHAW is assistant professor at Ohio State University. Her areas of research include visual cultural studies, art history, architecture and urbanism, and Turkish studies. She is the author of *Possessors and Possessed: Objects, Museums, and the Visualization of History in the Late Ottoman Empire.*

JEREMY STOLOW is a postdoctoral fellow in the faculty of social and political sciences, University of Cambridge. He is currently working on "Nation of Torah," a book manuscript about media and religiopolitics in the case of ArtScroll, a Jewish Orthodox publishing house.

SARAH THAL is assistant professor of history at Rice University. Her areas of research include the relationship between politics and popular religious practice in early modern and modern Japan and the industrialization of food in the twentieth century. Her article "Sacred Sites and the Dynamics of Identity" recently appeared in *Early Modern Japan.*

GAURI VISWANATHAN is professor of English and comparative literature at Columbia University. She is author of *Masks of Conquest: Literary Study and British Rule in India* and *Outside the Fold: Conversion, Modernity, and Belief.*

DARREN R. WALHOF is visiting assistant professor of political science at Gustavus Adolphus College. His research interests include early modern political thought, the history of liberalism, and philosophical and legal hermeneutics. He is currently writing on conscience and politics.

INDEX

217

Williams, Andy, 162
Williams, Peter, 159
Wilson, Bryan, 158

World War II, 111
Wright, Harold Bell, 156–157, 160, 162,
    164, 166